The first Boston Poultry Show is held in November, and one of its first exhibitors is Daniel Webster with his Javas and geese. Meanwhile, Queen Victoria makes a futile law banning cockfights.

Chicken wire is invented.

Black Giant
roduced.

Queen Victoria receives a gift of huge Cochin chickens from China, which creates a chicken craze.

The Barred Plymouth Rock chicken is bred.

L. C. Byce establishes the Petaluma Incubator Company, which allows artificial hatching of millions of chicken eggs.

A.D. 1841

A.D. 1846

A.D. 1854

A.D. 1870

A.D. 1875

A.D. 1885

A.D. 1843

A.D. 1849

A.D. 1856

A.D. 1874

A.D. 1878

A.D. 1887

Queen Victoria shows off her Cochins from China.

First commercial chicken hatchery established.

White Wyandotte chickens are introduced from Wyandotte, New York.

Dorking chickens come to America from England.

Rhode Island Red becomes an official breed of chicken.

The White Plymouth Rock chicken is bred.

CHICKEN

150 Great Recipes for All Seasons

by Elaine Corn

Illustrations by Sergio Baradat

"Chicken ain't nothing but a bird."
—Old Mississippi saying

CHRONICLE BOOKS

SAN FRANCISCO

Library of Congress Cataloging-in-Publication Data:
Corn, Elaine.
Chicken: 150 great recipes for all seasons/by Elaine Corn;
illustrations by Sergio Baradat.
p. cm.
Includes bibliographical references and index.
ISBN 0-8118-1772-5
1. Cookery (Chicken)   I. Title
TX750.5.C45   C67   1999
641.6'65—dc21   98—31672
CIP

Printed in the United States

Designed by Flux aka Steve Barretto Design.
Food styling for cover photograph by Erin Quon.

Distributed in Canada by Raincoast Books
8680 Cambie Street
Vancouver, British Columbia V6P 6M9

10 9 8 7 6 5 4 3 2 1

Chronicle Books
85 Second Street
San Francisco, California 94105

www.chroniclebooks.com

Thanks to Bill LeBlond and his big idea. Thanks to my agent, Martha Casselman. Thanks to the folks at Abraham Manchester,
Kathleen Abraham, Hilary Abramson, Pam Andersen, Dan Best, Louise Borke, Dr. Francine Bradley, Dr. A. W. Brant,
Ellie Brecher (for not cooking), Gerald Brecher, Vivienne Corn, Darrell Corti, Illa Corti, Toni Cox, the folks at Foster Farms,
Dotty Griffith, Barbara Haber, Gary Jenanyan, Chris Kimball, Peggy Kligman Sinofsky, Maine-ly Poultry, Fran McCullough,
Bob Munyon, Patricia Murakami, the folks at the National Broiler Council, Roxanne O'Brien, Lori K. Richardson, Marcie Rothman,
Sacramento's Town & Country Village farmers' market, Lowell Sherman, Martha Rose Shulman, Florence Spector, Teresa Urkofsky.
Hugs and kisses to my main leg men, David and Robert.

for *Monroe Corn*

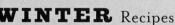

TABLE of CONTENTS

"Let's call it chicken. Everyone will eat it."

    —My friend Peggy, suggesting to her
    husband a good way to get the kids to eat
    dinner when she's cooked some kind
    of meat that's sort of white.

CHICKEN

150 Great Recipes for All Seasons

Introduction

You hold in your hands another cookbook about chicken.

It will last you all year. And the year after that.

Don't let the fact that there are fewer than 365 ways to cook chicken here fool you. The point isn't to eat chicken every day of the year but to pair chicken with fresh produce as the year goes by.

Considering that Americans now eat nearly 30 million pounds of chicken a year, many of us might actually look forward to a meal that isn't chicken. Such wasn't always the case. In the early 1900s, chicken cost about 20 cents a pound (adjusted to 3 dollars and 30 cents a pound in 1998 dollars), and was a luxury more expensive than beef. Today, agribusiness giants produce chickens in such numbers that we can afford to eat it at a rate of 96.8 pounds per person per year. We can't imagine not having chicken whenever we want it.

Devoid of its own season, our bird's special benign neutrality actually extends its variety. French philosopher and culinarian Anthelme Brillat-Savarin compared cooking a chicken to painting a canvas. A fashion maven might call chicken the basic black dress of cuisine (with seasonal produce as accessories). I think of chicken as a comic straight man. It absorbs whatever comes its way.

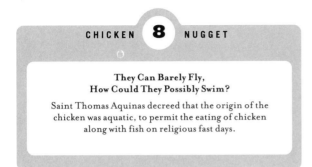

CHICKEN **8** **NUGGET**

**They Can Barely Fly,
How Could They Possibly Swim?**

Saint Thomas Aquinas decreed that the origin of the
chicken was aquatic, to permit the eating of chicken
along with fish on religious fast days.

Produce is the key to staying true to the seasons, although sometimes it's hard to tell the time of year by what's available in grocery stores. As actor and gourmand Vincent Price once wrote, shelf-stable cans, the refrigerator, and the freezer breached "the tyranny of the seasons" and freed cooks from seasonal dependency.

Look at the food-out-of-season concept today. Is it out of control? Agribusiness elongates growing seasons. Global wholesalers flip-flop hemispheres to bring summer fruit to winter climes, and the other way around. In truth, the world can feed on any food on demand no matter the actual season. Perhaps people who like autumn's food during autumn are experiencing the tyranny of shipping.

I love to rebel against many of the elements that make modern life just a little too slick—like tomatoes in winter. Staying seasonal, no matter what's at the store, is a grounding force that helps me to focus on what's real, what's in its right time and place.

I'm lucky to be able to shop at big farmers' markets all week, all year. But you can cook with the seasons, too, and this book will help you. Not only will you notice increased variety at dinner, but you'll develop an inner shop(ping) clock with an alarm that goes off when tomatoes show up in January. Where the heck did they come from? Most likely a greenhouse or tropical country. They're not illegal, just seasonally dishonest.

Making chicken seasonally correct is determined by two things: (1) the seasonal ingredients around the chicken, and (2) how hot the house gets.

Chicken allows many intimacies between its skin and flesh, from the strange to the predictable. In this book, a chicken will jump into a pan with just about anything—potato, tomato, apple, banana, mustard greens, curry, nuts, olives, Coke, wine, and the hard stuff. You'll find it with Bing cherries or favas in spring, tomatoes and corn in summer; chard or squash in autumn, and with ugly old root vegetables in winter.

The hotter the pot, the colder the season. Spring and summer recipes are fresh, quick, and fairly easy. Good spring examples are a quick stir-fry with asparagus and chicken braised in coconut milk with fresh peas. Summer grilling and chicken salads keep the house cool, as does a microwaved batch of chicken breasts. By autumn, we want the house steamed up from stocks and long-cooked recipes, such as chicken baked with fresh cranberry beans, a fine chicken paprikash with gypsy peppers, or even a big stuffed Thanksgiving chicken. And in winter the oven *and* stove top are kept busy fueling a variety of recipes designed to throw off enough heat, along with aromas, to warm up cold days, including chicken-in-a-pot, chicken pot pie, and chicken roasted with shallots in Chardonnay sauce.

While discovering the range of seasonal chicken cookery, I also found out more than I ever wanted to know about chickens themselves. In preparing this book I went to poultry shows, researched chicken's global history, learned a little about breeds, and collected nonsense in general, including chicken jokes, all recorded for you in these pages.

CHICKEN **35** NUGGET

Chickens Chat

A chicken's clucking is more than barnyard yadda-yadda-yadda. Peter Marler, director of the Animal Communication Laboratory at the University of California at Davis, went public in May 1997 with observations that chickens cluck to one another with meaning and intent. Their alarm cluck for a predatory raccoon is different from their warning for a hawk. Sly roosters give out the "food" call to attract a desirable hen when there's no food around. Is this cognition? Marler found that Golden Bantams had about 25 different vocal calls in their chicken vocabulary. And if one chicken sensed danger when no other chickens were around, the chicken didn't make a sound.

In truth, the chicken is the avian of the ages, richly imbued with symbolic intrigue, quirky social habits, and masses of devoted followers of the human persuasion. (In the following chapters, you'll discover some of that delicious trivia under the heading Chicken Nugget.) The chicken's questionable intelligence only adds to its charms. I have fallen for all its charms, particularly those that emanate from a sauté pan.

If you and your family eat chicken so much that, in the words of my mother's friend Florence, "We cluck," just follow the seasons. You'll have plenty of accessories to dress up your bird.

Getting to Know the Chicken

Where Do Chickens Come From?

The chickens we buy in stores and take home to cook are as removed from their origins as man is from the monkey. A reluctant consensus of poultry experts says that the first chicken was the wild Red Jungle Fowl, a two-pound critter believed to have originated in Southeast Asia. Beyond that, any discussion about where chickens came from and when and where they were domesticated resembles the chaotic din of a barnyard full of clucking hens.

A lot of stock is put in the belief that the little Red Jungle Fowl came to the end of his wild life when he was "domesticated" in the Indus Valley of today's west Pakistan. Some say it happened around 3000 B.C.; others more carefully date domestication by 2000 B.C. Confirming this information was no lesser an authority than Charles Darwin, who also concluded that of all the jungle fowls around at the time, the red fowl was the one involved in the domestication of the chicken.

Fast forward to 1994. A study complete with DNA tests pointed to an older bird going back ten thousand years to Thailand.

The truth is, no one is absolutely sure about the dispersion of chickens on their trajectories to nearly every country in the world and into the fires and stomachs of nearly every civilization.

They certainly didn't fly. There is strong evidence that they fanned out from India by sea to Egypt and by land to Persia, Greece, and Italy. There are even reports that they headed north to China as early as 6000 B.C. The names first used to describe chickens were those of a town or region where they showed up: Shanghai, Chittagong, Cochin, Peking, Castile, Minorca, Surrey, Sussex.

Today it's reasonable to credit *all* the jungle fowls for giving rise to our current chicken population—not necessarily only the red one.

If you want to see what some of those first chickens might have looked like, go to a poultry show nearly anyplace in the world and find a Malay. This beautiful bird that lays buff brown eggs and is bred by poultry fanciers who blow-dry their feathers is believed the only faintly tangible link to the progenitor.

While Southeast Asia figures prominently in the evolution of the chicken, the cradle of intellectual activity was Italy, where our wild jungle fowl got its Latin name, *Gallus gallus*. The world's earliest treatise recorded the habits, behavior, growth, physiology, and psychology of chickens in an obsessive circumspection written in 1600 by Ulisse Aldrovani, born in Bologna in 1522. Of Aldrovani's nine-volume magnum opus on animals, *Aldrovani on Chickens* took up an entire volume of the three he wrote about birds.

CHICKEN **9** NUGGET

What Made Abe Honest?

Abraham Lincoln got the nickname Honest Abe because he was known as a fair and forthright referee at cockfights. The winning cocks were known by the code "mortgage lifter."

It's taken many centuries to breed the chickens we buy today. Whatever shape chickens were in before man discovered them, they were quickly—and deliberately—altered. Greed drove the new chicken designs. For example, birds bred by the clever coupling of a hearty rooster and a mean old hen won the most money at cockfighting, which I'm sorry to say remains, as in ancient times, the world's biggest spectator sport.

The chicken came to America in 1607 with the Jamestown colonists. Eggs and chicken meat were essential sources of pioneer protein. Yet compared to other domesticated animals, the chicken seemed to receive little human gratitude (were chicken jokes far behind?). In wills, horses, cattle, sheep, and pigs were bequeathed with detailed instructions and beneficiary lists, but chickens were referred to only by how many there were at last count. In 1840, the first poultry census by the United States Department of the Interior counted about 99 million birds.

For two centuries Americans continually mixed chickens. Birds unwanted in the markets in Europe sailed here. They were added to coops and yards with other chickens, which hatched millions of chicks of accidental heritage. In the early years, most were dark skinned and laid brown eggs. Hardly any white chickens were sent to such markets as Faneuil Hall in Boston (or even to LaValee in Paris) because of a life span kept short by predators attracted to their whiteness (today, in contrast, most egg-laying poultry is white and so are their eggs).

Eventually the melting-pot chicken wore out its welcome. Poultry fanciers wanted clean strains. This was done by monitoring the roosters within a region. In the early 1800s, huge numbers of a reddish brown chicken began to dominate southern Massachusetts and all of Rhode Island, and the bird is known to this day as the Rhode Island Red.

In a few decades, knowing which chicken was which got downright confusing. *The American Poultry Book*, written in 1843 by M. R. Cock (this is not a joke, but the pen name for C. N. Bement), listed five poultry categories: Game Cock, Top Knot, Italian Hen, Malay, and Bantam.

But there came more. How did we keep them all straight? Is it a White Faced Black Spanish or a Barred Plymouth Rock or a White Rock? Drawings more detailed than the blueprint for

PLYMOUTH ROCK

How did we make a Plymouth Rock? It took several attempts. First Dr. John C. Bennet showed a cross of Asiatic fowl and the English Dorking using seven bloodlines to get his beast, which he called the Plymouth Rock. It was speckled dark brown with tips of gold on the feathers. Bennet believed he had invented a chicken by which all others would be judged. Unfortunately, it vanished from the scene, only to be replaced in 1868 by another Plymouth Rock developed by B. A. Upham of Worcester, Massachusetts. It looked more like the Barred (horizontally striped) Plymouth Rock chicken known today. This time careful breeding kept the line intact.

the Brooklyn Bridge were drawn of hens and their rooster mates. Some are worth a fortune today. The illustrations standardized the appearance of poultry, the new goal of breeding.

Like gourmands seeking the latest ingredient, poultry breeders sought cutting edge chicken exotica. Huge Cochin chickens from China caught the attention of Queen Victoria, whose interest initiated a global chicken mania. Americans were interested in the bushy Brahma and lovely Shanghai, breeds you see today at poultry shows all over the country.

What Is a Chicken Today?

Today's eating chicken is a bird of many other feathers, hybrids many times over. The Pioneer Seed Corn Company in Iowa came up with the first commercial chicken in 1942, the Hyline. Whatever else may be bred into them, all commercial chickens bear the bloodlines of Cornish chickens from England crossed with those of the White Rock.

As a form of technology, chicken production is right up there with the automobile. It supplies 20 billion dollars' worth of reliable and inexpensive food nearly around the clock. The formulas that predetermine fast growth and heavy meat are the intellectual property of poultry firms traded on the stock exchange.

There is no sign that the popularity of chicken will slow any time soon. Not even intermittent salmonella scares have daunted the demand for *Gallus domesticus*. In survey after poll after questionnaire, we say chicken is healthy, nutritious, cheap, a source of quality protein, tastes good, and is easy to cook. Considering the chicken doesn't fly, isn't very predatory, and is the butt of jokes, it turns out something of a winner and has been since those days back in the jungle. The difference is that today the chicken has won over that modern jungle we call the marketplace.

RHODE ISLAND RED

It's not in guidebooks. It's not on the map. And it's not on the Internet under "Rhode Island points of interest." But here I was, all the way from California to one of Rhode Island's southern fingers, to see for myself America's only monument to the chicken.

I'd read about the Chicken Monument in the poultry chapter of *The L. L. Bean Book of New New England Cookery* by Judith and Evan Jones. They'd located it in Adamsville. My imagination constructed a town center whose fulcrum was a tower topped by a sculpted chicken, or at the very least a fancy weathervane. If I got a snapshot of it maybe my editors would let me use it on the jacket of this cookbook.

With camera, notebook, and six-year-old son, I went there for myself.

Prior to 1900, Adamsville, today a lovely tree-shaded hamlet in the area known as Little Compton, was the Poultry Capital of the World. At the town's only intersection, the cross-roads of Main Street and Westport Harbor Road, is the Abraham Manchester Restaurant & Tavern built in the 1820s by the great-great-uncle of Franklin D. Roosevelt. I went inside to ask for directions because I hadn't encountered a single monument.

"I've come from California," I said, almost apologizing, "to find the monument to the chicken." The bartender pointed out the window in the direction of a big rock across the street. "That's it, right out there."

The term crestfallen couldn't fully underline our disappointment at this . . . this . . . rock. Washington, Jefferson, Lincoln: those are monuments. The one we'd found looked more like a prairie tombstone. We'd gone right by it because it was behind home plate of the Adamsville baseball diamond.

In 1925, a bronze plaque with a plumed chicken embossed into the center was nailed into the rock. The inscription on it reads:

> To commemorate the birthplace of the Rhode Island Red breed of fowl which originated near this location. Red fowls were bred extensively by the farmers of this district and later named "Rhode Island Red" and brought into national prominence by the poultry fanciers.
>
> This tablet is placed by the Rhode Island Red Club of America.
>
> With contributions of Rhode Island breeders throughout the world.
>
> On land donated by Deborah T. Manchester.
>
> 1925.

For thirty years this rock reigned as the primary tribute to the Rhode Island Red. But in 1954, the Little Compton area celebrated the centennial anniversary of the area's chicken. There were the usual clambakes, but this time a fit of minutiae forged a second monument a few miles away at Sisson Road and Long Highway, where oral historians say the Rhode Island Red really was hatched. Shortly after that, the Rhode Island Red officially became the state bird.

Pickin' Chicken

Hormones have not been fed to chickens for more than thirty-five years. Meat birds are never grown in cages. The recipes in this book were tested using conventionally raised grocery-store chickens. My decision to do this was based on the predictability that the chickens in a store near you will be of a similar quality—packaged fresh, hopefully never frozen, probably not as flavorful as a fresh-killed chicken from the country, but tender and assuredly up to the job. Price was also a factor. From time to time, when money was no object, I used a previously frozen Empire Kosher chicken or a free-range organic bird such as the Rocky the Range chicken from Petaluma, California.

No matter which chicken you use, the recipes will hold up. You can interchange grocery-store chicken, free-range chicken, organic chicken, kosher chicken, or even a chicken that's been previously frozen (by you). When recipes for stock call for a stewing hen (or chicken), it's because this older fowl yields a highly flavorful stock. It's not a rule, however. You can make delicious stock using a regular broiler-fryer.

What to Look For

On the East Coast, including the Delmarva Peninsula and throughout the Southeast, chickens are slaughtered smaller, with whole broiler-fryers weighing in at about three and a half pounds. Birds of the same designation on the West Coast are a little larger, ranging from three-and-a-half to four pounds plus.

Chickens should have more breast than leg and no blood spots or bruises. A whole bird should be short, not stretched out like a vaudevillian rubber chicken. If you're buying breasts, look for plump ones and avoid overly pointed ones. If fat globules are yellow, the chicken ate corn.

Look for chicken that's fresh and plump, that doesn't smell spoiled, and that is not sitting in bloody liquid. Chicken sells so quickly that turnover keeps our supply naturally fresh. If you have doubts, check the label for a freshness date.

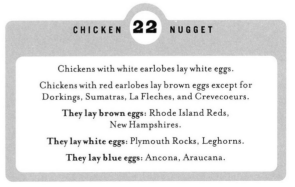

CHICKEN **22** NUGGET

Chickens with white earlobes lay white eggs.

Chickens with red earlobes lay brown eggs except for Dorkings, Sumatras, La Fleches, and Crevecoeurs.

They lay brown eggs: Rhode Island Reds, New Hampshires.

They lay white eggs: Plymouth Rocks, Leghorns.

They lay blue eggs: Ancona, Araucana.

Why name a chicken after a presumption of a cooking technique?

Before the 1930s, when hens stopped laying eggs they were summarily slaughtered and eaten. For the cook, the tacit understanding was that this bird was old and would require long stewing to make it tender.

By the 1940s, genetic selection began to breed chickens that grew fast and could be slaughtered young. Language was needed to alert cooks that these new young, tender chickens were different from those old laying hens.

Labeling a chicken a "fryer" or "broiler" implied that it was young enough to stay succulent if fried or broiled. In other words, the cook could bypass stewing, shaving hours off the usual journey to doneness.

Today, "broiler-fryer" is used interchangeably with "broiler" and "fryer" for a commercial chicken raised until it's 48 to 50 days old and weighs $3\frac{1}{2}$ to $4\frac{3}{4}$ pounds.

Labels Made Easy

Chickens get their label designations based on a number of elements, among them age at slaughter, weight at slaughter, sex, whether a male's been castrated, and whether a female is still laying eggs. Recent terminology takes the name of a cooking technique appropriate for a particular bird.

Chicken Terminology

Broiler Chick raised to 48 to 50 days old, the commercial chicken sold in stores, weighing $3\frac{1}{2}$ to $4\frac{3}{4}$ pounds.

Broiler-Fryer Another name for a standard broiler, above.

Broiler, Fast-Food Size Chick raised to about 42 days old, weighing $2\frac{1}{4}$ to slightly more than 3 pounds.

Broiler-Roaster Female chicks raised to 55 days old, weighing 5 to 6 pounds (see also Stewing Chicken).

Capon A castrated male chicken that's made the ultimate sacrifice for juiciness and is less than 15 weeks old.

Cockerel Male chicken less than a year old, after which it becomes a cock or rooster.

Cutlet Common East Coast term for boneless chicken breast, minus the tenderloin.

Fillet Boneless chicken breast minus the tenderloin.

Fryer Another name for a standard broiler, above.

Fowl A bird, but if the context is chickens implies an older female (see Spent Fowl).

Free-Range No regulations exist to govern the term "free range." The free-range chicken farmer is in a no-man's-land of self-determination, much like organic farmers were before certification programs were in place. Free range means the birds can go outside rather than remain enclosed in a brooder. Most free-range chickens are also raised organically (see Organic), although not all are.

Hen See Stewing Chicken.

Kosher The chickens reputed to have the best flavor are those raised and slaughtered according to Jewish dietary law. Empire Kosher of Liberty, New York, the largest kosher poultry plant in the world, won a number of chicken taste tests conducted by *New York* magazine and *Cook's* magazine. To be kosher, a chicken must be checked by a rabbi to make sure its vital organs are healthy. Slaughter is quick and painless and performed by hand. Because eating blood is forbidden, the blood in the birds is drained. Then the birds are soaked in a continual flow of cold water before being hand-salted. After draining again, the salt is rinsed away. These chickens are shipped frozen.

Natural A vague term whose minimum federal standard at this writing means only that chickens are grown with no artificial flavoring, coloring, or chemical preservatives and are minimally processed. It is legally possible to grow a "natural" chicken that has been fed antibiotics. Petaluma Poultry Processors, which produces the Rocky the Range and Rocky Jr. chickens, has proposed a set of stricter standards for natural chickens to the United States Department of Agriculture (USDA): no antibiotics, a diet of corn and soybeans (no animal fat or by-products), uncrowded living spaces in natural daylight, the ability to roam free, and humane handling.

Organic Chicken raised on a diet of certified organically grown feed.

Poussin French term for chicken no more than 24 days old and weighing 1 pound or less.

Pullet Female chicken, less than a year old, that lays eggs.

Roaster A standard broiler raised until it's 7 weeks old.

NOT A CHICKEN

Guinea fowls, which are native to Africa and were brought to Europe by the Portuguese in the Middle Ages, are closer kin to the pheasant. They have been seen a lot lately on trendy restaurant menus that cater to folks who like their delicate meat and vague wild flavor.

Spent Fowl Hens past egg-laying age that either came from breeder flocks or laid table eggs.

Stewing Chicken (or Hen) A female chicken about 15 months old, weighing 5 to 5½ pounds.

Suprême A boneless chicken breast that may or may not have the big wing bone attached. You don't find this interpretation of suprême in American stores, so you'll have to ask a butcher to do it for you, or do it yourself. It's a nice cut because the wing sticks up and acts like a little handle.

Tenderloin A long piece of meat that runs under the breast and may detach by itself, used to make chicken "tenders."

Parts Is Parts

Compared to the ten breakdown pieces for beef that yield more than forty retail cuts, a chicken has four anatomical areas with names that associate easily to human structure—breasts, wings, thighs, and legs.

About 50 percent of American chicken shoppers buy cut-up birds. It is surprising that with the popularity of whole roasted chicken at restaurants and in magazines, only 10 percent buy chickens whole. The remaining chicken purchases are for further processed parts, such as wings, thighs, or legs only. The most popular part is chicken breasts with bones and skin.

Does a Chicken Have One or Two Breasts?

One anatomical breast, yes, spread across the comparable area where a human has two breasts. The chicken's breast when whole is a delicious heart-shaped piece of meat, but it's almost always halved for selling.

For purposes of counting servings in this book, let's say that the chicken has two breasts. In recipes, I've shelved the clumsy "2 chicken breast halves" and opted for "2 chicken breasts." When the whole breast is requested, and it isn't very often here or in real life, I call for "1 whole chicken breast."

WHAT'S A PAILLARDE?

The use of the term *paillarde* on trendy West Coast menus gave the impression that a new chicken part had been discovered—the pay-yard. The term began at Paillard, a Parisian restaurant, named for its owner. Paillard's kitchen pounded veal thinly, what we'd call scaloppine. The locals began calling any thin veal scalloped a *paillarde*. Pounding chicken flat has the same tenderizing and even-cooking effects that the procedure has on veal. Chicken is more popular than veal. Now it's looking more understandable. Paillarde of chicken, therefore, implies the scaloppine treatment. It also avoids the word *breast*.

CHICKEN **40** NUGGET

Why Is a Rooster Called a Cock?

The answer is just what your dirty little mind is thinking, as Page Smith in *The Chicken Book* explains. Old Teutonic came up with *kok,* referring to the cluck the male bird makes. But in many languages, the word for male chicken is the word for penis. Cock is from the Anglo-Saxon for penis. During the Victorian era, Americans opted for the term *rooster* except in references to those fighting chickens.

WHOLE BREAST

If you can get the bones out of a whole breast, it makes a lovely heart-shaped roast. Or you can pound it just until it's an even thickness, roll it with a filling to look something like a pork loin, and roast on a rack at 350°F for about 45 minutes.

Buying the Chicken

My advice for buying a chicken is no different than it would be for buying clothing, cars, or bedding. *Buy the chicken on sale.* I couldn't have afforded to test all the recipes in this book without a certain, um, economic strategy. I watched the ads, bought chickens in bulk, cut them up at home, and froze them until my freezer looked like it was ready for retail!

A couple of weeks after Easter, when all the ham, ribs, and pork loins are sold, chicken comes in like a lion. Ten pounds of chicken could cost less than 10 dollars. Thighs may drop to 50 cents a pound. Wings priced lower than 40 cents a pound are a good choice for the family picnic. Unless chickens are having a bad year, low-price specials should last all summer and, in good weather, well into fall.

CORNISH GAME HEN

This little single-serving chicken is sometimes called a Rock Cornish game hen, Cornish game hen, Rock-Cornish Cross, or just game hen. There is nothing gamy about this chicken, except a game of words.

The USDA says a poultry product labeled Cornish must show that the bloodline carries true Cornish chicken from England somewhere in the heritage. The product began by crossing Cornish chickens with chickens of Plymouth Rock or White Rock bloodlines. Their small size is due to slaughtering at a youngish one month old.

Today, all major commercial chickens have Cornish and White Rock in them. Sorry to disappoint, but the game hen is just a chicken snatched from the brooder young—sort of what a baby carrot is to a carrot left in the ground until it's big. That's why chicken growers can raise chicks to 28 days old and call it a Cornish or a Rock hen.

The term *game* is confusing. A protected enclosed brooder isn't exactly the wilds, but the Cornish line was known as a game bird. As to the term *hen,* it's the default sex for chickens so sexually immature that it makes little difference in the tenderness of their meat. Game hens aren't even raised sex-separate. If the little "hen" were allowed to live another couple of weeks, "she" may, in fact, have become a rooster.

Some companies that have large Cornish hen programs, such as Perdue and Foster Farms, breed special chickens that fatten in 30 days, then continue with the rest of the flock until they've grown to fryer or roaster size.

CHICKEN **37** NUGGET

The English call the wishbone "merrythought." Breaking the wishbone is the origin of the term "lucky break."

Storing Chicken

So, you've located the chicken and brought it home. What comes next?

How to Cut Up Your Own Chicken

Mom used to cut up her own chickens. She did it over the kitchen sink. She learned to do this back in New Jersey when there was no other option. In those days you had to do everything to a chicken except kill it. She got used to the way the pieces were cut. When we moved to Texas, she disliked the local method of cutting the breast with part of the back still attached. She continued to cut her own birds even after she began to patronize Tony Haddad, one of the finest butchers in all of Texas, as she bought a month's worth of beef, lamb, veal, and poultry at one time. Mr. Haddad finally convinced her that he was able to do the job the way she preferred and for no extra charge.

Today's reasonably priced cut-up retail chicken is the best argument I can make for never having to cut up a chicken at home. However, when the price of *whole* chickens drops unbelievably low, it's worth your time to cut a couple of birds yourself.

There are many techniques for chopping up a chicken. The French slice. The Chinese hack. I do a little of both.

1 Take your time. Have ready a large cutting board, a paring knife, and a cleaver. If the chicken is slippery, hold on with a paper towel, which you can throw away after you're done.

2 Slit the skin between the thigh-drumstick and the body, then bend the thigh back until it cracks. Snip the one—and only—tendon that's holding the thigh in place. Keep bending back until the thigh piece comes free. Repeat on the other side.

3 Go to the wing. There's a low spot between the wing and the cavity opening. (To help you know what it feels like, finger it on *yourself* between your shoulder and neck.) Once located on the bird, slice through the area with the paring knife. Repeat for the other wing.

4 You're down to the body. Hold the body upright and hack out the back bones with a cleaver.

5 You're down to the whole breast. Skin up, hack through the center with the cleaver. If you like, hack the breasts in half crosswise.

6 Save extra skin, fat, and bones for stock.

Boning Raw Chicken Breasts

Complete this a few times and you'll figure out the anatomy of a half breast. Look, I don't love to do this. After years of boning my own chicken breasts I'd rate my skill as average. This level is good enough for any economy-minded home cook, too.

1 Have the pieces very cold. Use your fingers to slip between the bones and flesh.

2 Use a paring knife and hands to free the flesh.

3 Motto: Keep your eye on the bone; don't worry about the meat. Follow the bone and your chicken breast will come free.

4 When you hit a tendon—and you will, it's at the shoulder end—pick up a paring knife and cut it. With that barricade out of the way, you're clear again to finish the job.

Remember, chicken begins to dry out *when the skin and bones are removed*. The best practice is to remove skin from the cooked piece at the table. The second best is to skin and/or bone the chicken moments before you cook it.

Boning Cooked Chicken Breasts

Here's the trick to get juicy boneless chicken breasts for the cheaper price of buying them bone-in.

1 Cook them as you like—baked, for example.

2 When done, place one on a cutting board. Holding on with a towel or potholder, aim a knife at the thick side and follow the bone, cutting as you go (see Boning Raw Chicken Breasts, left).

3 Again, keep your eye on the bone; don't worry about the meat. Soon you'll have before you a plump chicken breast with the flavor benefit of having been cooked with the bone and the dining delight of eating it without the bone.

Boning an Entire Chicken

First cut up the chicken (see How to Cut Up Your Own Chicken, page 23). Next, bone the breasts (see Boning Raw Chicken Breasts, this page). Use a sharp paring knife to edge between the meat and bones of each thigh, then use knife and hands to free the meat completely. Use the paring knife to cut through the drumstick, down to the bone. Pull or scrape off meat. Repeat for wings. Use fingers to remove meat from the two small bones in each wing.

Grinding Chicken

Chicken Burgers (page 93) use ground breast meat. Chicken and Rice Stuffed in Grape Leaves (pages 120–121) uses ground dark meat. A number of other recipes use a blend of white and dark.

The blended product is easy to buy at the poultry case in your grocery store, but you can also "grind" chicken quickly at home in a food processor or by hand. Two or three breasts, depending on size, will yield about three cups.

To use a food processor, place up to 2 pounds rough-cut chicken pieces in the work bowl. Pulse until coarsely chopped. Overprocessing will turn the meat into a paste. To grind by hand, mince the boned chicken meat as you would an onion, using a large chef's knife and rocking it up and down over the meat until it's coarsely chopped.

Refrigerating Chicken

To store just-purchased chicken in the refrigerator, keep in its grocery-store packaging. If it's wrapped only in butcher paper, put it in a zip-style plastic bag or wrap it in plastic wrap. Place it on the lowest shelf—your refrigerator's coldest area—where it will keep for 1 to 2 days.

Freezing Chicken

Here's how to freeze chickens: Buy a waterproof marker pen and keep it in your kitchen. You must label, label, label! Write what chicken part is inside the wrapping and the date. For parts, use high-quality vapor-proof zip-style freezer bags. Squish out all excess air as you lock the top. Or, double wrap in plastic wrap. Freeze whole chickens in their grocery store packaging or in large, tightly sealed freezer bags. Stack the pack-

ages in the freezer. Packed like this, you'll have less bulk than if you kept it in its grocery-store packaging.

Once frozen in zip bags, chicken is easy to defrost. Open the bag and thaw in your microwave oven on the defrost setting. Or open partially, set the bag in a bowl to catch melting ice crystals, and allow to thaw in the refrigerator. If you're in a hurry, soak the chicken in its bag in lukewarm water for twenty to thirty minutes. Use the thawed chicken within a few hours.

A previously frozen chicken cooks nicely except for one bizarre thing—the bones turn red.

Storage Expectations for Carefully Wrapped Chicken

	Refrigerator	Freezer
Ground chicken	1 to 2 days	3 to 4 months
Chicken parts	1 to 2 days	9 months
Whole chicken	1 to 2 days	1 year

Bucket of Bones

In your freezer is a 2-quart plastic container with a tight-fitting lid. It is for freezing ragged pieces of raw chicken, bones, skin, and gizzards (but not livers) to use in making chicken stock. You're not likely to pack neatly, so a large bucket is necessary to allow for the wasted space between bones.

From the Chicken Folk Medicine Chest

Chicken broth from a young cock stops dysentery.

Broth from an old bird ends constipation.

Chicken fat as first-aid cream heals
ears and cures chapped lips.

Windpipes cures bed-wetting.

Brains rubbed on infant gums encourages teething.

Cocks' testicles stimulate lust, but ground up in water
are an antidote to epilepsy.

Whenever you have spare parts for whatever reason, it is a simple matter to open the container, add the pieces (no wrapping necessary), close the cover, and store nearly a year after when you started.

Yes, the quality of chicken deteriorates in the freezer. But bones and odds and ends won't give away their frozen heritage after hours of soup making (see Hacked Essence, page 46).

Once the bucket is full, you've got enough for a batch of Gelatinous Chicken Stock (page 47). If you can't make stock at this time, begin filling another bucket.

To Use the Bucket of Bones

In the microwave: Defrost uncovered in the microwave on the Defrost setting long enough for the bones to glide easily out of the bucket and into your stock pot.

In water: Defrost covered in a large bowl of cold tap water until the bones glide easily out of the bucket and into your stockpot.

Once in the stockpot, cover the bones with 4 to 6 quarts of water and bring to a simmer over medium heat. Skim off the scum and proceed with the above-mentioned recipes as directed.

TOUCH TEST

Everyone has a "doneness detector" on their body. Compare the feel of the breasts or thighs as they cook to the feel of the pad under your thumb. First, with your left hand, make the okay sign. The pad under the thumb will feel like meat cooked medium, fine for beef but not for chicken. The breasts will reach this touch stage when they're about half cooked. Now, touch your thumb to your pinkie. The pad under the thumb is taut. This is the comparative touch test for thoroughly cooked chicken breasts.

For breasts, use the thumb-to-pinkie touch test or juices-run-clear test. For a whole chicken, make sure the juices in the "crotch" between the thigh and body run clear, or a meat thermometer inserted in the inside of the thigh away from the bone registers 175° to 180°F. For other parts, use the juices-run-clear test.

Cooking Chicken

It's just a guess, but ever since the first cookbook was published in Italy just seventeen years before Columbus discovered America, cookbooks have contained more recipes for chicken than for any other source of protein. Unable to be eaten raw, chicken begs methods for getting it cooked.

Turning out white meat that's cooked but still juicy and dark meat cooked without overcooking the white meat—in the event that the two are being handled together—is a challenge unique to cooking chicken.

The flesh of chicken is muscle tissue. The muscle is about 75 percent water, 20 percent protein, and up to 5 percent fat. Bundles of muscle fibers are held together by connective tissue. The less connective tissue, the more tender the bird.

The differences between dark and white meat are anatomical. Dark meat—the drumsticks and thighs—has more connective tissue because these parts are the chicken's most active. Dark meat takes a little longer to cook and has more fat, which makes it juicy. White meat is quite lean and cooks quickly but is drier and has less flavor.

Most chickens are so young at the time of slaughtering that the dark meat's connective tissue hasn't matured enough to be tough. Ironically, free-range chickens, because of their activity, usually have more connective tissue, the trade-off for freedom.

When Is It Done?

No discussion about cooking any chicken, whole or cut-up, in this book or in general, can proceed without some dissonance on doneness. The government says chicken is safe if its internal temperature is 185°F on an instant-read thermometer. This isn't a law. And good thing. It's the opinion of people who like a juicy chicken that one cooked to 185°F is a mighty well-done bird.

The USDA's high recommended finishing temperature is the result of outbreaks of salmonella that originated in contaminated raw poultry. Salmonella organisms are destroyed when heated to 160°F and held at that temperature, or higher, for three minutes. While such organisms are destroyed at 160°F, the juices in the chicken will still be pink and the meat by no means cooked through. The good news for home cooks is that you will automatically prepare chicken that arrives at a finishing temperature high enough to kill microbial invaders if you simply cook it until the juices run clear.

Be reassured that the juices won't be clear until the breast meat registers between 170°F to 175°F and dark meat is around 175°F to 180°F. These temperatures produce breast meat that's succulent and white and dark meat that's rich and juicy, as well as safe.

"The Lord was inconsistent. Chickens should have been boneless to begin with."

—Chris Kimball, editor, *Cook's Illustrated* magazine

Whole Chicken

The obvious problem in cooking a whole chicken is that the requirements for doneness are different for breast meat and dark meat. The breast meat could dry out before the dark meat is done.

I'm sure you've seen recipes where the chicken is turned, flipped, flopped, and rotated to correct the dreaded overcooking of breast meat while it waits for the dark meat to catch up. Are these chickens juicier and more evenly cooked than a bird thrown in the oven and left there to react to heat in its own way in its own time?

The most exhaustive testing on this issue was performed by the staff of *Cook's Illustrated* magazine. The magazine's editor, Christopher Kimball, says yes. He came up with two methods. Both involve frequent intervention by the cook. Both also call for the cavity to remain unstuffed to allow air to circulate and to inspire the chicken to cook faster. And to prevent soggy skin, neither one permits basting.

Kimball's first method uses a constant 375°F throughout the roasting, but turning is crucial to insure that the thighs and breast are done at the same time. Required operating equipment are oven mitts (which will need washing that day), tongs, or many thicknesses of paper towels, or all three. The secret is to preheat the roasting pan, then set a buttered chicken seasoned with salt and pepper into the hot pan, placing the bird on one of its sides. Roast the first side for 20 minutes, turn the bird onto its other side for another 20 minutes, and then finish breast up for 20 to 25 minutes longer.

His other method avoids turning. The thighs are face up the entire time so their juices flow down and bathe the breast meat. This method uses low-temperature roasting after an initial high-heat booster to give the thighs a head start. Put the bird in at 400°F for about 20 minutes, then reduce the heat to 200°F and leave it there for about 1 hour. When the hour is over, the thighs should have cooked to the same playing field as the breasts. Finally, turn the temperature back up to 400°F to crisp the skin and finish the bird.

VERTICAL CHICKEN

Max Shulman, the author and comedic creator of the 1950s television series Dobie Gillis (and dad of my pal, Martha), was in a Los Angeles restaurant with the family looking at a menu that had a dish called Vertical Chicken.

Everyone at the table wondered, "What is a Vertical Chicken?" Max knew. "It's the one that got across the road."

Another way to roast a whole chicken is vertically. With a prong stuck up its cavity and its drumsticks down, the chicken appears to be standing. Heat flows around the bird to crisp all surfaces without having to flip it by hand. The fat under the skin melts and gravity gratefully directs it down and out into the baking dish.

New thought rearranges the chicken on the vertical roaster "butt" up (drumsticks on top), so juices from the dark meat can bathe the white meat during cooking. I tried both positions with equal trade-offs. With drumsticks up, the breast meat was juicy. With drumsticks down, the breast meat dried out but the skin got deliciously crisp.

My roasting setup is simple. It dispatches the chicken to its oven hiding place with little involvement from the cook. Set the chicken, breast up, on a rack inside a roasting pan. I like the effects of a rack because it allows heat to flow under those hard-to-cook thighs. I like the breast up so rack marks don't disfigure the sheen of the skin. Roast at 400°F for 15 to 20 minutes. Turn the heat down to 350°F and leave it there until the chicken is done, about 60 to 70 minutes longer. The juices should run clear between the thigh and the body. No turning, no flipping. But it's tasty and done.

Before we leave the whole chicken, remember that you don't have to roast it. A number of whole chickens in this book are "pot roasted" in a covered pot on top of the stove or in the oven. The bird might be seared first over high heat to give the skin some color, but all will be moistened by liquid such as stock, wine, or cider. It's easy to add vegetables or herbs to the in-progress chicken to make an easy one-pot meal. Such wet cooking prevents both the chicken and vegetables from drying out.

Cut-up Chicken

My dream bird is a flat-chested chicken with four legs. I've never been a white-meat type, not even as a kid. Our entire family—nuclear and most of the extended—lunged for drumsticks and thighs like a game of musical chicken parts.

Many, many, many years went by—and I mean *many*—and I got married. I noticed at restaurants that my husband-to-be was competing with me for the dark meat. Fourteen months after our wedding we had a son, who by age four became so swift at diving for dark meat that now I mostly buy hindquarters on sale. My husband, a Chinese chef, confirms that dark meat is what the Chinese call "good eating." The implied compliment is, if you like dark meat, you know good food.

I'll eat breasts, sure, preferably sautéed in butter or prepared by any of the recipes using chicken breasts in this book. I guarantee them all because they passed my own "juice detector."

Techniques That Cook Great Chicken

Any cooking technique ever invented can be used on cut-up chickens. The possibilities take us to combinations of white and dark meat, or to the cooking of white meat only or dark meat only.

When cooking a whole cut-up chicken, there are ways to outwit the white meat's tendency to finish first. If grilling, add breasts to the grill 10 minutes after the dark meat has started. (For ease, marinate the meats in two separate zip-style plastic bags.) If baking, start the breasts and dark meat at the same time, but remove the breasts earlier. If braising on top of the stove, the difference between the two meats isn't as critical. I find that if breasts sit in a lot of liquid, they turn out juicy even if they are cooked as long as the dark pieces. Still, James Beard liked to plop the breasts on top of the dark meat during the covered stage, which you can do if you've got a domed lid. Or you can nestle the breasts into a braised recipe a few minutes after the dark meat has begun to cook.

My favorite method for cooking chicken is stovetop braising. It combines sauté (see page 35) and boil (rather, its subsidiary "simmer") and dominates most of the recipes in this book. I call it . . .

Frickin' Chickassee

Of all the heat-bearing methods that have ever cooked chicken, the most versatile is the backbone of fancy menus, the mainstay of dinner houses, and one of the better habits at my house. Oh yes, it always makes its own sauce. Unfortunately, it doesn't have a name. But it's a revered process that deliciously cooks chicken all over the world, particularly in India, France, Spain, Hungary, Italy, China, and Southeast Asia.

It goes like this: The chicken pieces are sautéed in hot fat until browned. (They may be floured or not.) The pieces are temporarily taken from the pan in order for chicken stock or wine (or coconut milk, et cetera) to go in. This liquid sizzles and the pan's bottom is scraped with a spatula to get all the stuck-on chicken bits integrated into a rapidly forming sauce. Ultimately, the chicken goes back in the pan and cohabits with the sauce and new ingredients— tomatoes, mushrooms, potatoes, whatever.

The pan is covered and the chicken simmers over low heat (or is sent to a 350°F oven). It stays in this slow, steady situation until done and sitting in its own sauce. The chicken pieces can be removed and the sauce can be boiled down until it's as thick as the cook likes.

ABOUT FLOUR

Flour coats chicken for two reasons. One is that flour coating on a piece of meat being sautéed makes a nice crust for a dimension of texture. Two is that after the chicken is long gone from the pan, floury components left behind go to work to thicken the pan juices and give the resulting sauce some body.

Flour that has seen the chicken all the way through, from high heat to boiling in liquid, from a near-dry pan to being covered and braised, and then uncovered and cooked down, has gotten in sync with the dish and its flavors. Flour added to pan juices at the end of cooking makes gravy.

An alternative technique leaves the chicken in the pan after its initial browning. Liquid is poured directly over the chicken, the "extras" are piled in—the tomatoes, mushrooms, herbs, and spices—and the chicken simmers, covered or not, until it's done.

The only term that comes close to melding sauté, simmer, and braise is fricassee. And even this is technically inaccurate.

In America, it seems nearly all chicken sautés could turn into an unwitting fricassee. An unscientific person-on-the-street interview gleaned these definitions of fricassee:

A friend: "It's that dish my mother fixed every Friday night."

Her brother: "It's made with chicken leftovers."

A culinary librarian: "It's *gedemkeh*—cooking chicken through and through."

A New England cookbook: "It's a New England favorite."

A Southern cookbook: "It's a Southern favorite."

In just one afternoon at the Schlesinger Library in Cambridge, Massachusetts, I found hundreds of recipes called chicken fricassee. Few matched. One resembled chicken à la king, with boiled chicken shredded in white sauce. Others parboiled the chicken then braised it until it formed its own sauce.

The truth is, if chicken is sautéed lightly enough so it *doesn't* color and helps the final sauce be white, that's a true French fricassee. Everything else comes under the heading Chicken Conjecture, the delicious, juicy, tender one-pan sauté-braise affairs such as Riesling-Braised Chicken with Mushrooms and Chives (page 65); Chicken Braised in Coconut Milk with Peas and Lime Juice (page 72); Chicken Curry with the First Tomatoes of Summer (pages 128–129); and Beer-Braised Chicken with Red Cabbage and Apples (pages 248–249).

THE IMPORTANCE OF A STOVE-TO-OVEN SAUTÉ PAN AND LID

After an initial browning of chicken whole or in pieces, a not-so-unusual happenstance calls for the chicken to simmer in a liquid, covered. This is easily achieved on a burner, but you can also swing the pan into a 350°F oven for a period of brainless braising, provided all the parts of your pan can go in the oven.

When I asked my mom to test recipes for me, she realized that she didn't have the proper pan. One was fine for frying, but its plastic handle would melt in the oven. Another had a handle that would survive the oven but it didn't have a lid, so she fumbled with foil to crunch it around the rim.

Poaching

Poaching is more difficult than it sounds. Not boiling, not even simmering, it occurs when chicken—usually chicken breasts—submerged by an inch of stock, water, or wine is suspended for about 15 minutes in some recondite world between a simmer and nothing.

If you don't want to struggle with the perfect poach, here are three foolproof ways to "poach" juicy chicken breasts.

Microwaved "Poached" Chicken Breasts: When you need skinned and boned chicken breasts to come out juicy and white, as they appear in Chicken and Summer-Fruit Salad (page 154) or Chicken and Winter-Fruit Salad (page 269), the best way to proceed is over to the microwave oven.

Arrange 3 to 4 chicken breasts like spokes on a microwaveproof plate, sprinkle lightly with salt, and wrap tightly with plastic wrap. Microwave on High for 5 to 8 minutes. Chop or shred for use in recipes calling for cooked breast meat.

Microwaved "Poached" Chicken Breasts in Wine and Stock: Arrange 3 to 4 chicken breasts in a microwave-proof casserole with a lid. Pour in 1 cup chicken stock and ¾ cup white wine. Sprinkle lightly with salt. Cover and microwave at 50 percent power for 20 minutes for incredibly juicy breasts. Dice and use in chicken salads or other recipes calling for cooked breast meat.

Baked "Poached" Chicken Breasts: If you don't have a microwave oven, use this caterer's trick. Arrange chicken breasts on parchment paper on a baking sheet (jelly-roll pan). Sprinkle lightly with salt. Cover with plastic wrap, then wrap snugly with aluminum foil. Bake at 350°F for 20 minutes. These come out very, very moist, virtually steamed, and stay white—perfect for chicken salads, pot pies, or enchiladas.

Boiling

It is recommended that "boil" actually be toned down to "simmer." Boiling can toughen the chicken meat. The succulent meat that results from White-Cooked Chicken (page 50) and the chicken prepared for Green Chicken Enchiladas with Monterey Jack Cheese (pages 194–195) never see the boil. On the other hand, in braising situations, the liquid does come to a boil, just before it's covered and sustained at a simmer.

Broiling

Don't broil skinned chicken. It will dry out before it's done, making for a waste of money and a fat-ridding effort of questionable intent. Broiling is the indoor equivalent of grilling. Use a rack set on a piece of aluminum foil for easy clean up, and keep the chicken about 3 inches beneath the heat element. Preheat the rack and put the chicken on it skin side down first, which results in grill marks that make it look like you cooked outdoors. Turn and finish cooking. The juiciest broiling results come from periodic basting with juices or marinade.

Grilling

The recipes in this book use three methods for grilling chicken: (1) covered on a grill over indirect heat, (2) covered on a grill over direct heat, and (3) uncovered over direct heat.

Indirect heat turns your outdoor grill into an oven. I used this method to cook Chicken Grilled in Creamy Garlic-Herb Marinade (page 90) and Herbal-Rub Dark Meat Grill (page 115), among many others. Use a covered kettle-type grill. Light the charcoal briquettes, and when they are hot and ash white, arrange them in 2 equal beds on opposite sides of the bottom of the grill (its lower rack). Place a drip pan between the beds (or make a drip pan out of crimped heavy-duty foil). Put the cooking rack in place and cover the grill. Heat it about 5 minutes to burn off the gunk stuck on the rack from the last time you grilled. Scrape the rack with a steel brush, and it's ready. (After a couple of times the rack will transform into a sort of nonstick material, like a seasoned skillet. Before then you might have to brush it with vegetable oil.) Uncover and add the chicken, which will sizzle professionally. Then cover the grill, leaving the top and bottom vents three-quarters to fully open. Inside, the temperature will hover between 350°F to 400°F, just like your oven. If the grill is too hot, close the vents a little. If the chicken isn't cooking fast enough, open the vents to let in more oxygen.

If you don't feel like separating coals into two piles, they'll work fine in a single layer delivering direct heat. Direct heat inside a covered grill is fast and hot, more like cooking in an enclosed gas broiler than in an oven. You can see this method at work in Chicken-Pancetta Rolls with Basil Leaves (page 122) or Grilled Chicken with Mopped-on Rhubarb-Butter Sauce (page 87). Spread hot, white coals in a single layer. Top with the grill rack and cover the grill. Heat for about 5 minutes to burn off gunk stuck on the rack from

the last time you grilled. Scrape it with a steel brush. Uncover, add chicken, and watch it sizzle. Cover the grill with top and bottom vents three-quarters to fully open.

Open grilling is the old brazier style of grilling. It chars food and cooks it very quickly because the fire, exposed all over to oxygen, burns very hot. It does a good job on Chicken Kebabs in Cola-Cardamom Marinade (page 114). The advantage is it's great for small or thin pieces, such as satay or kebab, that cook fast and can handle the nice caramelizing and crisping that comes with intense heat. The disadvantage is its tendency to shoot flames up to the food, which can dry out chicken. You can douse the flames with a spray bottle of water. Spread hot, white coals in a single layer. Top with the grill rack and cover the grill. Heat for about 5 minutes to burn off gunk stuck on the rack from the last time you grilled. Scrape it with a steel brush. Uncover, add chicken, and grill it, uncovered.

Things the Recipes in This Book Tell You to Do

1 Cut the breasts in half.

When all the pieces of a cut-up chicken are laid in a sauté pan or baking dish, the large breasts quite undemocratically deny the others a good spot. If cut to the relative size of the thighs, they'll cook evenly and will be easier to eat. Once on the serving platter, your chicken will seem to have bred itself a generous two extra pieces.

To hack the breast pieces in half, give them a crosswise chop with a cleaver right through the bones, skin, and all.

2 Rinse the chicken.

A chicken direct from the butcher, even one on a Styrofoam tray and wrapped well in plastic, harbors bacteria from production, human handling, and simply from being a perishable product. Most bacteria are killed during cooking. Try to avoid cross-contamination in your kitchen. Rinse the chicken well under cool running water to flush away bacteria. Wash the cutting board and knife used on the raw chicken with hot, soapy water before using them again.

3 Pat the chicken dry with paper towels.

There are two important reasons to pat rinsed chicken dry. One, dry skin browns well and won't cause hot oil or butter to spatter upon contact. Two, if you'd like to smear soft butter or oil over your chicken prior to cooking, it will slither off if the skin is wet.

After washing a whole chicken inside and out with cool running water, sop up moisture inside the cavity with a wad of paper toweling, then pat the exterior very dry, too. In testing recipes for this book, I went through more than thirty rolls of paper towels. I'd feel guilty if my town didn't have mandatory recycling. Tamping moisture off a wet chicken with a cloth towel is a bad idea. It transports bacteria and makes for a very smelly towel.

4 Salt the chicken before you cook it.

This is my book, so I get to make personal statements about salt. Before, during, or after? My answer: Possibly all three, starting with before.

The word "seasoned" implies time, not quantity (as in "seasoned actor"). I learned from Udo Nechutnys, an exceptional chef who trained with France's Paul Bocuse, that the longer salt spends with its host food, the more the flavor of the host blooms. In fact, you might use less salt if you add it early. Still, you have to taste.

In this book raw chicken is sprinkled with salt before cooking. The seasoning deepens and mellows throughout the cooking, because it's been given the advantage of time. If the chicken is dredged in flour, a generous amount of salt will be in the flour.

It is expected that you will taste your evolving recipe as soon as it's safely edible and from

phase to phase until done. Sometimes you can tell halfway through that the initial salting was plenty. As cooking nears its end, you can make the decision to add more salt or not.

Whether you add salt in small amounts throughout the cooking or all at once at the end, chances are the quantities will end up the same. The results, however, are different. When you dump in a single load, your dish is defined only in terms of salt.

5 Sauté over high heat.

Unless otherwise instructed, keep the heat high. High heat is nothing to be afraid of, and it's important for the cause-and-effect nature of sautéed food.

Sautéed over high heat, chicken browns darker and crispier to fortify a sauce that's richer and darker. Chicken sautéed in a pan not so hot ends up stewing in its own pallid juices. Do not worry that high heat will burn butter. Butter may be melted in a good heavy pan over high heat until you notice bubbling followed by a slickening. Rather than turn down the heat, add the raw chicken, whose coldness will cool the pan. Keep it cranked high so the heat that was lost as the chicken went in can recover itself quickly. The higher the heat, the faster the chicken will cook. By the time the chicken is ready to be turned, the high heat will have pulled excess fats and some juices from the skin and flesh. Take a look. Your chicken won't be sitting in just butter anymore.

Reduce the heat only if it appears that the chicken might burn. Sorry, but if you're cooking in a thin, cheap pan, it probably will.

The exception to the high-heat rule? Sauté skinned chicken over medium-high heat.

6 As a general rule, bake or roast at 350°F.

I have a caterer friend who bakes everything at 350°F (pies and cookies are obvious exceptions). Neither she nor the staff forgets what temperature to set the oven. The 350-degree rule works just about all the time for chicken, unless otherwise noted. Sometimes you'll start a roast at higher heat for deep browning. Sometimes lower heat is used for longer, slower cooking. For these recipes, if you automatically twist the dial to 350°F, you won't be far off the mark.

7 Transfer the chicken to a platter.

This means one of two things: (1) The chicken has been partially cooked and is being temporarily taken from its cooking pan and held on a platter to allow you time to fiddle with the sauce. The chicken will be returned to the pan to finish cooking in the sauce you

made. (2) The chicken has been sautéed to doneness and is being permanently removed so you can continue cooking whatever is left in the pan without overcooking the chicken. The chicken will stay hot for a good ten minutes without even being covered.

8 Warm a serving platter in a 150°F oven.

You'll appreciate the warmed platter for the cooked chicken if you're still facing the sauce step. An oven with a pilot light or an electric oven heated to 150°F is sufficiently warm for an ovenproof platter. When covering the chicken for warmth, keep it loose. A too-tight wrapping will steam the chicken. This is especially disappointing to discover after you've gone to the trouble to sauté it for the sake of nice, crispy skin.

9 Cook the vegetables.

Just because an ingredient is fresh doesn't mean it should scarcely be cooked. I'm an opponent of undercooked vegetables and of the notion that there is such a thing as an al dente potato. You are on full alert that the vegetables included with my chickens do not come from the pan in a state of faux doneness.

A Chicken in Every Pot—
and Other Equipment

"A chicken in the pot on Sunday . . ."
—Henry IV of France

Before you cook chicken, you've got to have something to cook it in.

Pots and Pans

Sauté Pan and Skillet

For my purposes, the terms sauté pan and skillet are interchangeable. Strictly speaking, the sauté pan has straight sides and the skillet has sloping ones, but they play essentially the same role: They are wide, shallow pans that can handle high heat. It's good to have an assortment of them, ranging from 8 to 12 inches in diameter.

You think I'm going to mention the chicken fryer, the deep round pan with slightly flared sides and a lid. It's not my favorite, although it does fry chicken adequately. There are two serious problems with most chicken fryers. One, they're too small to fry a whole cut-up chicken, which means you'll stand there twice as long frying in batches. And two, cheap ones have plastic parts or are made of materials that wouldn't survive a half hour in an oven, where many presautéed chickens end up. If the recipe sends the pan of browned chicken to the oven, the cook using the chicken fryer will have to transfer the chicken to a baking dish, which have to wash.

No, there is no way around it. I am going to drop names. When recipes in this book call for a "wide, heavy sauté pan," or a "wide, heavy sauté pan with a tight-fitting lid" or a "wide heavy ovenproof skillet that has a tight-fitting lid," I am speaking of one article of cookware—a Le Creuset "buffet casserole." Made in France of enamel-coated cast iron and widely available in the United States, it serves as a sauté pan, baking dish, and covered casserole.

Yes, ol' Flame (its color is red-orange) has seen me through this entire book. I am impressed that a single piece of cookware so befits the cut-up chicken yet is nice enough to show up at the table.

There are many reasons why this pan, or others like it, is the ultimate in chicken-cooking equipment. Cast iron satisfies the preference for "heavy." Because it's heavy, it heats up slowly but stays hot, warding off hot spots so cooking is even. Cast iron cooperates on top of the stove over the highest heat or in the oven at any temperature. Because of its size, you can use it for large batches of voluminous vegetables. Because it's coated with white enamel, the pan doesn't have the usual sworn enemies of black cast iron. Spinach, pears, some wines, and cream all discolor in black cast iron. By not having to transfer browned chicken to a baking dish, and by not having to again transfer it to a serving platter, I've avoided washing twice.

"A chicken in every pot..."
—Herbert Hoover, during the 1932 GOP campaign
(which he lost)

As to the shape, the buffet casserole looks like a squat wok or a Dutch oven with the sides cut down. Many lines of cookware produce similarly designed pans that go by the following names: all-around pan, paella pan, international skillet, everyday pan, bistro pan, *sauteuse* (the classic French pan with straight rather than sloping sides). Whatever the name, look for a round pan at *least* twelve inches wide and two inches deep with two loop handles (rather than one long handle). It should be made of thick material and hold three quarts.

Avoid nonstick surfaces. Sticking is good—not ruination. Any particles that stick to the surface of a sauté pan or baking vessel are easily loosened by adding liquid, which when boiled literally will melt the bits away. In turn, the stuck-on bits will add flavor and color to your emerging sauce. Without those bits your sauce will be lifeless. You just can't get them using a nonstick pan.

Dutch Oven

This is the pot you'll use for making chicken chili and stew or for browning a whole chicken. You can also use it for "pot roasting" a whole chicken. It holds five to eight quarts and has small grasping handles on either side, and a tight-fitting lid. Sometimes it's called a French oven. New shapes and terms are replacing the Dutch oven of old, and you might consider items variously called chef's pan, with more rounded sides, or sauce pots, starting at about three and a half quarts.

Stockpot

A true stockpot always is taller than it is wide. A nonstick lining is useless in a stockpot. So, too, is an expensive rendition in copper. All you need is a sturdy stainless steel boiling pot, which will be a modestly priced lifetime buy. Look for eight- to twelve-quart sizes. Avoid plain aluminum. I used an aluminum stockpot for twenty years before I switched to stainless steel, but I've forgotten why. (Oh yes, the Alzheimer's connection.)

Steamer

If you don't have a designated steamer or a steamer inset that fits into a large pot, it's easy to rig up your own steamer. Here are three options: (1) Make a tower of 2 bamboo steamers lined with heavy-duty foil that you've pinched back in 4 places each to create steam "chimneys." Set the tower in a wok filled with a couple inches of water. Rather than cover the wok, cover the top basket. (2) Place a big bowl on a ring fashioned from a tuna fish can. Set the apparatus in a large pot filled with a few inches of water. (3) Place a wide, shallow-lipped plate on a rack set inside a large wok with a well-fitted cover. Fill the wok with a couple inches of water.

Roasting Pan (aka Baking Dish)

If you have only one, make it of a material that can go from stove to oven and back again—not glass (unless it's the Corning flameproof type) and especially not ceramic. I suggest stainless steel. Ceramic looks beautiful from oven to table but will shatter if placed on a burner to make sauce. Often after you've roasted a chicken, the pan holding the drippings (which hopefully have stuck) ends up over direct flame for the sauce step. If you've roasted in glass, the pan juices must be transferred to another pot. Not only do you lose the precious cooked particles in the transition, but you've got another pot to wash. A reasonable dimension for a roasting pan is nine by thirteen inches with sides no higher than about one and a half inches. It can also be round (for instance, the buffet casserole, page 37, minus its lid).

Broiler Pan

The one that came with your oven broiler is fine, with this caveat. To minimize clean up, line it with foil, set a cake cooling rack on top of the foil, preheat the rack inside the broiler, then add the chicken, skin side down. The chicken pieces will get nice grill marks as if grilled outdoors.

Chicken-Cooking Gadgets, Utensils, and Tools

Rack

I prefer the horizontal chicken, breast up so rack marks don't disfigure it. The bird roasts whole sitting tall, elevated out of the depth of its roasting pan. It's even better if the chicken completely clears the sides of the pan. The obvious reason is that heat can get way down on the bottom of the bird to speed the cooking of the dark meat and crisp the skin. Fats drip below the rack to be discarded or used at will in sauce. It's also easy to lift the rack out of the pan, chicken and all, in order to situate late-arriving vegetables underneath.

A rack can also be made of a bed of sturdy cut vegetables, as I did in the recipe for Thanksgiving Chicken (pages 204–206). Wedges of onion and chunks of carrot and celery strewn on the bottom give the chicken about an inch lift out of the pan.

Vertical Roaster

The most famous brand is the Spanek, which at 15 dollars for a couple of stiff soldered rods deserves to have cheap imitations, which it has in countless configurations, some of which flop over. (See page 29.)

Baster

Not really necessary, but nice to have instead of a spoon when the basting urge hits.

Knives

Sharp paring knife For boning chicken breasts or entire chickens, and for nicking tendons that get in the way while separating bone from flesh.

Extremely sharp chef's knife It should be long enough to extend two inches on either side of a chicken, so get one that's eight to ten inches long. Over time, the heat from the hot chicken will dull the blade. The sharpest knife I've ever owned is a Chinese knife (but not a true cleaver) autographed by Martin Yan. It cuts through the skin of raw chicken without pulling, slipping, or a hint of hesitation. Ironically, a knife this sharp is not for hacking the chicken into pieces through the bones. Hacking is a job for a heavy cleaver.

Heavy cleaver For hacking raw chicken through the bones into bite-sized pieces (also works for cooked chicken pieces). A good cleaver is heavy, and weighted just right for landing hard.

Cutting Board

Raw chicken is best handled on a cutting board rather than directly on countertops, because it's easier to get a cutting board clean of microorganisms with hot, soapy water, preferably in a dishwasher. I prefer space-age white plastic formations over wood precisely because such a material can go in the dishwasher. Food safety experts advise two cutting boards, one for meats, the second for everything else. In practice, I lose track and yank out whatever's handy, but always wash it very well.

You'll want a large wooden or plastic board with a trough around the rim to catch juices for cooked chicken, whether a whole roasted bird that needs a rest or just-sautéed breasts. The captured juices can be poured over the chicken to moisten it, or added to an in-progress sauce.

Lid

A slightly domed lid is good for covering chicken. Some manufacturers make clear lids. Beginners and experienced cooks alike love to see what's going on inside.

Poultry Shears

Also called kitchen scissors, and if you don't have a pair, get one. Remember, if you buy a whole chicken, at some point you will have to cut it up. You might want to do this before it's cooked or after. With poultry shears, you'll have no problem cutting up your bird at either end of the cooking.

Platters

When not serving chicken in the pan it's cooked in, show it off on serving dishes of all shapes and sizes. For a great presentation of chicken breasts, slice them on the diagonal, lift the slices as if the breast were still in one piece, fan them out on an oval platter, and spoon over the juices.

Wide, shallow bowls such as pasta serving bowls make great presentations for chicken cooked in a substantial sauce. The sweeping sides capture the sauce, but the bowl is wide enough to display all the chicken pieces.

Grill Frills

If you grill chicken often, these are must-haves, aside from the grill, which I will leave to personal preference. The following are easy to find near the grill departments of any hardware store and will make grilling easier and safer.

Grill brush Scrapes and cleans up the grill rack from the last time you grilled chicken.

Oversized V-shaped roasting rack Specially made for the grill and holds a whole bird.

Pastry brush For spreading bastes and marinades onto the chicken.

Long tongs To keep you a safe distance from intense heat.

BASIC RECIPES

That Will Come in Handy

Some of the recipes in this book will call for chicken building blocks: your basic chicken stock, your basic cooked chicken, and your basic smoked chicken. Making stock from chicken or its parts can be done quickly or the slow way, as you'll see in Hacked Essence (page 46) and Gelatinous Chicken Stock (page 47). The silkiest chicken meat comes from a Chinese technique in the recipe for White-Cooked Chicken (page 50) and can be used sliced, chopped, or shredded in a variety of recipes that call for cooked chicken. And you don't have to go to the deli for smoked chicken. You can make Smoked Chicken yourself quite easily in a wok (page 48). There's nothing like shredded smoked chicken in salad, risotto, or in soups. You can even decide what culture will contribute the smoked flavor—will it be Italian, Asian, or Texan?

This quick method—taking about an hour—makes a fine all-purpose stock. By sautéing shaggy bones and then simmering them, every molecule of chicken-ness is summoned into the liquid. I adapted this process (it's not really a recipe) from one by Pam Anderson of *Cook's Illustrated* magazine. She was tipped off to it in a book by Southern cook Edna Lewis.

HACKED ESSENCE

3 pounds chicken bones
and chicken-boning discards
(see Note)

1 large onion

About 8 cups boiling water

2 teaspoons salt

$1/4$ teaspoon white pepper

1 Use a cleaver to hack up the bones into 2-inch pieces. They don't have to be perfect. Rinse the bones, then place them in a large pot.

2 Chop the onion and add it to the bones. Turn the heat to medium-high and sauté the chicken until it's somewhat browned, about 15 minutes.

3 Pour in the boiling water. Add the salt and pepper. Simmer, cover askew, for 20 to 30 minutes. Taste. If it needs more salt or pepper, add now.

4 Strain the stock through a fine-mesh sieve into a clean container; discard the contents of the sieve. If you have time, set the stock in the refrigerator to force the fat to rise quickly. Skim off and discard the fat, then use the stock as desired. Or store covered in the refrigerator up to 3 days or freeze for up to 1 year.

Makes about 2 quarts

Note: I use this recipe when I've bought whole chickens at a ridiculously low price and have set aside the time to cut them into parts to freeze for later use. I end up with gobs of backs and wing tips, plenty of base for a great stock. I've even made this quick essence from the back and wing tips from just one bird. Chicken-boning discards from other recipes include backs, the tips off wings, bits pulled out of a cavity, extra fat, and any bones from leftover roasted chicken.

Large chickens, known regionally as broiler roasters, or stewing hens if they're female, store lots of flavor in their bones. Use this rich stock for steamed rice or risotto, as a base for soups, and in high-impact sauces.

GELATINOUS CHICKEN STOCK

1 chicken, 5 to 6 pounds
2 celery stalks, cut into chunks
2 carrots, cut into chunks
1 onion, peeled but left whole
Few fresh parsley sprigs
5 or 6 black peppercorns
1 teaspoon salt, or to taste

1 Rinse the chicken and place it in a tall stockpot. Add cold water to cover by 1 inch. Bring slowly to a simmer over medium heat, uncovered. Skim off any scum as it appears.

2 When the scum gives out, add all the remaining ingredients. Simmer, cover askew, for 1½ hours.

3 Lift out the chicken and place in a colander set over a bowl to catch the juices. Let cool, then skin and debone. Return the bones, skin, and any juices to the pot.

4 Simmer the bones, uncovered, for 30 to 45 minutes longer. Taste for salt and add more, if necessary.

5 Pour the stock through a fine-mesh sieve into a clean container; discard the contents of the sieve. Let rest at room temperature for 30 minutes. Cover with foil, poke with a few holes to allow steam to escape, and refrigerate until the fat rises.

6 Lift off the fat and discard. If the stock jiggles, you've got yourself a rich, gelatinous stock. Store covered in the refrigerator for up to 3 days, or freeze for up to 1 year.

Makes 3 to 3½ quarts

Note: Some culinary authorities would say that the chicken that sacrificed itself to the production of this stock is "spent" and not worth eating. I apologize for my upbringing, but my mother turned boiled stewing hens into a decent chicken salad for my school lunch. It has never crossed my mind that the hardworking bird from this pot is anything less than food, because we always happily ate it. If you can't bear to waste it, even if it is a little dry, stringy, and tasteless (it's an old bird, right?), shred it into a cream soup, a chicken salad, or roll it up in a burrito with beans and salsa.

Many recipes use chicken as if we deliberately caused leftovers. Smoked chicken is a mainstay of the grocery-store home-meal solutions, but you can smoke your own with little fuss but lots of fireworks. Rub it with the culinary destiny you have in mind for the chicken's final use. I have provided three possibilities here.

The use of heavy-duty aluminum foil makes this a fairly neat episode. Your kitchen will—repeat, will—get smoky. Your range hood will be tested to its limits, and if your smoke alarm stays off, the hood will have earned its worth. (I don't have a hood, just windows, and am undaunted by this style of stove-top smoking.)

SMOKED CHICKEN

1 chicken, 3½ pounds

FOR THE ITALIAN-SMOKED RUB:

2 tablespoons coarse salt

½ teaspoon black pepper

1 tablespoon minced fresh rosemary

2 tablespoons olive oil

¼ cup packed dark brown sugar for smoking medium

FOR THE ASIAN-SMOKED RUB:

1 tablespoon coarse salt

1 tablespoon brown sugar

2 tablespoons soy sauce

1 tablespoon peeled and minced fresh ginger

1 tablespoon minced garlic

¼ teaspoon white pepper

2 tablespoons vegetable oil

¼ cup packed dark brown sugar and 2 star anise for smoking medium

1 Select the rub of choice. In a bowl, combine all the ingredients except the smoking medium and mix until smooth. Have ready the ingredient(s) for the smoking medium.

2 Rinse the chicken and pat dry with paper towels. Rub inside and out with the entire rub mixture. Let stand at room temperature for 1 to 2 hours to allow the flavors to penetrate.

3 Meanwhile, line a large wok with heavy-duty foil. Similarly, line the underside of the wok's lid. Don't even think about using flimsy aluminum foil. It will tear and might burn through, making a real mess.

4 On another square of foil, place the ingredient(s) for the smoking medium. Fold the packet closed but not too tightly. Place the packet in the center of the foil-lined wok. Set a steamer rack or cake cooling rack over the packet.

5 Cover the wok and preheat it on high heat. When you see and smell smoke, open the wok and place the rubbed chicken directly on the rack. Cover, reduce the heat to medium, and smoke-cook until deeply bronzed, 40 to 45 minutes.

CHICKEN **43** NUGGET

Nowhere to Go from Here—But Up

Chicken and creativity have always gone together in the kitchen, but this combination needed a little work. Here's the recipe for Chicken Cheese, from *Favorite Recipes of Good Housekeepers,* Pawtucket, Rhode Island, 1893:

Boil 6 pounds of seasoned chicken until it's very tender, chop the skin and giblets very fine, and shred the chicken. Mix in the powdered yolks of 4 hard-boiled eggs and put the chicken back in the water in which it boiled. Line a mould [sic] with the sliced whites of the eggs. Pour in the chicken and allow to harden.

FOR THE TEXAN-SMOKED RUB:

2 tablespoons coarse salt

$^1/_2$ teaspoon coarse black pepper

2 tablespoons New Mexico chile powder

$1^1/_2$ teaspoons ground cumin

$1^1/_2$ teaspoons dried oregano

2 tablespoons vegetable oil

$^1/_4$ cup packed dark brown sugar and $^1/_4$ cup dry hickory or mesquite chips (optional) for smoking medium

6 Meanwhile, preheat an oven to 400°F. When the chicken is bronzed, transfer it to a baking dish and slip it into the oven to finish cooking, about 30 minutes. (Remove the wok from the heat immediately and discard the foil lining.) The juices should run clear between the thigh and breast.

7 Using tongs, transfer the chicken to a plate. Let the chicken and its juices cool. Shred the meat from the bones and use as the recipe directs.

Makes 1 chicken

The most beautiful bird in the world is the velvety, ivory-colored result of this Chinese technique. Use the especially juicy and tender meat in chicken salads, as the succulent pieces in a pot pie, or even plain with a green vegetable and rice. It's very easy, with a certain kindness in the procedure.

WHITE-COOKED CHICKEN

1 chicken, 3¹/₂ to 4 pounds

3 celery stalks, cut into chunks

3 carrots, peeled and cut into chunks

1 large onion, or 3 leeks

Handful of fresh parsley sprigs

1 bay leaf

5 white peppercorns

2 teaspoons salt

1-inch piece fresh ginger (about 1 ounce), unpeeled (optional)

¹/₄ teaspoon white pepper

1 Place all the ingredients in a stockpot. Add cold water to cover. Bring slowly to a simmer over medium heat, uncovered. Skim off any scum as it appears.

2 Simmer (no hotter) for 15 to 20 minutes. Turn off the heat, cover, and let the chicken cool in the broth for about 2 hours.

3 Lift out the chicken and place in a colander set over a bowl to catch the juices. Let cool, then skin and debone. Shred or cut the chicken into bite-sized pieces and set aside in whatever juices have collected. The cooked chicken may be covered and stored in the refrigerator for up to 3 days or frozen in zip-style freezer bags.

4 If you want to deepen the flavor of the stock, return the skin and bones to the pot and simmer, uncovered, for 40 to 50 minutes. Then pour the stock through a fine-mesh sieve into a clean container. (If you haven't simmered it with the bones and skin, you can skip this step.) Discard the contents of the sieve, and let rest at room temperature for 30 minutes. Cover with foil, poke with a few holes to allow steam to escape, and refrigerate until the fat rises. Lift off the fat and discard, then cover and refrigerate the stock for up to 3 days or freeze for up to 1 year.

Makes 1 chicken

SCHMALTZ

Schmaltz is a Yiddish word for rendered (melted) chicken fat. As inadequate definitions go, these words are just enough to spare us the gory details. When made right and clean, it's beautiful to behold, a high concept of flavored fat that permits sautéing or frying over the hottest fire.

It might sicken many that the idea behind schmaltz is to save fat you have deliberately removed to avoid eating it. For others, unwrapping a grocery-store chicken to find two big lobes of fat behind the thighs brings a smile. It's free after all. What cooking oil can you think of that is this cheap and fine?

Pull away any pieces of fat folded inside the chicken's cavity. Wrap in plastic wrap, then drop into a freezer-quality quart-sized zip-style plastic bag. If you believe that you won't recognize this in a week or two, label the bag with a waterproof marker. Every time you buy a whole chicken, you'll wrap another little package of fat and add it to the bag. When the bag is full, there is enough fat to justify making the schmaltz.

Defrost the frozen chicken fat and place it into a thick-bottomed pot. Chop up two large onions—the secret behind the best schmaltz—and add them to the fat. Set the pot over medium to medium-low heat and leave it there for perhaps 2 hours, maybe longer.

At first not much will happen. After an hour the fat will melt and submerge the onions. Stir now and then. By the end, the liquid fat will turn from yellow to golden and the onions may begin to brown somewhat. This is good. If the fat boils, lower the heat. It should scarcely simmer. At this point, someone may come home from work or school and say that the house smells good.

Strain the rendered fat, now officially schmaltz, through a fine-mesh sieve into a bowl. Return the solids to the pot and continue cooking them until they become crunchy and yield a little more liquid, then strain that, too.

Leave the fat to cool at room temperature. You'll see sediment on the bottom—leave it alone. You'll never use it. From that layer up will be beautiful, golden cooking fat.

When the schmaltz is cool, cover it and put it in the refrigerator. It will completely solidify to an off-white color, the sign of a truly saturated fat. It will keep indefinitely.

When you spoon out a tablespoon or so for sautéing and heat it, it will melt into the finest golden cooking oil you've ever seen. The smoking point of schmaltz is 400°F degrees, compared to 250°F for butter unskimmed of milk solids.

SPRING

Just because it's spring doesn't mean it's all sweetness and light outside. Blizzards, tornadoes, and hail often deliver a bitter beginning to spring, regardless of hemisphere. In the first days of the season, we're still in the mood for chicken stews and soup, and the stove and oven are still sending much needed warmth through the rest of the house.

Yet mere weeks bring daylight saving time, sometimes smack in the middle of a New England snow. Not content to wait until the last Sunday in April, the charcoal and grilling trades lobbied to send the date up to the first Sunday in April, giving them three extra weeks to encourage preseason barbecuing.

At the first warm evening, the grill does comes out. Chicken might be prepared slightly ahead of season with a spicy marinade built on ginger and chile and enjoyed with cold beer. You still feel that chicken with spinach and cheese sauce is a comfort.

In a day or two, true spring settles in. Aside from such stereotyped harbingers as artichokes, asparagus, mushrooms, and fava beans, spring begins with little because much of the seasonal harvest is still growing.

If it's a lucky early spring in California, the rest of the country will already have shipments of fresh peas, herbs, green beans, broccoli, cauliflower, spinach, chard, lettuces, all the early onions, and garlic. Outer leaves of artichokes and the fuzzy fava pods get the compost going. By the end of the season, the first cherries are off trees in California's hot valley areas, and by mid-June they're over (making them not a summer crop at all).

As spring turns into near-summer, the grill is stoked up more and more. Rhubarb comes along, as do the first peaches. You'll want to make chicken salad and have a picnic before summer is official.

SPRING

CIPES

Here is a chance to use up the excess red wine you received over the winter holidays and the first chives of spring. If the wine is in the pan with the chicken when it cooks, it's the wine to drink with the chicken when it's done, and it doesn't matter if the wine is dry, bone dry, or a little sweet.

CHICKEN BREASTS
in RED WINE SAUCE
with SPRING CHIVES

4 large boneless chicken breasts, skin on

1/2 cup flour mixed with 1 teaspoon salt and 1/2 teaspoon black pepper

1 tablespoon butter

1 tablespoon olive oil

1 to 1 1/2 cups red wine

1 tablespoon finely snipped fresh chives

1 Heat a serving platter in a 150°F oven.

2 Rinse the chicken breasts and pat dry with paper towels. Dredge them in the seasoned flour, shaking off the excess.

3 Melt the butter with the olive oil in a wide, heavy sauté pan with a tight-fitting lid over high heat. Add the breasts skin side down, and sauté, turning once, until well browned, 3 to 4 minutes on each side. Reduce the heat to medium-high if the chicken begins to burn.

4 Raise the heat to high and pour the wine around the breasts. Bring quickly to a boil, cover, reduce the heat to medium-low, and simmer until firm to the touch, 4 to 5 minutes longer. Transfer the chicken breasts to the warmed serving platter and keep warm.

5 Raise the heat to high, and bring the pan juices to a boil, scraping any browned bits from the pan bottom. Boil until thickened and reduced by a third.

6 Pour the sauce over the chicken. Sprinkle with the chives and serve right away.

Serves 4

This would be an anytime recipe unless you can get your hands on some fresh spring garlic, sometimes called green garlic. The bulbs are sold with long green tops attached, and the white parts have no sections. Otherwise, this is a nice, light dish perfect for a balmy spring evening.

EGG-BREADED
CHICKEN BREASTS
in GARLIC BUTTER

4 boneless chicken breasts, skin on

½ cup flour mixed with 1 teaspoon salt and ½ teaspoon black pepper

2 eggs, lightly beaten

⅓ cup bread crumbs (fresh or dried; see Note)

2 tablespoons butter

2 teaspoons minced garlic or spring garlic

1 cup dry white wine

1 Heat a serving platter in a 150°F oven.

2 Rinse the chicken breasts and pat dry with paper towels. Dredge them in the seasoned flour, dip into the eggs, then run through the bread crumbs, coating evenly.

3 Melt 1 tablespoon of the butter in a wide, heavy sauté pan over high heat. Add the breasts, skin side down, and sauté, turning once, until well browned and cooked through, 5 to 6 minutes on each side. Reduce the heat to medium-high if the chicken begins to burn. Remove the chicken breasts to the warmed serving platter and keep warm.

4 Reduce the heat to medium, add the garlic, and toss around the pan for about 15 seconds. Raise the heat to high again and scrape up any browned bits from the pan bottom as you pour in the wine. Boil until slightly thickened and reduced by half.

5 Remove from the heat and whisk in the remaining 1 tablespoon butter. Pour the sauce over the breasts and serve hot.

Serves 4

Note: The crumbliest bread crumbs are those you make yourself. If you're one of the million Americans who owns a bread machine, make crumbs out of any bread you've got. For this recipe, I make crumbs in a food processor from slices of nearly deceased plain white bread that has a tough crust. Rye would be fantastic, too.

CHICKEN **16** NUGGET

Chaucer's *Chanticleer and the Fox*, circa 1380, describes one of literature's first poultry-keeping scenes.

Quick, light, and universal, there's nothing like a sauce made with fresh herbs to do justice to boneless chicken breasts. You can make the chicken more appealing by being sure the skin side is beautifully browned.

60

CRUSTY CHICKEN BREASTS
in SPRING HERB SAUCE

4 boneless chicken breasts, skin on

½ cup flour mixed with 1 teaspoon salt and ¼ teaspoon black pepper

2 eggs, lightly beaten

2 tablespoons butter

¾ cup chicken stock or dry white wine

1 tablespoon minced mixed fresh parsley, thyme, and chives

1 Heat a serving platter in a 150°F oven.

2 Rinse the chicken breasts and pat dry with paper towels. Dredge them in the seasoned flour, dip into the egg, then run through the flour again, shaking off the excess.

3 Melt the butter in a wide, heavy sauté pan over high heat. Add the breasts, skin side down. Sauté, turning once, until well browned and cooked through, 5 to 6 minutes on each side. Reduce the heat if the chicken begins to burn. Remove the chicken breasts to the warmed serving platter and keep warm.

4 Spoon off all but 1 tablespoon of the fat from the pan. Raise the heat to high and scrape up any browned bits from the pan bottom as you pour in the stock or wine. Boil until slightly thickened and reduced by a third.

5 Add the herbs, whisk once or twice, then immediately pour the sauce over the chicken breasts and serve right away.

Serves 4

The dish is accented by capers and sometimes artichoke hearts. Although classically made with veal scaloppine, chicken breasts pounded thin and tender make a fine substitution.

CHICKEN PICCATA

4 boneless chicken breasts, skinned

1/3 cup flour mixed with 1/2 teaspoon salt and generous black pepper to taste

1 tablespoon olive oil

2 tablespoons butter

1/4 cup dry white wine or chicken stock

1 1/2 teaspoons chopped fresh parsley

1 tablespoon fresh lemon juice

1 tablespoon drained capers

1 Heat a serving platter in a 150°F oven.

2 Rinse the chicken breasts and pat dry with paper towels. One at a time, sandwich them between two sheets of waxed paper and pound (a rolling pin works great) until *very* thin.

3 Dredge the chicken scallops in the flour, shaking off the excess.

4 Heat the olive oil with 1 tablespoon of the butter in a wide, heavy sauté pan over high heat. Add the chicken breasts, skinned side down, and fry quickly, turning once, about 1 1/2 minutes on each side. Turn with tongs; don't stab the meat with a fork. Remove the breasts to the warmed serving platter and keep warm.

5 Continuing on high heat, immediately add the wine or stock and scrape up any browned bits from the pan bottom. Boil until reduced by half.

6 Remove from the heat, swirl in the last tablespoon of butter, then the parsley. Add the lemon juice and capers and pour over chicken. Serve immediately.

Serves 4

Skinned chicken breasts can become nice and crusty if they're floured first. The flour keeps working after the chicken comes out of the pan in making the star of the dish, a creamy, herbal sauce.

62

CHICKEN BREASTS
SAUTÉED with FINE HERBS, MUSTARD, and CREAM

6 boneless chicken breasts, skinned

½ cup flour mixed with 1 teaspoon salt and ¼ teaspoon black pepper

2 tablespoons butter

1 cup dry white wine

½ cup heavy cream or crème fraîche

1 tablespoon Dijon mustard

2 tablespoons mixed finely chopped fresh chervil, chives, parsley, and tarragon

1 Heat a serving platter in a 150°F oven.

2 Rinse the chicken breasts and pat dry with paper towels. Dredge in the seasoned flour, shaking off the excess.

3 Heat the butter in a wide, heavy sauté pan over high heat. Add the chicken breasts, skinned side down. Reduce the heat to medium-high and sauté until nicely browned and cooked through, 5 to 6 minutes on each side. Remove the breasts to the warmed serving platter and keep warm.

4 Spoon off all but 1 or 2 tablespoons of the fat from the pan. Raise the heat to high and scrape up any browned bits from the pan bottom as you pour in the wine. Boil until reduced by half.

5 Add 1 tablespoon of the herbs, then whisk in the cream or crème fraîche and mustard. Boil for a few seconds, then spoon over the chicken breasts. Garnish with the remaining herbs and serve hot.

Serves 6

Here is the authentic home-style version of this famous restaurant recipe. Once all the ingredients are prepared, it's an embarrassment of ease.

ASPARAGUS CHICKEN
with GINGER and BLACK BEAN SAUCE

FOR THE ONE-STEP SAUCE:

1 cup chicken stock

1 1/2 tablespoons bottled black bean sauce

2 tablespoons oyster sauce

3 tablespoons dry sherry

1/2 teaspoon sugar

1/4 teaspoon white pepper

2 tablespoons vegetable oil

2 boneless chicken breasts, skinned and cut into 1/2-inch-wide strips

1 onion, sliced

1-inch piece fresh ginger (about 1 ounce), peeled and minced

1 teaspoon minced garlic

1 pound asparagus, trimmed and cut on the diagonal into 1-inch lengths

Salt, if needed

1 tablespoon cornstarch mixed with 1/4 cup water

1 Heat a serving platter in a 150°F oven.

2 In a small bowl, combine all the ingredients for the one-step sauce, mixing well. Set aside.

3 Heat a wok or wide sauté pan over high heat. Add 1 tablespoon of the oil and continue heating until the oil shimmers.

4 Add the chicken and stir-fry for about 1 minute. Remove from the pan to a plate.

5 With the heat still on high, add the remaining 1 tablespoon oil, allow it to heat, and then add the onion and ginger. Stir-fry until the onion scarcely browns around the edges, about 1 minute.

6 Add the garlic and asparagus and give a few stirs. Return the chicken to the pan, tossing with the other ingredients.

7 Pour in the reserved sauce and bring quickly to a boil. Cover, reduce the heat to medium-low, and cook until aromatic vapors escape, about 1 minute.

8 Uncover and taste to see if you need to add a touch of salt. Quickly stir the cornstarch mixture, then add to the pan. Bring to a boil and cook until the sauce thickens, about 30 seconds. Remove to the warmed serving platter and serve right away.

Serves 4

Ah, fava beans and a nice Chianti, a lovely combination in the dreams of the imprisoned lunatic Hannibal Lechter in Silence of the Lambs. *I don't think he had this recipe in mind, but I believe a nice Chianti does go well.*

CHICKEN BREASTS
and FAVA BEANS
with GARLIC, SAGE, and OREGANO

2 pounds fava beans in the pod (see Note)

4 to 6 boneless chicken breasts, skin on

1 tablespoon olive oil

Salt and black pepper to taste

About 1/3 cup slivered red onion

1 tablespoon minced garlic

2 teaspoons minced fresh oregano

1 teaspoon minced fresh sage

1 Bring a pot of salted water to a boil. Meanwhile, shell the favas. You should have about 3 cups shelled. (The pods make wonderful compost!) Add to the boiling water and cook for about 30 seconds. Drain and rinse with cold water. Slip the beans out of their opaque skins and set aside.

2 Heat a serving platter in a 150°F oven.

3 Rinse the chicken breasts and pat dry with paper towels. Sprinkle generously with salt and pepper.

4 Heat the olive oil in a wide, heavy sauté pan over high heat. Add the breasts, skin side down. Sauté, turning once, until well browned and cooked through, 6 to 7 minutes on each side. Transfer the breasts to the warmed serving platter and keep warm.

5 Drain off all but 1 tablespoon fat from the pan. Raise the heat and add the onion and peeled favas. Sauté for about 1 minute.

6 Add the garlic, oregano, and sage, plus a little more salt and pepper. Stir for 1 to 2 minutes longer. Pour the favas over the chicken, or pile next to it, and serve immediately.

Serves 4 to 6

Note: Fava beans are more famous dried than fresh, but I only like them fresh. I once was treated to sautéed fresh favas at a banquet for nearly five hundred people, a feat for any chef. There are three preparation steps: 1) removing the beans from their huge fuzzy pods, 2) blanching the beans for about 30 seconds, and 3) peeling off a sort of "silver skin" bean by bean, to reveal a beautiful kelly green. The final step is to cook the prepared favas. The younger the favas, the quicker they'll cook.

This is one of those recipes I made with the wine leftover from a few evenings back. The slight sweetness of Riesling seems springlike to me, and makes the dish taste fresh.

RIESLING-BRAISED CHICKEN
with MUSHROOMS and CHIVES

1 chicken, 4 pounds, quartered

Salt and black pepper to taste

2 tablespoons butter

1 onion, chopped

1 teaspoon minced garlic

1½ cups Riesling

¾ pound fresh white mushrooms, sliced

½ cup cream

¼ cup snipped fresh chives

1 Heat a serving platter in a 150°F oven.

2 Rinse the chicken quarters and pat dry with paper towels. Sprinkle with salt and pepper.

3 Melt the butter in a wide, heavy sauté pan over high heat. Add the chicken, skin side down. Sear briefly, reduce the heat to medium-high, and sauté, turning once, until lightly browned, 3 to 4 minutes on each side. Drain off any excess fat.

4 Raise the heat to high, add the onion, garlic, and wine, and bring to a boil. Cover, reduce the heat to low, and simmer until the chicken is cooked through, about 25 minutes. Using tongs, remove the chicken to the warmed serving platter and keep warm.

5 Add the mushrooms to the pan juices, cover, and boil over high heat for 3 to 5 minutes. Uncover and boil until the liquid is reduced by half.

6 Stir in the cream and boil for 2 minutes longer, or until the sauce is as thick as you like.

7 Pour the mushroom sauce over the chicken and garnish with the chives. Serve hot.

Serves 4 to 6

As a kid I always loved spinach with potatoes, and that love match carries over here. Think creamed spinach made with cheese sauce plus chicken, and you'll have a good idea of how this dish ends up. Fresh asparagus spears would also be a nice touch of spring under this shallot-sweet cheese sauce.

SAUTÉED CHICKEN BREASTS
in JARLSBERG CHEESE SAUCE with SPINACH and POTATOES

2 pounds spinach, rinsed and stemmed

2 pounds Yukon gold potatoes, unpeeled, cut into wedges

6 boneless chicken breasts, skin on

Salt and black pepper to taste

1 tablespoon butter

1 large shallot, minced

Dusting of cayenne pepper or curry powder

2 tablespoons flour

2 cups milk, heated

¼ pound Jarlsberg cheese, shredded or cubed

1 Heat a wok or Dutch oven until very hot. Add the spinach with only the rinsing water clinging to the leaves, sprinkling with salt. Toss and cook until wilted, about 2½ minutes. Drain well in a colander and set aside.

2 Bring a saucepan of salted water to a boil. Add the potatoes, cover, reduce the heat, and simmer until a knife point easily pierces the a wedge, about 15 minutes. Drain into a colander. Set potatoes on a serving platter, wrap in foil, and keep warm in a 150°F oven.

3 Rinse the chicken breasts and pat dry with paper towels. Sprinkle generously with salt and pepper.

4 Heat the butter in a wide, heavy sauté pan over high heat. Add the chicken breasts, skin side down. Sear briefly, reduce the heat to medium-high, and sauté, turning once, until well browned and cooked through, 6 to 7 minutes on each side. Add the breasts to the serving platter and keep warm.

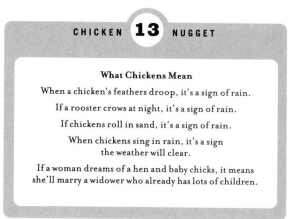

What Chickens Mean

When a chicken's feathers droop, it's a sign of rain.

If a rooster crows at night, it's a sign of rain.

If chickens roll in sand, it's a sign of rain.

When chickens sing in rain, it's a sign
the weather will clear.

If a woman dreams of a hen and baby chicks, it means
she'll marry a widower who already has lots of children.

5 Drain all but 2 tablespoons of fat from the sauté pan and place the pan over medium-high heat. Add the shallot and cayenne or curry powder and cook, stirring to coat, for about 30 seconds. Add the flour and warm milk, whisking until smooth. Simmer, stirring occasionally, until slightly thickened, about 3 minutes.

6 Just before serving, add the cheese to the sauce and stir until melted. Taste for salt.

7 Meanwhile, arrange the warm potatoes and mound the spinach around the chicken breasts. As soon as the cheese melts, pour the hot sauce over the chicken and spinach, then serve immediately.

Serves 6

Even though this recipe isn't authentically Indian, it calls for the spices and herbs commonly used in the cuisine. Serve these thighs with basmati rice and buttered green peas.

GRILLED INDIA
SPICE THIGHS

8 chicken thighs, skinned

3 tablespoons fresh or bottled lemon juice

6 garlic cloves

1-inch piece fresh ginger (about 1 ounce), peeled

1 small onion

2 tablespoons butter

1 teaspoon dried cilantro leaves

1 teaspoon pure chile powder such as New Mexico

½ teaspoon ground turmeric

½ teaspoon salt

¼ teaspoon ground cloves

Fresh cilantro leaves and lime wedges, for garnish

Flavorful Basmati Rice (recipe follows)

Buttered Sugar Snap Peas (recipe follows)

1 Make a few shallow slits in each thigh, then place in a roomy bowl. Add the lemon juice and toss well.

2 Rough-cut the garlic, ginger, and onion. In a food processor with the motor running, drop in the garlic and ginger through the feed tube and process until chopped. Add the onion and pulse until smoothly chopped.

3 Melt the butter in a small skillet over high heat. Add the onion mixture, reduce the heat to medium, and sauté, stirring, for 2 minutes. Add the dried cilantro, chile powder, turmeric, salt, and cloves and sauté for about 1 minute longer.

4 Empty the contents of the skillet into the bowl holding the thighs. Turn to coat and let stand for 10 to 30 minutes.

5 Meanwhile, prepare an indirect-heat fire in a covered charcoal grill (page 33).

6 Place the thighs on the grill rack, skin side down. Cover, open the top and bottom vents fully, and grill for 10 minutes. Turn the chicken, re-cover the grill with the vents nearly closed, and cook for 15 minutes. Turn the chicken again, re-cover, and cook with the vents wide open for the final 10 minutes.

7 Meanwhile, prepare the rice and peas.

8 Remove the thighs to a platter, garnish with fresh cilantro, and serve with lime wedges.

Serves 4

Flavorful Basmati Rice

1 cup raw
basmati rice

1 tablespoon butter

2 cups chicken stock

1. Sauté rice in butter until toasty, about 2 minutes. Add chicken stock, bring to a boil, cover tightly, reduce heat and simmer 20 minutes.

Buttered Sugar Snap Peas

1 pound
sugar snap pea pods

2 tablespoons butter

¼ teaspoon salt

1. Remove strings from pea pods, if any. Sauté rinsed and drained sugar snap peas in 1 tablespoon butter and 1 tablespoon water, plus salt, until bright green, about 3 to 4 minutes. Off the heat, stir in 1 tablespoon additional butter, and serve.

This beautiful white stew is made in a style loosely adapted from that used for making the French classic *blanquette de veau* but without the addition of cream or egg yolks. It is a welcome sight on the dining table during early spring when the weather is still cold and blustery. Serve with simply cooked asparagus spears. Everything else to complete the meal is already in the stew.

WHITE CHICKEN STEW
with PEAS

1 chicken, 4 pounds, cut into serving pieces

Salt and black pepper to taste

3 tablespoons butter

1 tablespoon vegetable oil

1 large white onion, finely diced

About ¾ cup finely minced celery (1 or 2 stalks)

1 cup Chardonnay or other fruity dry white wine

1½ cups chicken stock

2 bay leaves

1 bunch fresh parsley, tied with kitchen string

Pinch of ground nutmeg

1 pound small Yukon gold potatoes, unpeeled, cut into quarters or sixths, or new red potatoes

2 tablespoons flour

1 cup shelled peas

1 tablespoon dry sherry (optional)

1 Hack the breasts and thighs in half crosswise. Your chicken should now be in 12 smallish pieces. Rinse the chicken pieces and pat dry with paper towels. Sprinkle generously with salt and pepper.

2 Heat 1 tablespoon of the butter and the oil in a heavy pot over medium-high heat. Add the chicken pieces, skin side down, and sauté on all sides without coloring, reducing the heat to medium if browning occurs. This should take 12 to 15 minutes. Remove the chicken to a bowl.

3 Pour off all but 2 tablespoons of the fat from the pan. Return the pan to medium heat, add the onion and celery, and sauté until the onion is barely colored, about 4 minutes.

4 Raise the heat to high and add the wine. When it boils, return the chicken to the pot and add the stock, bay leaves, parsley bundle, and nutmeg. Cover, reduce the heat to medium-low, and cook for 10 minutes. Add the potatoes, cover, and cook until the potatoes are cooked through, about 15 minutes longer.

Are Chickens Stupid?

Chicken walkers are needed to walk through the hen-house on very hot afternoons to force hens to flap around and get their circulation going. The implied insult is that hens are too stupid to do this on their own.

A baby chick will follow any hen that comes along, thinking it's mom. Is this stupid?

5 Pour the stew into a colander placed over a large measuring pitcher or bowl, capturing all the cooking liquid. Discard the bay leaves and parsley. Measure the liquid; you should have about 3 cups. Set it briefly in the freezer to force the fat to rise, then skim off any visible fat. Return the contents of the colander to the pot.

6 Melt the remaining 2 tablespoons butter over high heat. Add the flour, whisking for a full minute. Slowly pour in the reserved cooking liquid, whisking constantly to form a sauce. Bring to a boil and cook for 2 minutes, stirring often. Taste; it will probably need salt, so add it now.

7 Pour the sauce into the stew. Add the peas and the sherry, if using, stir, cover, and heat through. The chicken should be tender and the sauce should be lightly thickened.

8 Bring the stew to the table and ladle into bowls.

Serves 4

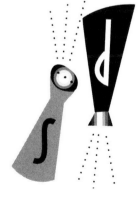

Get out the food processor to make one of the most aromatic mixtures ever to waft from the feed tube. You'll sauté a paste of shallots, garlic, red chiles, and fresh ginger just before adding turmeric-coated chicken. The combination cooks on top of the stove unattended while you pull the rest of dinner together—jasmine rice and cold beer.

CHICKEN BRAISED
in COCONUT MILK with PEAS and LIME JUICE

1 chicken, 4 pounds,
cut into serving pieces

1 teaspoon ground turmeric

1/2 teaspoon salt

FOR THE AROMATIC PASTE:

3 shallots, chopped

8 to 10 garlic cloves, chopped

3 or 4 small dried red chiles,
including seeds, or
1 teaspoon red pepper flakes

2-inch piece fresh ginger
(about 2 ounces),
peeled and cut up

1 teaspoon salt

1 tablespoon vegetable oil

1 can (13 1/2 ounces)
coconut milk

1/4 teaspoon white pepper

Pinch of sugar

1 cup shelled peas
(fresh or frozen)

Juice of 1 lime
(about 2 tablespoons)

Chopped fresh cilantro
or shredded green onion
for garnish

1 Hack the breasts in half crosswise. Rinse the chicken pieces and pat dry with paper towels. In a bowl, combine the chicken, turmeric, and salt, mixing until the chicken is evenly coated.

2 Place all the ingredients for the paste in a food processor and process until smooth, stopping to scrape down pieces flung onto the sides of the machine. Leave in the food processor until needed.

3 Heat the oil in a wide, heavy sauté pan (no black cast iron or aluminum) that has a lid over high heat. Add the paste, reduce the heat to medium, and sauté for 2 minutes.

4 Add the chicken pieces, skin side down, and sauté, turning once, until well browned, 3 to 4 minutes on each side.

5 Add the coconut milk, white pepper, and sugar and mix well. Cover and cook over low heat until the chicken is cooked through, about 30 minutes. The coconut milk should just barely simmer.

6 Add the peas, cover, and cook until tender, about 2 minutes if fresh and 3 to 4 minutes if frozen.

7 Uncover, squeeze lime juice all over the chicken, and scatter the cilantro or green onion over the top. Serve directly from the pan.

Serves 4 to 6

Yes, spring is the season for fresh artichokes, but I've used them canned here to bring spring to the table with ease of preparation and the juices they're packed in. This earthy dish is just a tad piquant from garlic and pepper flakes.

CHICKEN with ARTICHOKE HEARTS, TOMATO, and ROSEMARY

1/4 pound pancetta or bacon

1 chicken, 4 pounds, cut into serving pieces

1/2 teaspoon salt

Black pepper to taste

1 tablespoon minced garlic

1/2 cup dry white wine

1 can (14 ounces) artichoke hearts, undrained

1 can (15 ounces) crushed tomatoes

1/8 teaspoon red pepper flakes

2 fresh rosemary sprigs, each about 3 inches long

1 Select a wide, heavy sauté pan with a lid that will accommodate the chicken. Fry the pancetta or bacon in the pan over medium heat until no longer pink, 5 to 6 minutes. Remove to paper towels to drain, then crumble when cool. Pour off all but 1 tablespoon of the fat from the pan.

2 Meanwhile, hack the breasts in half crosswise. Rinse the chicken pieces and pat dry with paper towels. Sprinkle with the salt and pepper.

3 Return the sauté pan to medium-high heat. Add the chicken, skin side down, and sauté, turning once, until well browned, about 4 minutes on each side.

4 Add the garlic. Raise the heat to high, add the wine, and bring to a boil. Add the artichoke hearts (halve them if large) with their liquid and the tomatoes. Dust the chicken with the pepper flakes and tuck in the rosemary sprigs. Bring to a boil, cover, reduce the heat to medium-low, and simmer until the chicken is cooked through, about 20 minutes.

5 Remove the chicken to a serving platter, arranging skin side up. Continue boiling the sauce until reduced by half, 5 to 8 minutes. Pour the sauce, vegetables, and rosemary sprigs over the chicken. Sprinkle with the crumbled pancetta or bacon and serve hot.

Serves 4 to 6

The secret to preparing little artichokes is to snap
off the green leaves until you reach the yellow leaves.
(That's how you handle big artichokes, too.)
Yes, you'll have this really small artichoke in your hand
and a pile of debris (for me, valued compost!), but
the results are worth it. If you see these little ones in your
store, get them. They have a season of about a minute.

74

CHICKEN BREASTS
with SMALL FRESH ARTICHOKES and CAULIFLOWER with DILL-MINT FLAVOR

¼ cup bottled lemon juice
or juice of 2 lemons

10 little artichokes

4 to 6 boneless
chicken breasts, skin on

4 tablespoons butter

1 head cauliflower, about
1½ pounds, cut into florets

½ cup flour mixed with
1 teaspoon salt and generous
black pepper to taste

1½ cups chicken stock

1 tablespoon mixed chopped
fresh dill and mint

¼ cup fresh lemon juice

1 Fill a big bowl about three-fourths full of water. Add the bottled lemon juice or the juice of 2 lemons and their squeezed rinds.

2 Cut off the top third of each artichoke, placing the artichoke into the lemon water as you go. Then remove 1 artichoke at a time from the water and snap off all the outer leaves until you reach the yellow leaves. Trim the stem, quarter the artichoke lengthwise, and return to the lemon water.

3 Rinse the chicken breasts and pat dry with paper towels. One at a time, sandwich them between two sheets of waxed paper and pound them a little (a rolling pin works great), just until evenly thick.

4 Heat a serving platter in a 150°F oven.

5 Heat 2 tablespoons of the butter in a wide, heavy sauté pan with a lid over medium-high heat. Drain the artichokes and add to the pan. Sprinkle with salt and sauté for about 10 minutes, browning all sides. Using tongs, remove from the pan to a plate.

6 Add 1 tablespoon more butter to the pan and then add the cauliflower. Sauté over medium-high heat until lightly browned, about 10 minutes. Remove to another separate plate.

7 Dredge the chicken breasts in the seasoned flour, shaking off the excess. Add the remaining 1 tablespoon butter to the pan over medium-high heat. Then add the chicken breasts, skin side down, and sauté until golden, about 4 minutes on each side.

8 Remove the chicken to the warmed serving platter and keep warm. Raise the heat to high and pour in the chicken stock, stirring well. Bring to a boil, add the browned cauliflower and artichokes, cover, and cook for about 5 minutes.

9 Uncover, add the dill and mint, and boil for about 1 minute. Add the ¼ cup fresh lemon juice, boil for another minute until reduced slightly, and pour over the chicken. Serve right away.

Serves 4

Although these artichokes are small, they require relatively long cooking to be tender. That's why they're twice-cooked here.

76

CHICKEN BRAISED

with SMALL ARTICHOKES, LEMON, and WINE

¼ cup bottled lemon juice or juice of 2 lemons

10 little artichokes

1 chicken, 4 pounds, cut up

About 1 cup milk

½ cup flour mixed with 1 teaspoon salt and generous black pepper to taste

2 tablespoons butter or olive oil

1 cup dry white wine

1 fresh rosemary sprig, or ½ teaspoon dried rosemary

1 Heat a serving platter in a 150°F oven.

2 Fill a bowl about three-fourths full with water. Add all but 3 tablespoons of the lemon juice.

3 Cut off the top third of each artichoke. Place the artichokes into the lemon water as you go. Then remove 1 artichoke at a time from the water and snap off all the outer leaves until you reach the yellow ones. Trim the stem, quarter the artichoke lengthwise, and return to the lemon water.

4 Rinse the chicken pieces and pat dry with paper towels. Dip each piece in the milk and then roll each piece in the seasoned flour.

5 Heat the butter or olive oil in a wide, heavy sauté pan over high heat. Add the chicken, skin side down. Sauté, turning once, until browned, about 4 minutes on each side. Using tongs, remove the chicken to a plate.

6 Drain the artichokes and add to the fat remaining in the pan. Sauté, turning as necessary, until golden brown on all sides. Add the wine and bring to a boil. Nestle the pieces of dark meat in the artichokes, cover, and simmer 8 to 10 minutes. Add the breasts, re-cover, and continue cooking until the chicken is cooked through, about 15 minutes longer. Remove the chicken to the warmed serving platter and keep warm.

7 Tuck the rosemary into the sauce and boil it, tasting for salt and sprinkling with lemon juice, until reduced by a third. Pour the sauce and artichokes over the chicken and serve.

Serves 4

We are pea crazy at our house. We grow all kinds of peas in a little strip of soil that runs along the driveway. Peas are more nutritious than beans, and they're simple to grow. This recipe uses shelled peas. Sugar snap peas would be equally delicious.

PROSCIUTTO-WRAPPED
CHICKEN BREASTS in MARSALA SAUCE
with SPRING PEAS

6 boneless chicken breasts, skinned

6 long, thin prosciutto slices

6 small fresh sage leaves

Salt and generous black pepper to taste

1 tablespoon olive oil

1 tablespoon butter

¼ cup dry Marsala

1¼ cups shelled peas (fresh or frozen)

1 Heat a serving platter in a 150°F oven.

2 Rinse the chicken breasts and pat dry with paper towels. One at a time, sandwich them between two sheets of waxed paper and pound them a little (a rolling pin works great), just until evenly thick.

3 Lay out the prosciutto pieces on a work surface. Top each with a breast piece, underside up. Lay a sage leaf in the center of each breast. Sprinkle with salt and pepper. Roll up, tucking a toothpick into the seam to secure.

4 Heat the olive oil and butter in a wide, heavy sauté pan with a lid over high heat. Add the rolls, reduce the heat to medium-high, and sauté, turning to brown the top and bottom, for about 3 minutes on each side. Then turn to brown the sides for about 2 minutes each. Remove the rolls to a plate.

5 Pour off all but 1 tablespoon of the fat from the pan and return the pan to high heat. Add the Marsala and boil for 1 minute or so, drawing a spatula across the bottom of the pan to dislodge the browned bits. Return the chicken rolls to the pan, cover, and simmer for 3 minutes. Remove the rolls to the warmed serving platter and keep warm.

6 Add the peas to the pan and toss and cook for 2 minutes over high heat if fresh and 3 to 4 minutes if frozen. Pour the peas and sauce around the rolls and serve immediately.

Serves 4 to 6

I worried that the Italian method of cooking chicken weighted under a brick on the stove top might be some gimmick perpetuated by chefs desperate to be trendy. I asked my friend Patricia, who is of pure Sicilian extraction and now an exceptional pastry chef, if she had ever heard of cooking chicken under a brick.

Of course, she said. Her family did it all the time. "Why?" I asked. "Because it makes the chicken incredibly browned." "Where do you get the bricks?" I asked. "Elaine," she said, "I'm from New Jersey. We'd just find an abandoned building and go home with a coupla' bricks."

She wraps the bricks in foil before placing them on top of the chicken. For these thighs I use two bricks across a twelve-inch pan, and rotate them from time to time. Patricia is right. The thighs brown very nicely.

CHICKEN UNDER A BRICK
with POLENTA, PORCINI, and PARSLEY

¾ ounce dried porcini mushrooms

8 chicken thighs

Salt and black pepper to taste

A little olive oil

Soft Polenta (recipe follows)

About ¼ cup fresh flat-leaf (Italian) parsley leaves

1 Heat a serving platter in a 150°F oven.

2 Place the porcini in a bowl with warm water to cover by 1 inch. Set aside to soak. Wrap 2 garden-variety bricks in heavy-duty aluminum foil.

3 Rinse the thighs and pat dry with paper towels. Sprinkle generously with salt and pepper.

4 Pour enough olive oil into your heaviest, widest skillet to form just a film on the bottom and place over high heat. When hot, place the thighs in it, skin side down. Top with the bricks. Immediately reduce the heat to medium. Let cook for 20 minutes.

5 Remove the bricks. With tongs, turn the thighs over, replace the bricks, and cook 10 minutes longer.

6 During this time, lift the porcini from the soaking liquid. Chop if the pieces are large. Rinse the mushrooms in running water, squeeze out excess water, and keep handy. Strain the soaking liquid through a sieve lined with a small piece of wet cheesecloth or paper towel, and keep the liquid handy, too. You'll need ¾ cup. At this point, prepare the polenta.

Soft Polenta

½ teaspoon salt

1 cup coarse yellow cornmeal

Black pepper to taste

¼ cup Parmesan cheese

1. Microwave method: Combine 3 cups water, the salt, cornmeal, and black pepper in a microwaveproof bowl. Cover and microwave on High for 5 minutes. Uncover, stir well, and microwave for 4 to 5 minutes longer, uncovered. Stir in the butter and cheese. Spoon the soft polenta onto serving plates immediately.

2. Stovetop method: Bring 3 cups water to a boil in a heavy saucepan. Add the salt, then slowly add the cornmeal in a fine stream, stirring quickly. When all the cornmeal is added, sprinkle with a little black pepper. Cook at a simmer, stirring constantly, for about 15 minutes. Off the heat, stir in the butter and cheeses. Spoon the soft polenta onto serving plates immediately.

7 Again remove the bricks. Pour off all the fat. Return the pan to medium-high heat, turn the chicken thighs so the skin side is down, replace the bricks, and cook for 5 minutes longer over medium-high heat. Remove the chicken to the warmed serving platter, arranging it to one side, and keep warm.

8 Raise the heat to high and add the rinsed mushrooms to the skillet. Sauté for about 1 minute. Add ¾ cup porcini liquid and the parsley and cook down to ¼ cup. Taste for salt, and add if necessary.

9 Spoon the polenta to the side of the chicken. Spoon the porcini and sauce over the polenta and chicken thighs and serve immediately.

Serves 4 to 6

When you are making this recipe, the oven vapors will positively open your sinuses. Once cooked, however, there is no pounce, just the elegant flavor of chicken with tarragon—and from a rather quick and easy dish.

TARRAGON VINEGAR CHICKEN

1 chicken, 4 pounds, cut into serving pieces

Salt and black pepper to taste

1 tablespoon butter or olive oil

1 tablespoon butter

1 small white onion, quartered and thinly sliced

1 teaspoon finely minced garlic

2 fresh tarragon sprigs, or 1/2 teaspoon dried tarragon, plus sprigs for garnish (optional)

1/2 cup tarragon vinegar

1 Preheat an oven to 350°F. Have ready a 9-by-13-inch baking dish with a cover.

2 Hack the breasts in half crosswise. Rinse the chicken pieces and pat dry with paper towels. Sprinkle with salt and pepper.

3 Heat the butter in a wide, heavy sauté pan over high heat. Add the chicken pieces, skin side down and sauté, turning once, until golden brown, about 4 minutes on each side. Transfer the chicken pieces to the baking dish.

4 Drain off all but 1 tablespoon of the fat from the pan. Return to medium heat. Add the onion to the pan and sauté gently until softened, about 4 minutes. Add the garlic and tarragon sprigs or dried tarragon and sauté for about 1 minute.

5 Raise the heat to high, add the vinegar, and bring to a boil, scraping up the browned bits from the pan bottom. Pour the vinegar sauce over the chicken.

6 Bake, covered, basting frequently after the first 15 minutes, until the chicken is cooked through, about 30 minutes.

7 Arrange the chicken pieces on a serving platter and spoon some of the sauce over the top. Garnish with a few tarragon sprigs, if using, and serve immediately.

Serves 4

This mildly sweet sauce is reminiscent of a sauce paired with duckling. It's important to use red wine with good pigment, such as Cabernet Sauvignon or Zinfandel (an especially good match with cherries), that won't turn gray or pale as the sauce cooks. Added brightness comes during the deglazing step from a splash of balsamic vinegar.

BING CHICKEN

4 cups pitted Bing cherries

2 tablespoons sugar

1 cup red wine such as Cabernet Sauvignon or Zinfandel

1/4 teaspoon ground cinnamon

1/8 teaspoon ground cloves

1/8 teaspoon ground allspice

Salt and white pepper to taste

1 chicken, 4 pounds, cut into serving pieces

2 tablespoons butter

1/4 cup balsamic vinegar

1 Heat a serving platter in a 150°F oven.

2 In a saucepan, combine 3 cups of the cherries with the sugar, wine, cinnamon, cloves, allspice, and an ever-so-small pinch of salt. Place over medium heat, bring to a boil, reduce the heat to low, and simmer until nearly broken up, about 10 minutes. Remove from the heat, let cool a little, then puree in a blender. Strain.

3 Rinse the chicken pieces and pat dry with paper towels. Sprinkle with salt and white pepper. Heat the butter in a wide, heavy sauté pan with a lid over high heat. Add the chicken pieces, skin side down, and sauté, turning once, until golden brown, about 4 minutes on each side. Remove the chicken to a plate.

4 Pour off all but 1 tablespoon of the fat from the pan and place it over high heat. Pour in the vinegar, let it sizzle, and then boil it, scraping up browned bits from the pan bottom, until reduced by half.

5 With the heat still on high, stir in the strained cherry sauce. Return the chicken to the pan, skin side up, and nestle it in the sauce. Spoon the sauce over each piece. When the sauce boils, cover the pan, reduce the heat to low and cook for 15 minutes. Remove the chicken to the warmed serving platter and keep warm.

6 Boil the sauce over high heat until reduced by a third. Stir the remaining 1 cup cherries into the boiling sauce and cook for 1 minute. Pour the sauce over the chicken and serve.

Serves 4

A great dish for company, especially when the little hens are on sale. Once the hens are in the oven, you've got 1 1/2 hours to fix the rest of the meal, or relax.

82

CORNISH GAME HENS
ROASTED with PORTOBELLO MUSHROOMS for COMPANY

6 Cornish game hens

10 fresh portobello mushrooms

2 teaspoons dried oregano

Salt and black pepper to taste

1/2 teaspoon red pepper flakes

1/2 cup good olive oil

1 Preheat an oven to 350°F. Line two 9-by-13-inch baking pans with heavy aluminum foil. Set 3 birds in each pan. Tuck the mushrooms, gills down, in and around the birds.

2 Sprinkle the birds with the oregano, salt, black pepper, and red pepper flakes. Drizzle the olive oil over the top.

3 Roast, uncovered, basting with pan juices during the final 30 minutes, until the hens are cooked through, 1½ hours. When done, the juices between the breast and thigh should run clear.

4 Remove the hens to a big platter and surround them with the mushrooms. The hens will be soft enough to break apart with hands or limited cutlery. Give each guest a mushroom and a piece of hen.

Serves 8 to 10

Each spring, when the first shoots of thyme appear, by some miracle the spring lemons are ready, too. That's when I roast this chicken. The roasting and the resting time will give you about one-and-a-half hours to plan the rest of the dinner.

LEMON-AND-THYME-
TESTED CHICKEN

1 chicken, 4 pounds

Salt and black pepper to taste

Generous handful of fresh thyme sprigs

1 lemon, sliced paper-thin

3 large garlic cloves, sliced paper-thin

1 tablespoon butter, at room temperature, or olive oil

1 Position a rack in the lower third of an oven. Preheat to 450°F.

2 Rinse the chicken and pat dry with paper towels.

3 Season the bird's cavity with salt and pepper and then loosely pack it with the thyme sprigs.

4 Loosen the skin over the breast by slipping your fingers or the slender handle of a wooden spoon between the skin and the flesh. Without lifting too much, slide the lemon and garlic slices evenly under the skin.

5 Smear the chicken with the butter or oil, then sprinkle with salt and pepper. Set the chicken on a rack inside a baking pan.

6 Roast for 15 minutes. Reduce the heat to 350°F and continue roasting until the chicken is cooked through, 1¼ hours longer. Remove the chicken to a cutting board with a trough to catch the juices. Let rest for 15 minutes.

7 Pour the pan juices into a small pot, scraping up the browned bits stuck to the pan and adding them as well. If there is time, place the pot in the freezer for a few minutes to force the fat to rise, then skim it off and discard.

8 Put the pot of juices over high heat and boil until reduced by one-fourth.

9 Carve the chicken (or cut apart with poultry shears), adding the juices captured on the cutting board to the pot. Pour all the pan juices into a pitcher and serve with the chicken.

Serves 4

What a wonderful early spring dish—easy yet sustaining
with powerful flavors from a short list of ingredients.
The oregano-laced sauce gets a generous addition of *finely*
grated (the emphasis is on *finely*) Parmesan cheese.
The cheese dissolves into the sauce and makes it thick.

ROASTED OREGANO-LEMON
CHICKEN with PARMESAN POURING SAUCE

1 chicken, 4 pounds

1 smallish lemon, pricked in
several places with a fork

Several fresh oregano sprigs

1 tablespoon butter,
at room temperature

Salt and black pepper to taste

FOR THE SAUCE:

1 tablespoon skimmed
chicken fat, from roasting pan

1 teaspoon flour

¼ cup dry white wine

2 teaspoons finely minced
fresh oregano

Salt and black pepper to taste

¾ cup finely grated
Parmesan cheese

1 Position a rack in the lower third of an oven. Preheat to 450°F.

2 Rinse the chicken and pat dry with paper towels.

3 Place the lemon in the cavity of the chicken. Add a few fresh oregano sprigs. Tuck the wing tips under themselves. Rub the entire chicken with the butter, then sprinkle with salt and pepper. Set the chicken on a rack inside a baking pan.

4 Roast for 15 minutes. Reduce the heat to 350°F and continue roasting until the chicken is cooked through, about 1¼ hours longer. Remove the chicken to a cutting board with a trough to catch the juices. Let rest for 15 minutes.

5 Pour the pan juices into a measuring cup, scraping up the browned bits stuck to the pan and adding them as well. Set in the freezer for 5 to 10 minutes (don't worry, the chicken will stay hot) to force the fat to rise.

6 To make the sauce, skim off 1 tablespoon of the fat from the top of the juices and place in a small pot. Skim off and discard the remaining fat from the juices, removing as much as possible. To the juices remaining in the measuring cup, add water to equal ½ cup.

CHICKEN **5** **NUGGET**

When Americans eat out, about 83 percent of them are eating chicken.

CHICKEN **3** **NUGGET**

Women with high incomes eat chicken at least two or three times a week.

7 Heat the chicken fat over high heat. Add the flour, whisking until a beige paste forms, about 1 minute. Add the wine and minced oregano and boil for 30 seconds. Add the pan juices and any more juices captured by the board. Add salt and pepper and boil until slightly thickened, 2 to 3 minutes. Remove from the heat.

8 Carve the chicken into serving pieces (or cut apart with poultry shears) and arrange on a platter.

9 Just before serving, stir the cheese into the hot sauce. Pour the sauce over the chicken, garnish with additional oregano sprigs, and serve immediately.

Serves 4

Sage is one of the first herbs to wake up from winter. The small new leaves have a delicate flavor that I love with gooey melted Fontina cheese. A little pocket cut inside a chicken breast is a nice place to put both.

CHICKEN BREASTS
STUFFED with SAGE and FONTINA CHEESE

4 boneless chicken breasts, skin on

4 slices Fontina cheese

4 to 8 small fresh sage leaves

1 tablespoon butter or olive oil

Salt and black pepper to taste

1 Preheat an oven to 350°F.

2 Rinse the chicken breasts and pat dry with paper towels.

3 Slit the side of each breast horizontally to form a pocket. Stuff each pocket with a slice of Fontina and 1 or 2 sage leaves, depending on their size. Close the breasts and sprinkle with salt and pepper.

4 Melt the butter in an ovenproof sauté pan over high heat. Add the breasts, skin side down, and sauté until browned, about 3 minutes.

5 Transfer the pan to the oven and bake until the breasts are fully cooked and the cheese oozes, about 10 minutes. Serve immediately.

Serves 4

CHICKEN **7** NUGGET

The first deliberately fattened chicken is believed to have lived on the Greek island of Kos.

"Rhubarb-e-cue?" Rhubarb is the base of an easy, sticky sauce that glues itself to chicken. Slap the sauce onto a springtime bird for a sweet-tart bite cooked on the grill.

GRILLED CHICKEN
with MOPPED-ON RHUBARB-BUTTER SAUCE

1 chicken, 4 pounds, cut into serving pieces

1¼ pounds rhubarb

1 onion, chopped

4 tablespoons butter

2 tablespoons sugar

Salt and black pepper to taste

1 Prepare a direct-heat fire in an open charcoal grill (pages 33–34).

2 Strip off any leaves from the rhubarb stalks and discard. Slice the stalks and place in a saucepan with the onion, butter, and sugar. Place over medium heat for about 15 minutes, giving a few stirs. The mixture will thicken. Transfer to a large bowl and let cool a little.

3 Rinse the chicken pieces and pat dry with paper towels. Sprinkle with salt and pepper.

4 Add the chicken to the rhubarb sauce and stir to mix. If you like, tuck a little sauce between the chicken's skin and flesh.

5 Add the dark meat to the grill rack, skin side down, and grill for 10 minutes. Add the breasts and wings, skin side down, and grill for 15 minutes longer. Turn all the pieces and continue to grill, dabbing any remaining rhubarb sauce onto the chicken during the last 10 minutes of grilling, until cooked through, about 15 minutes. Sprinkle the skin with a little more salt and pepper.

6 Remove to a platter and serve hot or warm.

Serves 4

Spring rains bring mushrooms. They can be plain white mushrooms, exotic chanterelle or oyster mushrooms, or veritable hallucinogens. This fabled dish is called *moo goo gai pan* in Cantonese. *Moo goo* means mushrooms, *gai* is chicken, and *pan* means slices. The recipe comes from my husband, David SooHoo, a master Chinese-American chef who learned how to make it from his father and uncle, both Chinese restaurateurs and chefs.

CHICKEN, SNOW PEAS,
and MUSHROOMS
over PANFRIED NOODLES

½ pound white chicken meat, sliced (about 2 breasts)

¼ teaspoon salt

⅓ teaspoon sugar

⅛ teaspoon white pepper

1 tablespoon cornstarch

FOR THE ONE-STEP SAUCE:

Scant ½ teaspoon salt

Rounded ½ teaspoon sugar

⅛ teaspoon white pepper

2 tablespoons oyster sauce

1 teaspoon brown coloring such as Kitchen Bouquet brand

1 In a small bowl, mix together the chicken, salt, sugar, white pepper, and cornstarch, stirring well.

2 To make the sauce, measure all the ingredients into a measuring cup. Stir to mix.

3 To prepare the noodles, heat a serving platter in a 150°F oven. Heat a wok, a wide skillet, or griddle over high heat. When hot, add the oil and continue heating.

4 Spread the cooked noodles in an even layer in the pan, reduce the heat to medium-high, and let the underside brown, about 5 minutes.

5 Flip the noodles like a pancake, maneuvering the entire mass of noodles in a single flip. Brown the second side, about 5 minutes longer.

6 Loosen the browned "pancake" a little, then transfer to the warmed serving platter and keep warm.

FOR THE PANFRIED NOODLES:

2 tablespoons vegetable oil

½ pound thin egg noodles, boiled according to package instructions and drained

2 tablespoons vegetable oil

½ cup sliced onion

6 ounces small fresh mushrooms such as white button or a mixture of shiitake, chanterelle, oyster, and whatever is available, in any combination

2 ounces snow peas, trimmed

1 cup chicken stock

2 tablespoons cornstarch mixed with 3 tablespoons cold water

7 Heat a wok or heavy skillet over high heat until almost smoking. Add the oil; when it smokes, add the chicken. Sauté until lightly browned.

8 Add the onion, stirring quickly. In about 30 seconds, the onion will brown and release its aroma. Add the mushrooms, snow peas, and stock, cover, and when the steam escapes, reduce the heat to low and cook, covered, for 2 minutes.

9 Uncover and stir in the sauce. Bring to a boil.

10 Add the cornstarch mixture a little at a time, as needed, and boil until the sauce coats the chicken and vegetables.

11 Ladle over the panfried noodles. Serve immediately.

Serves 4

CHICKEN GRILLED
in CREAMY GARLIC-HERB MARINADE

½ cup roughly chopped
fresh curly or flat-leaf
(Italian) parsley or
¼ cup roughly chopped
fresh tarragon, basil,
thyme, or oregano

1 head garlic, peeled

1 teaspoon salt

1 tablespoon fresh lemon juice

Black pepper to taste

¼ cup olive oil

¼ cup vegetable oil

1 chicken, 4 pounds,
cut into serving pieces

1 Place all the ingredients except the chicken in a food processor and process until smooth and creamy.

2 Rinse the chicken pieces and pat dry with paper towels.

3 Combine the chicken and garlic mixture in a bowl and toss to coat evenly. Leave at room temperature for 2 hours, or cover and refrigerate for up to 1 day. (You can also store the chicken in a large zip-style plastic bag.)

4 Prepare an indirect-heat fire in a covered charcoal grill (page 33).

5 Set the dark meat on the grill rack, skin side down. Cover, open the top and bottom vents fully, and grill for 10 to 15 minutes. Add breasts and wings, skin side down, and continue grilling for 15 minutes longer. Check underneath. If not nicely browned, give the chicken another 10 minutes on the skin side.

6 Turn the pieces over. Spoon any excess marinade over the skin side, cover the grill, and continue to grill until cooked through, about 25 minutes longer.

7 Transfer to a serving platter and serve hot or warm.

Serves 4

This much-loved soup makes good use of leftover tortilla chips and chicken and the last nub of cheese. If you don't have Mexican cheese, use Monterey Jack.

TORTILLA SOUP
with CHICKEN SHREDS

2 tablespoons butter

1 white onion, chopped

1 tablespoon minced garlic

1 tablespoon flour

1 can (15 ounces) tomato sauce

3 or 4 ancho chiles

4 cups chicken stock, heated

1 teaspoon dried Mexican oregano

$\frac{1}{2}$ teaspoon salt

Black pepper to taste

Handful fresh mint sprigs

Handful fresh cilantro sprigs

FOR GARNISH (VERY IMPORTANT!):

1 cup corn tortilla chips (real ones!)

$\frac{1}{2}$ pound *queso blanco* (dry Mexican cheese), crumbled

Diced avocado

About 1$\frac{1}{2}$ cups shredded cooked chicken

4 lime wedges

1 Melt the butter in a large pot over medium heat. Add the onion and garlic and sauté until softened, about 8 minutes. Don't let the onion brown.

2 Sprinkle the flour over the onion, stirring the resulting paste for 1 minute. Stir in the tomato sauce and the whole anchos and bring to a boil, stirring constantly.

3 Slowly add the warm stock. Then add the oregano, salt, and pepper. Simmer, uncovered, for 15 to 20 minutes. Stir now and then, checking that the bottom doesn't scorch. Add mint and cilantro sprigs and continue to simmer until the flavors are blended, another 15 minutes. Remove and discard the sprigs.

4 To serve the soup, place the tortilla chips directly into soup bowls. Leaving the anchos in the pot, ladle the soup over the chips, then top decoratively with the cheese, avocado, and chicken. Serve immediately with lime wedges.

Serves 4

No other avocado—Fuerte or those stringy cannonballs from Florida—can hold up to the smooth lushness and fine flavor of the Haas. This satiny Haas-based soup is built on a simple formula for each serving: $1/2$ avocado, 1 tablespoon lemon juice, $1/2$ cup chicken stock, $1/4$ cup cream, and salt and white pepper to taste. Here is the arithmetic for 6 servings.

THICK AVOCADO SOUP

3 cups chicken stock

3 ripe (not too mushy) Haas avocados, pitted, peeled, and cut up

6 tablespoons fresh lemon juice

$1^{1}/_{2}$ cups cream

$1/2$ teaspoon salt

$1/8$ teaspoon white pepper

FOR GARNISH:
Chopped tomato
Chopped fresh cilantro
Freshly cut corn kernels
Minced jalapeño chile

1 Pour 2 cups of the stock into a saucepan and heat until hot.

2 In a blender, combine the avocado pulp, lemon juice, and the hot chicken stock. Blend until very smooth. Pour into a large bowl.

3 Whisk in the remaining 1 cup stock, and then the cream, salt, and pepper. (If your chicken stock is light on salt, you may need to add more to this soup to smooth out any acidic edge.) Cover and chill at least 2 hours.

4 Ladle into bowls and top each serving with as many of the garnishes as you choose.

Serves 6

I cannot brook dry chicken meat. That is precisely what comes to mind at the mention of chicken-breast patties that use a solid piece of meat. When breast meat is ground and then mixed with seasonings and a bit of egg, they're juicy and flavorful along with all the other attributes we like about cooking chicken, namely, that it's quick and easy.

CHICKEN BURGERS

1¹/₂ pounds boneless breast meat, skinned (about 5 breasts)

¹/₄ cup chopped onion

¹/₂ cup bread crumbs (fresh or dried; see Note, page 59)

1 egg, lightly beaten

1 tablespoon Worcestershire sauce

1¹/₂ teaspoons Dijon mustard

¹/₂ teaspoon black pepper

1¹/₂ teaspoons salt

1 tablespoon vegetable oil

4 buns of choice (whole wheat, regular hamburger buns)

FIXIN'S:
Ketchup, mustard, pickle relish, mayonnaise, onion slices, tomato slices, lettuce leaves

1 Turn the chicken breasts into "ground" chicken (page 24–25).

2 Place the chicken in a bowl and add all the remaining ingredients. Mash together with your hands. Form into 4 patties, each 1 inch thick.

3 Heat the oil in a nonstick skillet over high heat. When hot, add the patties. Sear briefly, reduce the heat to medium-high, and fry, turning once, until well browned and cooked through, about 5 minutes on each side. Alternatively, grill over a charcoal fire or slip under a preheated broiler (about 3 inches from the heat source) for about the same amount of time.

4 Serve on buns with your favorite fixin's.

Serves 4

Note: In your efforts to make these chicken burgers, I hope that you use chicken breast meat you've saved and frozen, or that at least you will purchase the bone-in, skin-on breasts and do the skinning and boning yourself. As burgers go, the ones made from those pretty chicken breasts already skinned and boned aren't much of a bargain.

ALLIUM FAMILY
CHICKEN TART

FOR THE PASTRY:

1 1/2 cups flour

1/4 teaspoon salt

Dash of sugar

7 tablespoons chilled butter, cut up

1 egg

1 tablespoon ice water

FOR THE FILLING:

3 tablespoons butter

1 yellow onion, cut into 1/4-inch-thick rings

1 red onion, cut into 1/4-inch-thick rings

2 leeks, white part only, thinly sliced

1/2 head garlic, minced

3/4 cup shredded cooked chicken meat (smoked is good, page 48)

2 eggs

2 cups heavy cream or half-and-half

1/4 teaspoon salt

Black pepper to taste

1 To make the pastry, in a food processor, combine the flour, salt, and sugar and pulse briefly to mix. Top with the butter, and process until crumbly.

2 Mix the egg and ice water in a measuring cup with a spout. With the motor running, pour the egg mixture into the processor and run until the mixture becomes a loose ball. Stop the machine immediately.

3 Gather the dough onto a big piece of waxed paper. Flatten as much as you can, wrap up, and chill for at least 30 minutes or as long as overnight.

4 Preheat an oven to 350°F. Roll out the cold dough into an 11-inch round and fit into a 9-inch tart pan with a removable bottom and 1-inch sides. Trim the edges and prick the pastry in several places with the tines of a fork. Line the dough with the same waxed paper you used to wrap it, and weight it down with a layer of raw rice, macaroni, or dried beans. Bake for 15 minutes, until pale. Remove from the oven.

5 Pull up on the waxed paper to lift out the weights. Raise the oven temperature to 450°F. Let the crust cool slightly.

Ouija Chick

The Romans were so superstitious that they let a chicken peck out their fortunes: They watched while the bird pointed to letters in an alphabet carved in the dirt.

6 While the crust is baking and cooling, make the filling: Melt the butter in a sauté pan over medium-high heat. Add the yellow and red onions, the leeks, and the garlic. Reduce the heat to medium-low, cover, and cook, stirring now and then, until wilted, about 20 minutes. Uncover and cook for a few minutes longer to dry out any pan juices. Pour into a sieve and discard the liquid. Place the contents of the sieve in a bowl.

7 Add the shredded chicken and set aside to cool slightly.

8 In another bowl, whisk together the eggs, cream, salt, and pepper to taste.

9 Spread the onion-chicken mixture in the partially baked tart crust, then slowly pour the egg mixture evenly over the top, allowing it to soak in.

10 Set the tart pan on a baking sheet to catch any drips. Bake for 5 minutes. Reduce the oven temperature to 325°F and bake for 25 to 30 minutes longer. The tart is done when a knife inserted halfway between the center and the edge comes out clean. Let cool for 10 minutes before slicing into wedges, or serve at room temperature.

Serves 4 to 6

I got the idea for this when I saw a leftover chicken breast in the refrigerator after a weekend of zealous grilling with mesquite-flavored charcoal, although leftover baked, wok-smoked, or sautéed chicken would be good, too. A trip to a farmers' market garnered dainty, young green beans.

SMOKED CHICKEN, GREEN BEANS, GARLIC, and PARMESAN FRITTATA

1/3 pound young, tender green beans, trimmed

6 eggs

2 tablespoons milk

1/2 teaspoon salt

Black pepper to taste

3 tablespoons olive oil

1 teaspoon minced garlic

1 smoked chicken breast, boned and skinned, sliced into strips

1/4 cup shredded Parmesan cheese

1 Preheat a broiler.

2 If the beans are thick, cut them into 1-inch lengths; if they are small, young, and tender, leave them whole.

3 In a bowl, combine the eggs, milk, salt, and pepper but don't whisk yet.

4 Heat the oil in a nonstick skillet that has an ovenproof handle over high heat. Add the beans and sauté until bright green, 1 to 1½ minutes. Add the garlic and chicken and sauté for 1 minute longer.

5 Whisk together the eggs and milk and pour them into the skillet. After a moment, reduce the heat to medium and lift the edges of the egg to let uncooked portion flow under.

6 When the edges are set but the center is still runny, sprinkle the surface with the Parmesan and quickly slip the frittata under the broiler. Broil until it puffs, about 30 seconds.

7 Slide the frittata onto a serving platter, cheese side up. Serve hot or cold, cut into wedges.

Serves 4

Here, Brie and herbs are combined in a
beautiful ring mold, to make a cool appetizer
for spring parties and celebrations.

BRIE MOUSSE
with CHICKEN and HERBS

1 bunch green onions

1 envelope plain gelatin

3 tablespoons fresh lemon juice

$^3/_4$ cup boiling water

$^1/_2$ pound Brie cheese,
at room temperature

$^1/_2$ pound cream cheese, at
room temperature

$^1/_2$ cup mixed finely chopped
fresh herbs such as parsley,
tarragon, rosemary, basil,
thyme, and chervil; or
$^1/_4$ cup mixed dried herbs; or a
combination of fresh and dried

$1^1/_2$ cups finely minced
cooked chicken

$^3/_4$ cup fat-free chicken stock

Salt and white pepper to taste

4 egg whites

$^1/_2$ cup heavy cream

Small toasts for serving

1 Chop white and green parts of the green onions separately. Sprinkle the green parts over the bottom of a 5- to 6-cup tube pan.

2 In a large bowl, stir together the gelatin and lemon juice. Let the mixture stand for 5 minutes to soften the gelatin. Add the boiling water, stir, and let cool.

3 In a food processor, combine the white parts of the green onions, the Brie and cream cheeses, and the herbs. Process until well mixed. Add to the gelatin, stirring to blend well, then add the chicken, stock, salt, and pepper.

4 In a bowl, beat the egg whites until stiff peaks form. In another bowl, whip the cream until medium-stiff peaks form. Fold the whites into the cheese mixture just until combined, then fold in the cream. Pour into the prepared tube pan, cover, and refrigerate until set, about 3 hours.

5 To unmold, dip the base of the tube pan in a bowl of hot water for 1 or 2 seconds, then immediately invert onto a round serving platter. (The mold can then be returned to the refrigerator for up to 2 days before serving.) Serve as an appetizer for spreading on small toasts.

Serves 10 to 12

Real people eat quiche, and real cooks make them. You can make quiche with chicken on purpose, or wait for the leftovers. The quiche's softness does well as a backdrop for the velvety White-Cooked Chicken (page 50).

DEEP-DISH
CHICKEN-SPINACH QUICHE

FOR THE PASTRY:

1½ cups flour

Dash of salt

Dash of sugar

7 tablespoons chilled butter, cut up

1 egg

1 tablespoon ice water

FOR THE FILLING:

1 tablespoon butter

3 leeks, white part only, sliced

1 pound spinach, rinsed and stemmed, or 1 package (10 ounces) frozen spinach, thawed

2 tablespoons olive oil

2 cups diced cooked chicken meat

1 tablespoon minced garlic

¾ cup shredded Parmesan cheese

4 whole eggs

3 yolks

2 cups half-and-half

½ teaspoon salt

Black pepper to taste

Pinch of nutmeg

1 To make the pastry, in a food processor, combine the flour, salt, and sugar and pulse briefly to mix. Top with the butter, and process until crumbly.

2 Mix the egg and ice water in a measuring cup with a spout. With the motor running, pour the egg mixture into the processor and run until the mixture comes together in a rough mass. Stop the machine immediately.

3 Gather the dough onto a big piece of waxed paper. Flatten as much as you can, wrap up, and chill for 30 minutes.

4 Preheat an oven to 350°F. Roll out the cold dough into an 1-inch round and fit into a 9-inch tart pan with a removable bottom and 2-inch sides. Trim the edges and prick the pastry in several places with the tines of a fork. Line the dough with the same waxed paper you used to wrap it, and weight it down with a layer of raw rice, macaroni, or dried beans. Bake for 15 minutes, until pale. Remove from the oven.

5 Pull up on the waxed paper to lift out the weights. Increase the oven temperature to 450°F. Let the crust cool slightly.

6 While the crust is baking and cooling, make the filling: Melt the butter in a sauté pan over medium heat. Add the leeks and sauté until soft, about 5 minutes. Set aside.

Pecking Order

The social behavior established by roosters is called The Order of the Peck. It was first detected in chickens by a sixteenth-century Italian, Ulisse Aldrovani.

7 Meanwhile, if using fresh spinach, add it wet to a very hot wok or Dutch oven. Stir quickly until partially wilted, about 2 minutes. Drain and press out the water. If using frozen spinach, press out excess moisture

8 Heat the olive oil in a sauté pan over high heat. Add the wilted or thawed spinach and sauté for 30 seconds. Add the chicken and garlic, stir a few times, and remove from the heat.

9 Sprinkle the Parmesan over the bottom of the partially baked crust. Top with the cooked leeks and then the spinach-chicken mixture.

10 In a bowl, whisk together the whole eggs, egg yolks, half-and-half, salt, a generous amount of pepper, and the nutmeg. Slowly pour the egg mixture over the spinach-chicken mixture, allowing it to soak in.

11 Set the tart pan on a baking sheet to catch any drips. Bake until a knife inserted halfway between the center and the edge comes out clean, 70 to 80 minutes. Let stand for 10 minutes before cutting into wedges.

Serves 6 to 8

SCRATCH

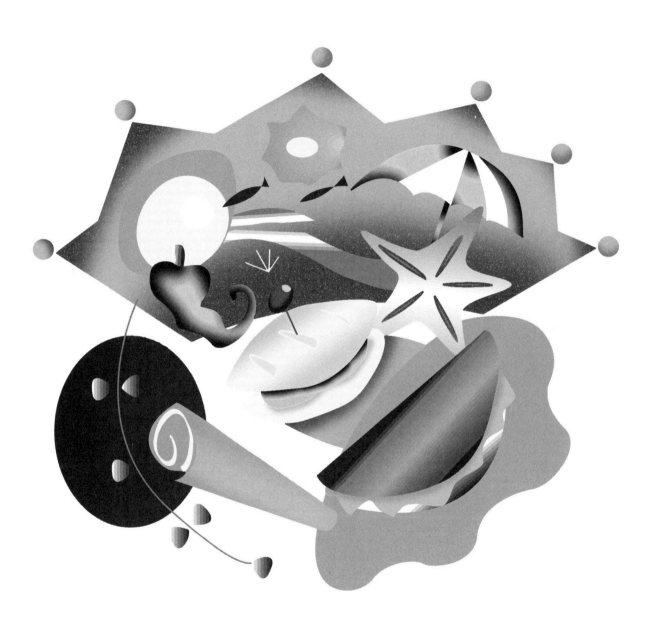

SUMMER

Summer heat encourages culinary heat, just like in countries where the weather and the food are simultaneously hot. This is the season to cook chicken in quick stove-top sautés or out on the grill, and serve it hot, at room temperature, or cold.

Imagine a sultry evening with chicken coated in the refreshing flavors of cardamom, lemon, lime, or coconut. Cook skewered chicken with yogurt marinade, peanut butter, and all kinds of spices and even a baste based on Coke. Fill grape leaves with chicken for an appetizer of dolmades.

By midsummer, the glorious stereo-types of tomatoes and basil overpower us. Ratatouille stuff shows up. The sight of tomatoes and okra at the same time means gumbo must be made, even if it makes the house hot. Chicken welcomes eggplant, peppers, and all kinds of summer squashes. If you've got red roses, the petals make a fragrant marinade.

We also cook with summer's fruit: chicken and peaches, chicken and plums, chicken with mango and banana. By now the house is hot and chicken salad must be made. And that California cliché of goat cheese and sun-dried tomatoes is out in full force.

Summer seems to hang on long after its official end. There's corn to spare, romano beans, eggplant, and melon still hanging around. The grape harvest begins, and they're good with chicken, too. Don't put the grill away yet.

SUMMER

R E

CIPES

Boneless chicken breasts get a crunchy coating from bread crumbs. If you don't make the crumbs yourself out of stale bread, use store-bought crumbs—it won't make any difference to the chicken. But homemade crumbs have an irregularity that browns the breasts in appealing multiple tones, from dark on the outermost edges to a twinkling of light and beige gazing in.

EGG-BREADED
CHICKEN BREASTS
in NATURAL SAUCE

4 boneless chicken breasts, skin on

½ cup flour mixed with 1 teaspoon salt and ½ teaspoon pepper

2 eggs, beaten

⅓ cup fresh bread crumbs (see Note, page 59)

2 tablespoons butter

½ cup chicken stock

1 tablespoon chopped fresh parsley

1 Heat a serving platter in a 150°F oven.

2 Rinse the chicken breasts and pat dry with paper towels. Dredge them in the seasoned flour, shaking off the excess, dip in egg, then run through the bread crumbs generously.

3 Melt 1 tablespoon of the butter in a wide, heavy sauté pan over high heat. Add the breasts, skin side down. Reduce the heat to medium-high and sauté, turning once, until well browned and cooked through, 5 to 6 minutes on each side. Remove the chicken breasts to the warmed serving platter and keep warm.

4 Spoon off all but 1 tablespoon fat from the pan and return to high heat. Add the stock, scraping up any browned bits from the pan bottom. Boil until slightly thickened and reduced to about ½ cup.

5 Remove from the heat. Whisk in the remaining tablespoon butter until melted. Pour the sauce over the chicken breasts, sprinkle with the parsley, and serve hot.

Serves 4

Sweet 100s are tiny cherry tomatoes that are a favorite in supermarkets and backyard gardens. The gardener's patio tomato is a close second. If you end up using slightly larger cherry tomatoes, cut them in half.

CHICKEN BREAST

SAUTÉ with SWEET 100s, GARLIC, and BASIL

4 boneless chicken breasts, skinned

¹/₄ cup flour

¹/₄ cup bread crumbs (fresh or dried; see Note, page 59)

3 tablespoons grated Parmesan cheese

Salt and black pepper to taste

1 tablespoon olive oil

2 tablespoons butter

1 tablespoon minced garlic

1 cup (about ¹/₂ pint basket) Sweet 100s or Patio tomatoes, stemmed (see recipe introduction)

7 or 8 fresh basil leaves

¹/₂ cup chicken stock

1 Heat a serving platter in a 150°F oven.

2 Rinse the chicken breasts and pat dry with paper towels.

3 In a shallow bowl, mix together the flour, bread crumbs, cheese, and dashes of salt and pepper.

4 Heat the oil and 1 tablespoon of the butter in a sauté pan over medium-high heat. Roll each chicken breast in the flour-crumb mixture, lowering each one into the pan as you go. Reduce the heat to medium and sauté until browned on the first side, 4 to 5 minutes. Turn, add the remaining 1 tablespoon butter, and cook until browned on the second side and cooked through, 4 to 5 minutes. Transfer to the warmed serving platter and keep warm.

5 Add the garlic, tomatoes, and basil leaves to the pan. Sauté for a few seconds until you can smell the garlic. With the heat cranked to high, pour in the stock. Stir and boil until somewhat thickened, 1 to 2 minutes.

6 Pour over the sautéed breasts and serve right away.

Serves 4

Here, the heart-shaped *whole* chicken breast is grilled, much as you'd treat a flank steak. The resulting slices are tender and juicy.

110

GRILLED WHOLE CHICKEN BREASTS
with GARLIC and LIME

2 whole boneless
chicken breasts, skin on

Juice of 5 limes (about $^2/_3$ cup)

$^1/_2$ cup olive oil

Salt and black pepper to taste

4 large garlic cloves, slivered

Lime wedges

1 Rinse the whole chicken breasts and pat dry with paper towels.

2 In a bowl, combine the lime juice, olive oil, salt, and pepper. Add the chicken breasts, turning to coat. Cover and marinate for 2 hours at room temperature or overnight in the refrigerator.

3 Prepare a direct-heat fire in an open charcoal grill (pages 33–34).

4 Just before cooking, remove the breasts from the marinade, reserving the marinade. Using your fingers, loosen the skin on both breasts and slip the slivers of garlic under the skin.

5 Place the breasts on the grill rack, skin side down, and grill for about 7 minutes, basting often with the marinade.

6 Turn the chicken breasts, sprinkle lightly with salt and pepper, and grill, continuing to baste, until cooked through, about 6 minutes longer.

7 Remove to a cutting board with a trough to catch the juices. Cut on the diagonal into juicy ¼-inch-thick slices. Remove to a serving platter. Collect any juices and serve as a sauce.

Serves 4 to 6

THE SAME RECIPE,
BROILED

...5 Set a broiler rack inside a broiler pan, brush the rack with vegetable oil, insert the apparatus in the broiler about 3 inches from the heating element, and preheat the rack.

6 When hot, add the marinated chicken breasts to the rack, skin side down. They'll sizzle as if on an outdoor grill. Broil for about 5 minutes, skin side down, basting with the marinade. Turn, sprinkle with salt and pepper, and broil the second side, continuing to baste.

7 Pour the pan drippings into a pitcher and serve with the chicken breasts.

Much of the preparation for these pretty chicken-and-vegetable sandwiches is done grillside, which keeps the kitchen clean. You can serve them whole as a hot main course, or chill them, slice them on the diagonal to reveal the layers inside, and eat them as an appetizer held together with toothpicks.

CHICKEN BREASTS
STUFFED with GRILLED EGGPLANT and ROASTED RED BELLS

6 boneless chicken breasts, skin on

1/2 cup olive oil, plus olive oil for brushing

1/4 cup fresh lemon juice

1 tablespoon minced garlic

1/2 teaspoon salt

1/8 teaspoon black pepper

2 red bell peppers

1 eggplant

Minced fresh or dried oregano to taste

Salt and black pepper to taste

6 small fresh oregano sprigs (optional)

1 Rinse the chicken breasts and pat dry with paper towels. Slit the breasts across as if to butterfly them, leaving one side attached like a hinge for opening and closing.

2 In a shallow bowl, combine the 1/2 cup olive oil, the lemon juice, garlic, salt, and pepper. Add the chicken and leave to marinate. Prepare a direct-heat fire in an open charcoal grill (pages 33–34).

3 Grill the bell peppers, turning with tongs, until the skins are black and blistered on all sides. Transfer to a plastic or paper bag to cool. Using your fingers, peel off the skins and discard the stems and seeds. Cut into sections about the same size as the chicken breasts.

4 At grillside, slice the eggplant into rounds 1/4 inch thick. Have ready a small bowl of olive oil and a pastry brush. Place the eggplant rounds on the grill rack, then brush with olive oil and sprinkle with salt, pepper, and oregano. Grill, turning once, until black grid marks show on both sides and the slices are tender, about 4 minutes total. Transfer to a plate. Keep the grill hot.

5 Fill the slit breasts with layers of grilled eggplant and red pepper. Sprinkle each with salt and pepper, insert a sprig of fresh oregano, if using, and then drizzle a little olive oil inside. Close each breast.

6 Place the stuffed breasts on the grill rack and grill, turning once, until cooked through, about 5 minutes on each side. Serve as directed in the recipe introduction.

Serves 4 to 6

This is a good dish for company on a hot evening. It's easy and exotic, quick and refreshing, with enough of a spice jolt to make its presence known. Thai red curry paste is easily found at Asian stores.

GRILLED COCONUT-CURRY
CHICKEN

2 chickens, 3¹/₂ to 4 pounds each, cut into serving pieces

1 can (13¹/₂ ounces) coconut milk

2 tablespoons Thai red curry paste

²/₃ cup packed brown sugar

¹/₂ cup chopped fresh cilantro

1 tablespoon chopped fresh mint

2 jalapeño chiles, seeded and minced

¹/₂ teaspoon salt

1 Rinse the chicken pieces and pat dry with paper towels.

2 In a big bowl, combine all the remaining ingredients. Add the chicken and mix with your hands until well coated. Cover and marinate in the refrigerator for at least 3 hours or as long as overnight. Remove the chicken from the refrigerator 1 hour before grilling.

3 Prepare an indirect-heat fire in a covered charcoal grill (page 33).

4 Add the dark meat to the grill rack, skin side down. Cover, position the top and bottom vents three-quarters open, and grill for 15 minutes longer. Add the breasts and wings and continue grilling, covered, for 15 minutes longer. Turn all the pieces, re-cover, and grill on the second side until golden and cooked through, about 20 minutes.

5 Remove to a serving platter and serve hot or warm.

Serves 8

CHICKEN **52** NUGGET

Why did the chicken cross the road?

Karl Marx: Because as a function of dialectical materialism the chicken owned the road.

Coke (is there another kind of cola?) does a nice job of tenderizing chicken. Combined with vinegar for power and cardamom for fragrance, the flavor of this marinade holds up well during cooking. Ground cardamom is available in supermarket spice departments. Serve with rice and a cucumber salad.

CHICKEN KEBABS
in COLA-CARDAMOM MARINADE

6 boneless chicken breasts, skinned (about 2 pounds)

1 can (12 ounces) Coca-Cola®

3 large garlic cloves, minced

$\frac{1}{4}$ cup balsamic vinegar or red wine vinegar

$\frac{1}{2}$ teaspoon ground cardamom

2 teaspoons coarse salt

1 teaspoon coarsely ground black pepper

3 lemon zest strips, each 1 inch wide

1 Rinse the chicken breasts and pat dry with paper towels. Cut into $1\frac{1}{2}$-inch cubes.

2 In a bowl, combine all the remaining ingredients. Add the chicken, stir to coat, cover, and marinate for 2 hours at room temperature or as long as overnight in the refrigerator.

3 Prepare a direct-heat fire in an open charcoal grill (pages 33–34).

4 Remove the chicken pieces from the marinade and thread onto metal skewers. Pour the marinade into a small pot.

5 Place the marinade over high heat, bring to a boil, and boil until reduced to $\frac{1}{2}$ cup, about 12 minutes. The marinade will darken and thicken.

6 Arrange the skewers on the grill rack and grill, turning once and basting frequently with the boiled marinade, until cooked through, 8 to 10 minutes.

7 Remove to a serving platter and serve.

Serves 4 to 6

The rough-crushed spices stand up nicely to the big flavor of grilled dark meat. If you don't have a mortar and pestle, put the spices in a zip-style bag and bang on it with a rolling pin.

HERBAL-RUB
DARK MEAT GRILL

4 large garlic cloves

1 teaspoon coarse salt

¹/₄ cup chopped fresh parsley

¹/₂ teaspoon black peppercorns

2 teaspoons dried thyme

2 shallots, finely minced

8 chicken thighs

3 bay leaves

1 In a mortar, crush together the garlic, salt, parsley, peppercorns, and thyme. Add the shallots and crush into the spices.

2 Rinse the thighs and pat dry with paper towels.

3 Using your fingers, carefully loosen the skin on the thighs and tuck some of the herbal rub under the skin. Load the thighs, any remaining rub, and the bay leaves into a sturdy zip-style plastic bag. Refrigerate overnight or for up to 2 days.

4 Prepare an indirect-heat fire in a charcoal grill (page 33). Place the thighs on the grill rack, skin side down, cover, open the vents fully, and grill for 15 minutes. Turn, re-cover, and grill until cooked through, about 15 minutes longer.

5 Remove to a serving platter and serve.

Serves 4

This is so easy that all you need is a slicing knife and a fork. If you have peanut butter in the house, that should inspire you to go out and buy the few exotics to finish making the dish.

116

PARTY CHICKEN SATAY

with PEANUT DIPPING SAUCE

6 boneless
chicken breasts, skinned

Juice of 4 limes

2 tablespoons vegetable oil

3 tablespoons chopped fresh
cilantro

2-inch piece fresh ginger (about 2
ounces), peeled and minced

$1/2$ teaspoon cayenne pepper

2 large garlic cloves, minced

Salt and black pepper to taste

FOR THE PEANUT DIPPING SAUCE:

$1/3$ cup peanut butter

2 tablespoons fresh lime juice

$1/4$ teaspoon cayenne pepper

1 teaspoon sugar

2 teaspoons soy sauce

1 tablespoon peeled and minced
fresh ginger

$1/4$ cup water

1 Rinse the chicken breasts and pat dry with paper towels. Cut the chicken into 1-inch squares.

2 In a zip-style plastic bag, combine the chicken with all the remaining ingredients. Seal the top, then turn the bag to mix well. Refrigerate overnight.

3 Prepare a direct-heat fire in a covered charcoal grill (pages 33–34).

4 To make the peanut sauce, in a bowl, combine all the ingredients and stir with a fork.

5 Remove the chicken from the marinade, reserving the marinade. Thread the chicken onto metal skewers. Arrange on the grill rack, cover, open the vents fully, and grill, drizzling some of the marinade over the skewers as they cook, until browned on the first side, about 4 minutes. Turn and grill on the second side until browned and cooked through, about 4 minutes longer. Discard the remaining marinade.

6 Serve immediately with the peanut dipping sauce.

Serves 6 to 8

An easy make-ahead meal. The marinade's dose of lemon freshens the flavor of the yogurt base.

CHICKEN AND SUMMER-VEGETABLE SKEWERS in YOGURT MARINADE

FOR THE YOGURT MARINADE:

1 cup plain yogurt

3 tablespoons olive oil

1 tablespoon honey

1 teaspoon finely minced garlic

1 teaspoon dried oregano

Finely minced zest of 1 lemon

$1/2$ teaspoon salt

$1/8$ teaspoon white pepper

1 pound boneless chicken breasts, skinned (about 3 breasts)

1 red bell pepper

1 yellow bell pepper

1 zucchini

About 12 fresh white mushrooms

$1/2$ large red onion, cut into wedges

1 In a bowl or food processor, combine all the marinade ingredients. Stir or process until well mixed. Divide evenly between 2 bowls.

2 Rinse the chicken breasts and pat dry with paper towels. Cut into 1-inch squares. Add the chicken to 1 of the bowls, turning to coat. Cover and marinate for 2 hours at room temperature or as long as overnight in the refrigerator. (You can store the chicken in a zip-style plastic bag if it goes into the refrigerator. Cover and refrigerate the second bowl of marinade as well.)

3 Seed the bell peppers and cut into 1½-inch squares. Cut the zucchini into 1½-inch lengths. Add the peppers, zucchini, and mushrooms to the remaining bowl of marinade, turning to coat. Cover and marinate at room temperature for 2 hours.

4 Prepare a direct-heat fire in an open charcoal grill (pages 33–34).

5 Remove the chicken and vegetables from their marinades. Discard the chicken marinade and reserve the vegetable marinade. Thread the chicken onto skewers alternately with the vegetables.

6 Place the skewers on the grill rack over a very hot fire. Grill, turning once and dabbing with the reserved vegetable marinade, until cooked through, about 5 minutes on each side.

7 Remove to a serving platter and serve.

Serves 4

While the chicken grills, you can go back to the kitchen and quickly sauté and broil a batch of buttered spiced corn, which hopefully is cut fresh from the cob.

118

SPICE-RUBBED GRILLED CHICKEN
with BUTTERED CORN
and RED CHILE

1 chicken, 4 pounds,
cut into serving pieces

¼ cup olive oil

1 tablespoon pure chile powder
such as New Mexico

2 teaspoons paprika

2 chipotle chiles in adobo
sauce, minced

½ teaspoon ground cumin

¼ teaspoon salt

FOR THE CORN:

2 tablespoons butter

2 cups corn kernels
(fresh or frozen)

½ teaspoon red pepper flakes

Salt and black pepper to taste

¼ cup plain yogurt,
sour cream, or crème fraîche

2 tablespoons buttered bread
crumbs (see Note, page 59)
or cracker crumbs

1 Rinse the chicken pieces and pat dry with paper towels.

2 In a bowl, combine the oil, chile powder, paprika, chipotle chiles, cumin, and salt. Add the chicken pieces, turning to coat, cover, and marinate at room temperature for 2 hours or for as long as overnight. (You can store the chicken in a large zip-style plastic bag if it goes in the refrigerator.)

3 Prepare an indirect-heat fire in a covered charcoal grill (page 33). Place the dark meat, skin side down, on the grill rack, cover, position the top and bottom vents three-quarters open, and grill for 10 minutes. Add the breasts and wings, skin side down, re-cover, and continue grilling for 10 minutes. Turn all the chicken, re-cover, and grill on the second side until cooked through, about 20 minutes.

4 While the chicken grills, preheat a broiler and butter a small flameproof baking dish. Melt the butter in a sauté pan over high heat. Add the corn and sauté until tender but not mushy, 2 to 2½ minutes. Add the red pepper flakes and season with salt and pepper. Cook for a minute or two more. Remove from the heat, stir in the yogurt, sour cream, or crème fraîche, and transfer to the prepared baking dish. Sprinkle with the crumbs.

5 Just before the chicken is ready, run the baking dish under the broiler to brown lightly. Bring outdoors and eat grillside with the chicken.

Serves 4

Here, whole breasts get grilled and sliced as if they were London broil. Mind you that the word fajita means "little belt" or "sash" and is the term used for skirt steak, a piece commonly discarded by many folks in the past. Fajita now implies any grilled meat snuggled into a flour tortilla, although the concept "chicken belt" is a struggle. The original beef fajita was not marinated but seasoned with salt and pepper and served with *pico de gallo* (salsa), guacamole, and sour cream. Here the chicken is marinated and we keep the fixin's. It doesn't matter if the beer is flat; it will be shortly.

CHICKEN FAJITAS

2 whole boneless chicken breasts, skin on

Juice of 2 limes

2 large garlic cloves, minced

1/4 cup chopped fresh cilantro

2 tablespoons mesquite smoke flavoring

1/4 cup beer

2 teaspoons Worcestershire sauce

Dash of Tabasco or other hot-pepper sauce

3 tablespoons vegetable oil

8 small flour tortillas, heated

Salsa of choice

Guacamole (optional)

Sour cream (optional)

1 Rinse the chicken breasts and pat dry with paper towels.

2 In a small bowl, combine the lime juice, garlic, cilantro, smoke flavoring, beer, Worcestershire sauce, Tabasco sauce, and oil. Slip the chicken breasts into a large zip-style plastic bag, pour in the lime juice mixture, seal the top, and turn the bag to coat the chicken evenly. Marinate overnight in the refrigerator.

3 Prepare an indirect-heat fire in a covered charcoal grill (page 33).

4 Remove the chicken breasts from the marinade, reserving the marinade. Place the chicken, skin side down, on the grill rack. Cover, position the top and bottom vents three-quarters open, and grill for 8 minutes, basting with the reserved marinade. Turn, re-cover, and grill on the second side, basting occasionally, until cooked through, about 8 minutes longer.

5 Remove the chicken from the grill. You may remove the skin at this point, if desired. Thinly slice the chicken while it is still hot.

6 Place about 1/4 cup of the chicken in each warmed tortilla. Top with salsa and with guacamole and sour cream, if desired. Wrap like burritos and serve at once.

Serves 4

A long time ago I went to Greece and learned how to make dolmades, stuffed grape leaves, in the home of a friend's mother on the island of Rhodes. She used lamb. She would never have used chicken, and until I began writing this book, it didn't cross my mind that the dark meat of chicken would be just as rich and delicious. At any rate, I was astounded (actually, jealous) that she was privileged to reach out her kitchen's second-floor window to yank grape leaves off a vine.

At the time of my trip, my home was back in Texas. When I returned, I was able to make dolmades just as she did because everything I needed grows as profusely in America as it does in Greece. Did you know there are wild grape leaves growing all over the place—in alleys, through the cracks in sidewalks, flopping over hedges? Keep your eyes open for them every June.

Now that I live in California I have a grapevine of my own—not for wine, but for grapes we eat for snacks. When the vine gets too pushy, I give it a few whacks and stuff the leaves. When they make contact with the boiling water, the house smells like wine.

CHICKEN AND RICE
STUFFED in GRAPE LEAVES

FOR THE GRAPE LEAVES:

40 (or so) fresh or bottled grape leaves

1 teaspoon baking soda, if using fresh leaves

1 If using fresh vine leaves, rinse well. Pour water to a depth of 4 inches into a Dutch oven or other large, deep pot. Bring to a boil, adding the baking soda, and then drop in the leaves. Boil for about 3 minutes. Drain off the liquid, rinse the leaves again, and drain well. If using bottled grape leaves, rinse off the brine and boil the leaves for 5 minutes without baking soda.

2 Select 6 to 8 of the largest leaves and use to line the bottom of the same Dutch oven. Snip out the thick bottom stem of each remaining leaf, making an incision in the shape of an inverted V. (You may not have to do this with the bottled leaves.)

3 To "grind" the meat for the filling, mince it with a chef's knife as you would any other food, or place in a food processor and pulse, using 20 short-long bursts. Transfer the chicken to a bowl and add all the remaining ingredients except the lemon. Mix well.

FOR THE CHICKEN FILLING:

1 pound boneless chicken
thighs or drumsticks

1 large onion, minced

1 teaspoon minced garlic

¹/₂ cup pine nuts

¹/₂ cup minced fresh mint

¹/₂ cup minced fresh dill

¹/₄ cup minced fresh parsley

2 teaspoons ground cinnamon

¹/₂ cup olive oil

2 teaspoons salt

¹/₂ cup long-grain white rice

Juice of 1 lemon

FOR THE EGG LEMON SAUCE:

Juice of 4 lemons

3 egg yolks

2 tablespoons cornstarch

4 Lay out a few of the leaves, underside up, on a work surface. Place 1 tablespoon of the chicken-rice mixture near the base of a leaf. Fold over the base, fold in the sides toward the center, and then roll up the leaf toward its point into a snug packet. Place seam side down in the pot. Repeat until all the leaves and filling are used up.

5 Pour in enough water to cover the packets barely. Sprinkle with the lemon juice.

6 Weight down the packets with a heavy heatproof plate (or top a regular heatproof plate with a heavy can of food). Cover and simmer over low heat for 45 minutes to 1 hour.

7 Using tongs, (you'll be using the cooking liquid), transfer the dolmades to a rack to drip dry. Lift out and discard the leaves lining the pot.

8 To make the sauce, in a bowl, whisk together the lemon juice, egg yolks, and cornstarch until smooth. Return the Dutch oven to medium heat and bring to a simmer. Whisk the egg yolk mixture into the warm cooking liquid until the sauce thickens, about 1 minute. You should have about 2½ cups sauce. Remove from the heat immediately and pour into a small bowl.

9 Serve the dolmades warm or chilled with the sauce chilled or at room temperature.

Makes about 3 dozen

Pancetta, an Italian bacon, is used here as an item of interest inside a rolled up chicken breast.

122

CHICKEN-PANCETTA ROLLS
with BASIL LEAVES

6 boneless
chicken breasts, skinned

Salt and black pepper to taste

12 fresh basil or sage leaves

6 pancetta slices

1 Prepare a direct-heat fire in a covered charcoal grill (pages 33–34).

2 Rinse the breasts and pat dry with paper towels. One at a time, sandwich them between two sheets of waxed paper and pound (a rolling pin works great) until thin.

3 Place the breasts on a work surface, smooth side down. Sprinkle with salt and pepper. Lay a slice of pancetta on each breast, then place 2 basil leaves, end to end, over the pancetta.

4 Roll up the breasts, and hold in place with wooden toothpicks.

5 Place the rolls on the grill rack, cover, open the top and bottom vents fully, and grill, turning once, until cooked through, about 8 minutes on each side.

6 Let cool slightly, then slice into spirals and arrange on a platter.

Serves 6

Bone-in chicken breasts enjoy fantastic sales in summer. The cooking time is about twice as long as for boned, skinned breasts, but the peppers need the extra time, anyway, to soften fully. For the pickled garlic, buy a jar of whole cloves pickled in some kind of spicy backdrop. There are many brands. I use Holler's from Stockton, California.

CHICKEN BREASTS
with SUMMER PEPPERS and SPICY PICKLED GARLIC

4 chicken breasts (about 2 pounds)

Salt and black pepper to taste

2 tablespoons butter

$^1/_2$ onion, sliced

$^3/_4$ pound assorted summer peppers (bell, gypsy, mild Italian), seeded and cut into long strips $^1/_3$ inch wide

$^1/_2$ cup chicken stock

8 to 10 large pickled garlic cloves, coarsely chopped, plus 1 tablespoon of the juice

1 Heat a serving platter in a 150°F oven.

2 Rinse the chicken breasts and pat dry with paper towels. Sprinkle with salt and pepper.

3 Melt the butter in a wide, heavy sauté pan over medium-high heat. Add the chicken breasts, skin side down, and sauté, turning once, until well browned, 4 to 5 minutes on each side. Remove to a plate.

4 Add the onion to the pan and sauté for 1 minute over medium-high heat. Then add the peppers, raise the heat to high, and sauté for 1 minute. Reduce the heat to medium and sauté until softened, about 5 minutes.

5 Return the chicken to the pan, skin side up. Raise the heat to high, and add the stock. Scatter the garlic over the chicken and drizzle with the garlic juice. Cover, reduce the heat so the liquid simmers, and cook until the breasts are cooked through, 5 to 8 minutes longer.

6 Remove the chicken breasts to the warmed serving platter. Bring the peppers and juices in the pan to a boil and boil for 1 minute or so, to thicken the juices slightly. Pour the juices and peppers over the chicken and serve hot.

Serves 4

The Mexican trilogy of corn, beans, and squash here comes to the table quite un-Mexican except for the addition of Mexican oregano. A huge amount of shredded Monterey Jack cheese goes over the vegetables and is allowed to melt—not bake—in a hot turned-off oven.

CHICKEN SAUTÉ
with ROMANO BEANS, CORN, and SQUASH

1 chicken, 4 pounds, cut into serving pieces

Salt and black pepper to taste

1 tablespoon butter

1 tablespoon vegetable oil

³/₄ pound romano beans, cut on the diagonal into 1-inch lengths

Kernels from 1 ear of yellow or white corn

2 tomatoes, peeled, seeded, and cut into chunks (see Peeling Tomatoes, page 177)

1 tablespoon minced garlic

3 assorted summer squashes, such as dark green zucchini, crookneck, and light green zucchini, quartered lengthwise and cut into thick slices

2 teaspoons dried Mexican oregano

³/₄ pound Monterey Jack cheese, shredded

2 tablespoons white wine, water, or stock

1 Hack the breasts in half crosswise. Rinse the chicken pieces and pat dry with paper towels. Sprinkle with salt and pepper.

2 Butter a 1½-quart baking dish or soufflé dish. Preheat an oven to 350°F.

3 Heat the butter and the oil in a wide, heavy sauté pan over high heat. Add the chicken, skin side down. Sear briefly, reduce the heat to medium-high, and sauté, turning once, until well browned, about 4 minutes on each side. Remove to a bowl.

4 Add the beans to the fat remaining in the pan and sauté over medium-high heat for a good 3 minutes. Scoop out the beans with a slotted spoon, letting the excess fat drip back into the pan, and place in a bowl.

5 Pour off all but 1 tablespoon of the fat from the pan and return the pan to medium-high heat. Add the corn, tomatoes, and garlic and sauté for 1 minute. Add the squashes and sauté for 1 minute longer. Return the beans to the pan and sprinkle all the vegetables with salt, pepper, and 1 teaspoon of the oregano. Cover and cook over medium-low heat for 1 minute.

Brazil Is Number Two

Brazil is the second-largest producer of poultry meat
in the world. A typical Brazilian poultry company
owns the breeding farm, hatchery, processing plant,
and feed mill.

6 Transfer the vegetables to the prepared dish. Sprinkle evenly with the cheese and set in the oven. Turn off the oven and leave the vegetables in it until you're ready to serve.

7 Return the sauté pan to high heat and return the chicken to the pan, including any juices that have collected in the bowl. Sprinkle the chicken with the remaining 1 teaspoon oregano. Add the wine or other liquid, bring to a boil, cover, reduce the heat to low, and simmer until cooked through, about 10 minutes.

8 Serve the chicken directly from the pan or on a platter. Offer the vegetables alongside.

Serves 4

In Greek, *arista* means "the best," particularly when rosemary, garlic, and olive oil are present. This is a great company recipe for cooking outdoors. Serve with something green—a salad or sautéed green beans or zucchini.

GRILLED CHICKEN ARISTA

8 chicken breasts
(about 4 pounds)

3 tablespoons minced garlic

1/4 cup finely minced
fresh rosemary

1/4 cup sherry

1 tablespoon salt, plus extra
for grilling

3/4 teaspoon white pepper,
plus extra for grilling

6 tablespoons olive oil

1 Rinse the chicken breasts and pat dry with paper towels.

2 In a small bowl, combine the garlic, rosemary, sherry, I tablespoon salt, and 3/4 teaspoon pepper. Stir to form a paste.

3 Find the spot where the breast meat meets the rib bones. Slide your finger between the two, and stuff as much paste into each chicken breast as possible.

4 Place the stuffed breasts in a big bowl. Pour in the olive oil and turn to coat. Let stand for 15 minutes.

5 Prepare an indirect-heat fire in a covered charcoal grill (page 33).

6 Place the chicken breasts, skin side down, on the grill rack and grill, uncovered, for 4 minutes. Cover, open the top and bottom vents fully, and grill for 6 minutes longer. Uncover, turn the chicken, sprinkle with salt and pepper, re-cover, and grill until cooked through, another 10 minutes, for a total of 20 minutes.

7 Remove to a platter and serve hot.

Serves 6

Made in the style of the roasted suckling pig found in central Italy, these juicy packets are fabulous chilled, sliced, and layered inside a bulky-bread sandwich. Even knowing that serving the slices cold is best, once when I made this I couldn't wait and served them hot. No complaints.

CHICKEN THIGHS
STUFFED with HERBAL OLIVE PASTE

FOR THE OLIVE PASTE:

1 cup drained, pitted black olives (labeled "medium")

1 tablespoon finely minced garlic

1/2 cup chopped flat-leaf (Italian) parsley

1/2 teaspoon fennel seeds

1 tablespoon finely minced fresh rosemary

1 teaspoon finely minced fresh sage

1/4 teaspoon salt

1/8 teaspoon black pepper

FOR THE CHICKEN:

8 boneless chicken thighs, skin on

1/2 cup flour mixed with 1 teaspoon salt and black pepper to taste

1 1/2 tablespoons butter

5 juniper berries

1/3 cup gin

1 To make the olive paste, put all the ingredients in a food processor and process until a pebbly paste forms. Alternatively, mince as finely as possible by hand. Set aside.

2 Rinse the chicken thighs and pat dry with paper towels.

3 Fill the underside of each thigh with about 1 tablespoon of olive mixture. Roll up and tie each thigh with kitchen string into a tidy rectangular packet.

4 Dredge the packets in the seasoned flour, shaking off the excess.

5 Melt the butter in a heavy sauté pan over medium-high heat. Add the chicken packets and sauté, turning once, until well browned, about 5 minutes on each side.

6 Toss the juniper berries into the pan and pour in the gin. Bring to a boil, cover, reduce the heat to low, and simmer until cooked through, about 20 minutes. If in doubt, slice one open to check.

7 Remove from the pan, let cool, cover, and refrigerate until well chilled. Cut the strings, then slice across the packets to reveal the spiral inside. Serve chilled in a sandwich or as an appetizer.

Serves 8

One of my favorite ways to use fresh tomatoes, this dish is based on a recipe from a fifties cookbook series that included *Indian Cooking* by Savitri Chowdhary. I bought the book at a garage sale from a teacher who used it for a home economics class. In the book, the London author made her own yogurt and cooked chicken a really long time. This version fits nicely into my family's dinner hour. For a companion, there is none finer than a steamed vat of the longest-grain rice you can find. Look for basmati or a basmati hybrid, such as Texmati. You'll have plenty of sauce for sopping.

CHICKEN CURRY
with the FIRST TOMATOES of SUMMER

7 or 8 chicken thighs, preferably skin on

4 or 5 garlic cloves

1-inch piece fresh ginger (about 1 ounce)

1 large onion, coarsely cut

1 tablespoon clarified butter (see Note)

1 1/2 teaspoons ground turmeric

1 1/2 teaspoons garam masala

1 teaspoon salt, or maybe more

1/8 teaspoon cayenne pepper, or 1/4 teaspoon hot paprika

1/4 cup coarsely chopped fresh cilantro

3 large, ripe tomatoes

1/4 cup plain yogurt, stirred

1 Rinse the chicken thighs and pat dry with paper towels.

2 Turn on a food processor and drop the garlic and ginger through the feed tube. Process until minced. Turn off the processor, add the onion, and, using about 20 short-long pulses, chop finely. Leave in the work bowl.

3 Heat the clarified butter in a wide, heavy skillet over high heat. When it's hot, empty the contents of the processor bowl into the skillet. Fry gently for a few minutes.

4 Add the turmeric, garam masala, salt, cayenne or paprika, and cilantro. Stir to blend and fry for a few minutes longer.

5 Add the chicken, skin side down. If you've skinned the chicken, put it in with the side that got skinned facing down. Cook, turning once, until well browned, about 5 minutes on each side. Cover, reduce the heat to low, and simmer for 10 minutes. If the pan seems dry, add a few tablespoons water.

6 While the chicken cooks, halve, seed, and chop the tomatoes. After 10 minutes, add the tomatoes to the pan, re-cover, and simmer until the chicken is cooked through, about 10 minutes longer. Taste; it may need more salt.

7 If the sauce is soupy, uncover and cook for about 5 minutes longer.

8 Remove from the heat and spoon some of the sauce into the yogurt. Stir well, then pour over the chicken, stirring into the rest of the sauce.

Serves 6

Note: Clarified butter is butter from which the milk solids have been removed, making it possible to use it over high heat without burning. To clarify 4 tablespoons of butter, melt it slowly in a small pot. You'll notice whitish foam. Spoon it away. What's left is clarified butter.

CHICKEN **32** NUGGET

Chickens Like Classical Music

At the suggestion of a psychologist, an Israeli chicken farmer played Beethoven and Brahms in the henhouse and increased egg laying by 6 percent.

This recipe has been a family staple since I first made it for my husband-to-be to impress him when he came to dinner. It's gone through lots of adjustments, but this is the way it has been for a long time. Now our son loves it and has eaten it since he was three years old. Cook some long-grain rice, maybe adding a little orange zest, almonds, and saffron.

SAFFRON-YOGURT CHICKEN
with FRESH RED TOMATOES

FOR THE MARINADE:

2 tablespoons fresh lemon juice

Salt and black pepper to taste

1 teaspoon ground cumin

1 teaspoon ground coriander

1 cup plain yogurt, stirred

3 green onions, sliced

1 tablespoon chopped fresh cilantro

1 To make the marinade, in a large bowl, combine all the ingredients.

2 Skin the chicken pieces. Hack the breasts in half crosswise. Rinse and pat dry with paper towels.

3 Add the chicken pieces to the marinade and mix well with your hands. Cover and set aside at room temperature for about 1 hour while you prepare the rest of the ingredients.

4 In a small bowl or coffee cup, stir together the cumin, turmeric, coriander, saffron, paprika, and the cardamom, if using ground.

5 Melt the butter in a wide, heavy sauté pan over high heat. Add the onion, garlic, and ginger and sauté for 1 minute. Reduce the heat to medium and sauté until soft, about 5 minutes longer.

6 Add the spice mixture, cinnamon stick, and the cardamom pods, if using. Stir around until you can smell the spicy aroma, about 1 minute.

CHICKEN **21** NUGGET

Celebrity Chickens

Clark Gable and Carol
Lombard raised chickens.

Babe Ruth raised Rhode
Island Reds.

1 chicken, 4 pounds,
cut into serving pieces

2 teaspoons ground cumin

1 tablespoon ground turmeric

1 tablespoon ground coriander

About $\frac{1}{8}$ teaspoon
saffron threads

2 teaspoons paprika

$\frac{1}{2}$ teaspoon ground cardamom,
or 3 whole cardamom pods

2 tablespoons clarified butter
(see Note, page 129)

1 large yellow onion, chopped

1 tablespoon minced garlic

1-inch piece fresh ginger
(about 1 ounce),
peeled and minced

1 cinnamon stick, 2 inches long

1 cup chicken stock

2 cups seeded and chopped
tomatoes (about 6)

$\frac{1}{2}$ cup plain yogurt, stirred

Fresh cilantro sprigs

7 Lift the chicken pieces from the marinade and place in the pan, skin side down, directly on top of the spices. Spoon out some of the green onions from the marinade and use to top the chicken. (Discard the rest of the marinade.) Sauté over medium-high heat, turning once, until well browned, about 4 minutes on each side.

8 Raise the heat to high and add the stock and tomatoes. Bring to a boil, cover, reduce the heat to low, and simmer until cooked through, about 20 minutes.

9 Remove the chicken to a casserole-style serving dish with sides high enough to hold sauce.

10 Meanwhile, turn the heat back to high and keep the sauce boiling until reduced by half. Pour the sauce over the chicken, then pour the stirred yogurt over the sauce. Garnish with cilantro sprigs and serve.

Serves 6

Notes: You can make this with 3 pounds skinless thighs (about 8 thighs) instead of a whole chicken. They turn out a very rich dish. It's also interesting that the softer the tomatoes (or if using canned tomatoes), the redder the sauce. If chopping firm tomatoes, such as a plum (Roma) type, the sauce remains yellow-gold specked with the red tomato pieces.

The premise of this recipe is to use up the contents of bottles and jars in the cupboards and refrigerator. It doesn't matter what's on hand to Gerald Brecher, the creator of this concept, just so the mix has citrus, mustard, something tomato based, some soy sauce or a cousin, and, because he lives in New England, maple syrup to help it thicken. Gerald, who works at home, poaches the chickens in the morning before the temperature outside gets too hot, then finishes them on the grill. The brief poaching shortens the grilling time, which ensures the birds will be moist—a fine, old deli technique if you have the luxury of time to do it.

GERALD'S QUICK
SUMMER CHICKEN
with ODD PACKAGED THINGS

2 chickens,
3½ to 4 pounds each

¾ cup mojo griollo sauce (Vitarroz or Goya brand) or adobo sauce

4 or 5 shakes Taste of Thai brand fish sauce or other fish sauce

½ cup fresh citrus juice of choice

¼ cup maple syrup

3 tablespoons ketchup

¼ cup balsamic vinegar

3 tablespoons mustard

1 Bring a large pot filled three-fourths full of water to a boil. Drop the whole chickens into boiling water. Reduce the heat so the water is at a bare simmer and poach the chickens for 10 minutes. Remove the chickens from the water and set aside to cool. Discard the water.

2 When the chickens are cool, pat them dry with paper towels. In a very large bowl, combine all the remaining ingredients. Add the chickens and turn them by hand to coat them completely with the marinade. Let soak for about 20 minutes while you prepare an indirect-heat fire in a covered charcoal grill (page 33).

3 Place the chickens on V-shaped racks or directly on the grill rack, cover, open the top and bottom vents fully, and grill until juices between the thigh and body run clear, about 1 hour.

4 Remove to a cutting board that has a trough to catch the juices. Carve or cut with poultry shears and serve immediately. Pour the juices into a pitcher and serve at the table.

Serves 4

Any fragrant red rose will transform its petals into an exotic marinade, regardless of whether the nap on the petals is deep or light. My rose for this recipe is the scented climber Don Juan.

GRILLED CHICKEN
MARINATED in ROSE PETALS and BRANDY

12 red roses of medium size

1 cup fresh orange juice

¼ cup sugar

2 tablespoons minced fresh mint leaves, or 1 tablespoon mint jelly

¼ cup brandy

1 chicken, 3½ to 4 pounds, cut into serving pieces

1 Pluck the petals off the roses, then rinse gently one at a time.

2 In a saucepan, combine the rose petals, orange juice, sugar, and mint or mint jelly. Bring to a simmer over low heat, stirring to dissolve the sugar. Then simmer, uncovered, for about 30 minutes, until thickened and caramelly.

3 Strain the rose mixture through a sieve into a bowl, let cool slightly, and add the brandy.

4 Hack the breasts in half crosswise. Rinse the chicken pieces and pat dry with paper towels. Place in a zip-style plastic bag. Add the rose-orange mixture, seal the top, turn the bag to coat the chicken, and marinate for 2 hours at room temperature or as long as overnight in the refrigerator.

5 Prepare an indirect-heat fire in a covered charcoal grill (page 33).

6 Lift the chicken from the marinade, reserving the marinade. Place the chicken, skin side down, on a grill rack, cover, position the top and bottom vents three-quarters open, and grill for 25 minutes. Turn, baste the chicken with any remaining marinade, and grill until cooked through, about 20 minutes longer. Serve hot.

Serves 4

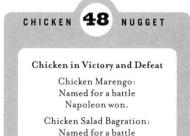

CHICKEN **48** NUGGET

Chicken in Victory and Defeat

Chicken Marengo: Named for a battle Napoleon won.

Chicken Salad Bagration: Named for a battle Napoleon lost.

The jewel-toned sweet-sour sauce is made with the same flavors as true Chinese plum sauce. The chicken joins the spiced plums with its skin side down to stain it the color of rubies. The plums' natural pectin thickens the sauce.

CHICKEN SAUTÉED
with SPICED SUMMER PLUMS

FOR THE SPICED PLUMS:

6 plums such as Santa Rosa, Friar, or red-fleshed Elephant Heart

$1/8$ teaspoon ground cloves

$1/4$ teaspoon ground cinnamon

$1/4$ teaspoon dry mustard

$2/3$ teaspoon ground ginger

$1/4$ teaspoon white pepper

$1/4$ cup sugar

FOR THE CHICKEN:

4 chicken hindquarters, or 4 drumsticks and 4 thighs

Salt and white pepper to taste

2 tablespoons butter, plus 1 tablespoon, if needed

2 tablespoons minced garlic

$1/2$ cup distilled white vinegar

1 To make the spiced plums, cut the plums in sections off their pits into a bowl (no need to peel). Add all the spices and the sugar, mixing well. As you go through the following steps, return to the bowl and mix a few times.

2 Warm a serving platter in a 150°F oven. Rinse the chicken pieces and pat dry with paper towels. Sprinkle with salt and white pepper.

3 Melt the 2 tablespoons butter in a wide, heavy sauté pan over medium-high heat. Add the chicken, skin side down, and sauté, turning once, until well browned, about 6 minutes on each side. Remove the chicken to a plate.

4 Pour off all but 2 tablespoons of the fat from the pan. Return the pan to high heat, add the garlic, and stir for 1 minute. Pour in the vinegar, which will sizzle, and boil until reduced to $1/4$ cup.

5 Add the spiced plums and then top with the chicken, skin side down. Dust with a little more salt. Cover, reduce the heat to medium-low, and simmer for 6 minutes.

6 Uncover and turn the pieces skin side up. Raise the heat to high and cook, uncovered, until the chicken is cooked through and the juices start to thicken, about 3 minutes. Remove the chicken to the warmed serving platter and keep warm.

7 Boil the sauce for another 2 minutes or so. The pectin in the plums will thicken it naturally. If the sauce tastes too sharp, remove from the heat and whisk in the remaining 1 tablespoon butter. Pour the sauce over the chicken and serve while hot.

Serves 4

The tandoori effect here is just that, an effect gotten from a dry spice rub and not an authentic tandoori chicken at all. The grill does a nice job of vaguely replicating what happens in the dire heat of the tandoor oven, however. Look for the garam masala—northern Indian spice blend—in a shop that caters to Indian cooks.

TANDOORI
CHICKEN SALAD

FOR THE CHICKEN:

1 chicken, 4 pounds

1 tablespoon garam masala

¼ teaspoon hot paprika

⅛ teaspoon ground turmeric

½ teaspoon salt

FOR THE DRESSING:

1 cup plain yogurt

¼ cup mayonnaise

¼ teaspoon ground cumin

½ teaspoon ground coriander

Pinch of ground cardamom or cinnamon

About ⅛ teaspoon saffron threads

2 tablespoons fresh lemon juice

Salt, if needed

FOR THE SALAD:

2 green apples, cored and chopped

1½ cups chopped celery (about 3 stalks)

5 or 6 green onions, sliced

½ cup chopped cashews

½ cup dried currants

⅓ cup chopped fresh cilantro

1 Prepare an indirect-heat fire in a covered charcoal grill (page 33).

2 Skin the entire chicken. Cut about a dozen shallow slits into the flesh.

3 In a small bowl, stir together the garam masala, paprika, turmeric, and salt. Rub into the chicken, covering the surface.

4 Place the chicken on a V-shaped roasting rack or set directly on the grill rack. Cover, open the top and bottom vents fully, and grill, for 1½ hours.

5 Remove the chicken from the grill and let cool. Bone the chicken and shred or tear the meat.

6 While the chicken is cooling, make the dressing. Combine all the ingredients in a bowl, and set aside.

7 To make the salad, in a bowl, combine the chicken, apples, celery, green onion, cashews, currants, and cilantro. Stir to mix. Add the dressing and mix well. Cover and chill before serving.

Serves 8

Two whole chicken breasts become exotic roasts.
You'll have a great time making this dish if you
use some of the choice ingredients to fix yourself
a stove-side rum and Coke with lime.

INDIES-STYLE CHICKEN
with MANGO, BANANAS, COFFEE BEANS, and RUM

1 large, ripe tomato, peeled, seeded, and chopped (see Peeling Tomatoes, page 177)

1 onion, minced

2 teaspoons minced garlic

1/2 jalapeño chile, seeded and minced

2 bananas, peeled and sliced

1 mango

2 large whole boneless chicken breasts, skin on

1/2 cup flour

1 teaspoon salt

1/4 teaspoon cayenne pepper

1/2 teaspoon ground allspice

Generous pinch of black pepper

1 tablespoon butter

1 cinnamon stick

1 teaspoon dark-roast coffee beans (9 or 10)

2 tablespoons dark or light molasses or brown sugar

1/3 cup rum

1/2 cup Kahlúa or other coffee-flavored liqueur

Fresh cilantro and/or basil leaves

1 Preheat an oven to 375°F.

2 In a bowl, combine the tomato, onion, garlic, jalapeño, and bananas. Set aside. Peel, pit, and dice the mango and place it in another bowl.

3 Rinse the chicken breasts and pat dry with paper towels.

4 In a shallow bowl, mix together the flour, salt, allspice, and both peppers. Dredge the chicken in the flour, shaking off the excess.

5 Melt the butter in a large, heavy, ovenproof sauté pan over medium-high heat. Add the breasts, skin side down, and sauté, turning once, until well browned, 4 to 5 minutes on each side. Remove to a platter.

6 Add the tomato-banana mixture, cinnamon stick, and coffee beans to the pan and sauté over medium heat until melded, about 5 minutes. Stir in the molasses or sugar.

7 Raise the heat to high, add the rum, and ignite with a match. When the flame dies out, fold in the mango, return the chicken to the pan, and spoon the sauce over the pieces. Cover, transfer to the oven, and bake until cooked through, about 10 minutes.

8 Transfer the breasts to a cutting board with a trough to catch the juices. Return the sauté pan to the stove top over high heat and boil for about 30 seconds to thicken.

9 Add the liqueur and any chicken juices from the cutting board. Stir and remove from the heat. The sauce will be thick and the bananas will be nearly broken up.

10 Slice the breasts on the diagonal and arrange on a serving platter. Top with sauce. Garnish with cilantro or basil—or both. Serve hot or at room temperature.

Serves 6

I don't use the term "delightful" very often, but that's what comes to mind as I make and eat this dish. It's perfect for summer and a great way to use up squash if you've got too much in the garden.

138

CHICKEN and SUMMER SQUASH SAUTÉ with PARMESAN

4 boneless chicken breasts, skin on

Salt and black pepper to taste

2 tablespoons butter or olive oil

2 summer squashes such as zucchini, pattypan, yellow

½ teaspoon dried oregano

2 teaspoons minced garlic

¼ cup grated Parmesan cheese

1 Rinse the chicken breasts and pat dry with paper towels. Sprinkle with salt and pepper.

2 Heat 1 tablespoon of the butter or oil in a large, heavy sauté pan over medium-high heat. Add the chicken breasts, skin side down, and sauté, turning once, until well browned and cooked through, 6 to 7 minutes on each side. Remove the breasts to a cutting board with a trough to catch the juices.

3 Add the remaining tablespoon of butter or oil to the pan and place over high heat. Add the squashes and stir into an even layer. Reduce the heat to medium and cook, stirring occasionally, for 3 to 4 minutes.

4 Meanwhile, slice the cooked breasts on the diagonal and arrange on plates or a platter, saving the juices.

5 Sprinkle the squashes with salt, pepper, oregano, and garlic. Stir and cook until the squashes are lightly browned, about 1 minute longer. Drizzle with any released juices from slicing the chicken.

6 Spoon the squash mixture next to the chicken and sprinkle with the Parmesan. Serve hot.

Serves 4

It's all right that this throw-together occurred in New York on the hot summer day my uncle died. We weren't really hungry, but I made dinner anyway. A quick survey of the refrigerator and cabinets in my aunt's apartment produced the ingredients for this dish, including the fine bottle of Santa Margherita Pinot Grigio from northern Italy hidden in back.

CHICKEN BREAST SAUTÉ
with TOMATOES, MUSHROOMS, and PINOT GRIGIO

4 boneless chicken breasts, skinned

1 egg, beaten

Seasoned dried bread crumbs mixed with 1/4 teaspoon dried oregano

2 tablespoons butter

1/2 cup Pinot Grigio or other dry white Italian wine

1 large, ripe tomato, seeded and chopped

3/4 pound small, fresh white mushrooms

1 tablespoon minced garlic

Salt and black pepper to taste

3/4 cup chicken stock

1 Heat a serving platter in a 150°F oven.

2 Rinse the chicken breasts and pat dry with paper towels. Dredge them in the egg, then in the bread crumb mixture.

3 Melt the butter in a large sauté pan over medium-high heat. Add the chicken breasts and sauté, turning once, until browned well and cooked through, about 6 minutes on each side. Remove to the warmed serving platter and keep warm.

4 Raise the heat to high and add the wine, scraping up any browned bits on the pan bottom. Boil down to about 2 tablespoons. Add the tomato, mushrooms, garlic, salt, and pepper. Sauté for 1 minute, then add the stock. Simmer for 10 minutes. Check the flavor and add salt and pepper, if needed.

5 Pour the sauce over the chicken breasts and serve right away.

Serves 4

The only element of this recipe unsuited to summer is long cooking. But when okra and tomatoes are in season at the same time, the gumbo imperative is hard to ignore.

Okra is one of nature's most effective thickeners. If present throughout the gumbo process, it assumes the role of the traditional oil-flour roux, while providing nutritional muscle. Cajun chef Paul Prudhomme uses the okra in batches, and I've taken a cue from the Louisiana master. A large portion of okra goes in early literally to break down into the base of the simmering stew. The rest goes in at the end to give the gumbo a nice fresh taste and appearance. Serve over fluffy long-grain white rice.

CHICKEN GUMBO
with OKRA and TOMATOES

FOR THE CHICKEN:

1 chicken, 4 pounds, hacked into bite-sized pieces

½ cup flour

1 teaspoon salt

½ teaspoon white pepper

1 teaspoon paprika

1 teaspoon garlic powder

Vegetable oil for frying

1 Rinse the chicken pieces and pat dry with paper towels.

2 In a paper bag, combine the flour, salt, white pepper, paprika, and garlic powder and shake to mix. Working in batches, add the chicken pieces to the bag and shake to coat.

3 Pour oil into a Dutch oven or other big pot to a depth of 1 inch. Heat over high heat until hot. Add the chicken pieces and sauté, turning as necessary until well browned, a good 10 minutes. Remove the chicken to paper towels to drain, cover loosely with foil, and set aside.

4 To make the gumbo, pour off all but 2 tablespoons of the oil from the pot. Return the pot to high heat. Set aside one-third of the okra to be used at the end of the gumbo making. Add the remaining two-thirds while scraping up browned bits from the pot bottom. Add the salt, black pepper, and cayenne, reduce the heat to medium-high, and sauté until softened, 5 to 7 minutes. Add the onion and sauté until the mixture is soft, about 5 minutes longer.

FOR THE GUMBO:

1 pound medium-length okra, stemmed and sliced

½ teaspoon salt

½ teaspoon black pepper

¼ teaspoon cayenne pepper

1 large onion, chopped

6 cups chicken stock

3 large, ripe tomatoes, peeled, seeded, and chopped (see Peeling Tomatoes, page 177; save the juices!), or 2½ cups chopped canned tomatoes, with juices

2 celery stalks, chopped

1 green bell pepper, seeded and chopped

5 Add 1 cup of the stock and all the tomatoes and their juice. Bring to a boil and stir until you see that the okra is dissolving, about 5 minutes. Add the celery, bell pepper, and the remaining 5 cups stock and bring to a boil. Reduce the heat to medium-low and simmer, uncovered, until thickened, about 40 minutes. Add additional salt now, if needed.

6 Add the reserved okra and return the chicken to the pot. Simmer until the okra is tender and the chicken is cooked through, about 10 minutes longer.

7 Serve hot.

Serves 8

This recipe and the one that follows use nearly the same ingredients but with different cooking methods. Here, chicken and vegetables bake for nearly 2 hours. This makes a great casserole for company or for taking to a potluck.

CHICKEN BAKED
with RATATOUILLE INGREDIENTS

About 6 pounds chicken pieces, including 3 thighs, 3 drumsticks, 3 wings, and 3 breasts

3 tablespoons fresh lemon juice

Salt and black pepper to taste

1 pound summer squashes, cut into large chunks (see Note)

1/3 pound bell peppers of any color (except purple), seeded and cut into large chunks

1 1/4 pounds large, ripe tomatoes, peeled, seeded, and cut into large chunks

1 onion, cut into eighths

1 pound eggplant, cut into 1-inch chunks

1 tablespoon minced garlic

1 1/2 teaspoons salt, plus extra to taste

1 teaspoon black pepper, or more to taste

3 tablespoons olive oil

1/4 cup chopped flat-leaf (Italian) parsley

2 sprigs fresh thyme or 1/2 teaspoon dried thyme

1 Rinse the chicken pieces and pat dry with paper towels. Hack the 3 chicken breasts in half crosswise.

2 In a bowl, combine the chicken pieces with the lemon juice and salt and pepper to taste. Set aside.

3 Position a rack in the lower third of an oven and preheat to 350°F.

4 In a large bowl, mix together the squashes, bell peppers, tomatoes, onion, eggplants, and garlic. Add the 1 1/2 teaspoons salt and the pepper. Gently mix in the olive oil.

5 Place the chicken in an ovenproof Dutch oven. Top with all the vegetables. Sprinkle with the parsley and tuck in the thyme sprigs or sprinkle with dried thyme. Sprinkle once more with salt to taste.

6 Cover and bake for 45 minutes. Uncover and continue to bake, stirring now and then, until the chicken is cooked through and the vegetables are very tender, 45 minutes to 1 hour longer. Transfer the Dutch oven to a rack to cool, then cover and refrigerate for serving the next day.

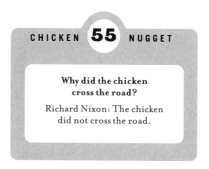

CHICKEN **55** NUGGET

**Why did the chicken
cross the road?**

Richard Nixon: The chicken
did not cross the road.

7 Lift off the fat that has solidified on top and discard. Serve the chicken and vegetables cold or at room temperature.

Serves 10, with leftovers

Note: The veggie amounts are by weight to let you select any member of the squash, pepper, or eggplant families that appeals during the season. For example, for the summer squashes, I used yellow and sea-green pattypans and a ball-shaped zucchini called Roly-Poly. For the eggplants, I interspersed a white eggplant called Casper and small eggplants with light purpling called Asian Bride. The peppers were red, yellow, green, and orange. Some were bell peppers, some were mild Italian peppers. Whatever you use, if the vegetables are cut too small they'll disintegrate, so be sure they are in rather large, ungainly chunks.

This recipe demonstrates how browning the chicken first helps the dish develop a fuller flavor.

144

SAUTÉED RATATOUILLE
BAKED with BROWNED CHICKEN

About 6 pounds chicken, including 3 thighs, 3 drumsticks, 3 wings, and 3 breasts

Salt and black pepper to taste

5 tablespoons olive oil

1 onion, cut into eighths

1 tablespoon minced garlic

1½ pounds large, ripe summer tomatoes, peeled, seeded, and cut into large chunks

1 pound eggplant, cut into 1-inch chunks

1 pound summer squashes of any variety, cut into large chunks

⅓ pound bell peppers of any color (except purple), seeded and cut into large chunks

¼ cup chopped fresh flat-leaf (Italian) parsley

2 fresh thyme sprigs, or ½ teaspoon dried thyme

1 Rinse the chicken pieces and pat dry with paper towels. Hack the 3 chicken breasts in half crosswise. Sprinkle with salt and pepper.

2 Heat 1 tablespoon of the oil in a large, heavy sauté pan over medium-high heat. Working in batches, add the chicken pieces and sauté, turning as necessary, until well browned, about 8 minutes total. Remove to paper towels to drain.

3 Add the onion, garlic, and tomatoes to the fat remaining in the pan and sprinkle with a pinch of salt. Sauté over medium-high heat until somewhat thickened, about 10 minutes. Pour the mixture into a large bowl.

4 Add 2 tablespoons of the oil to the pan. Add the eggplant, sprinkle with salt, and sauté over medium-high heat until nicely colored, about 10 minutes. Transfer to the bowl holding the tomato mixture.

5 Add the remaining 2 tablespoons oil to the pan. Add the summer squashes and peppers and sauté until bright and soft, about 10 minutes. Transfer to the bowl.

CHICKEN 54 NUGGET

Why did the chicken cross the road?

Charles Darwin: It was the next logical step after coming down from the trees.

6 Meanwhile, position a rack in the lower third of an oven and preheat to 350°F.

7 Arrange the chicken in the bottom of an ovenproof Dutch oven. Gently stir together the sautéed vegetables, adding a touch more salt and pepper. Pour over the chicken. Sprinkle with the parsley. Tuck in the thyme sprigs or sprinkle with dried thyme.

8 Cover and bake for 30 minutes. Uncover and continue to bake, stirring now and then, until the chicken is cooked through and the vegetables are very tender, about 45 minutes longer. Transfer the Dutch oven to a rack to cool, then cover and refrigerate for serving the next day.

9 Lift off the fat that has solidified on top and discard. Serve the chicken and vegetables cold or at room temperature.

Serves 10, with leftovers

Reminders of home in the Southwest don't get more to the point than squash, cream cheese, chiles, and herbs. If you want to punch up the flavor, this is a good opportunity to make Texan Smoked Chicken (pages 48–49).

CHICKEN SALAD
with ZUCCHINI, ROASTED CHILES, AVOCADO, and CREAM CHEESE

FOR THE SALAD:

4 green Anaheim or poblano chiles

3 cups cubed cooked chicken

2 zucchini, each of a different color, thinly sliced

2 yellow crookneck squashes, thinly sliced

1 red onion, halved and sliced

1 jalapeño chile, seeded and finely minced

2 avocados, pitted, peeled, and cubed

½ pound cream cheese, cubed

FOR THE DRESSING:

¼ cup red wine vinegar or balsamic vinegar

Juice of 1 lime

3 garlic cloves

1 tablespoon dark brown sugar

1 tablespoon chopped fresh mint

4 to 6 fresh basil leaves

½ teaspoon salt

¾ cup olive oil

1 To make the salad, preheat a broiler. Place the whole chiles on a baking sheet and broil, turning as needed, until the skins are black and blistered on all sides. Wrap in a kitchen towel or drop into a plastic or paper bag until cool, then peel, seed, and slice into long strips.

2 In a large bowl, combine the chicken, roasted chiles, zucchini, crookneck squashes, onion, and jalapeño.

3 In a food processor or blender, combine all the dressing ingredients except the oil. Process for a few seconds to blend. With the motor running, slowly pour in the oil, then stop the machine.

4 Add the dressing to the chicken mixture and toss gently. Add the avocado and cream cheese and again toss very gently. Cover and chill before serving, if desired, or serve at room temperature.

Serves 8

Potatoes grow almost all year round. In summer, the waxy ones make great potato salad, because after boiling they hold any shape you care to give them—slices, cubes, chunks. The green pistachios and red radishes brighten and add crunch to the salad.

FAMILY-SIZED CHICKEN
and RED-POTATO PICNIC SALAD

2 pounds red potatoes, unpeeled

White-Cooked Chicken (page 50), cooled and shredded

4 hard-cooked eggs, peeled and cut into chunks

1 teaspoon minced garlic

½ teaspoon Dijon mustard

8 to 10 red radishes, cubed

½ cup freshly shelled unsalted roasted pistachios

¾ teaspoon salt

Black pepper to taste

About 2 tablespoons fresh lemon juice or apple cider vinegar

¾ cup mayonnaise or plain yogurt, or a mixture

1 Bring a saucepan of salted water to a rapid boil. Add the potatoes, cover, reduce the heat to medium, and cook until a knife glides into the flesh, 12 to 15 minutes. Drain and immerse in cold water to halt the cooking.

2 While the potatoes are cooking, combine all the remaining ingredients in a big bowl, mixing well.

3 Cut the potatoes into chunks. Fold them gently into the chicken mixture, then serve. Also good the next day.

Serves 8 to 10

Sometimes you have to go to a lot of trouble for a great recipe. While no step is difficult, the final dish has many cooked parts. Most are best made a day before. The actual serving of this salad is really only a matter of assembly.

148

COMPOSED CHICKEN SALAD
with RIVIERA FLAVOR

About 6 ripe tomatoes, peeled, seeded, and chopped

1/2 cup chopped pitted Niçoise or other flavorful olives

4 large garlic cloves

2 anchovy fillets packed in olive oil

1 tablespoon finely minced fresh tarragon

1 chicken, 3 1/2 pounds, cut into serving pieces

Salt and black pepper to taste

2 teaspoons olive oil

2 tablespoons Cognac or other brandy

About 1/8 teaspoon saffron threads

1 In a bowl, combine the tomatoes and olives.

2 In a small bowl, mash together the garlic and anchovy fillets to form a paste. Stir in the tarragon.

3 Rinse the chicken pieces and pat dry with paper towels. Sprinkle with salt and pepper.

4 Heat the oil in a wide, heavy sauté pan over medium-high heat. Add the chicken, skin side down, and sauté, turning once, until well browned, about 5 minutes on each side. Remove to paper towels to drain.

5 Add the garlic-anchovy paste to the pan, raise the heat to high, and fry for 1 minute. Return the chicken to the pan, pour Cognac over the chicken, and ignite with a match.

6 When the flame dies out, add the tomato-olive mixture and the saffron. Cover, reduce the heat to medium-low and cook for 15 minutes. Uncover, raise the heat to medium, and continue to cook until the chicken is cooked through, about 12 minutes. Remove the chicken pieces to a shallow bowl or storage container.

7 Raise the heat to high and boil the sauce about 30 seconds longer. Pour over the chicken. Let the chicken cool in the sauce, or cover and refrigerate overnight.

FOR THE VINAIGRETTE:

3 tablespoons
white wine vinegar

$\frac{1}{8}$ teaspoon salt

Black pepper to taste

$\frac{1}{2}$ cup olive oil

FOR THE SALAD:

5 red potatoes, peeled

$\frac{1}{2}$ pound green beans, trimmed

Butter or romaine lettuce leaves

6 hard-cooked eggs, peeled
and cut into wedges

2 ripe tomatoes, cut into wedges

8 To make the vinaigrette, in a small bowl, whisk together the vinegar, salt, and pepper. Whisk in the oil.

9 To assemble the salad, bring a saucepan of salted water to a rapid boil. Add the potatoes, reduce the heat to medium, cover, and cook until a knife glides into the flesh, 12 to 15 minutes. Drain the potatoes, let cool, and slice. Place in a bowl, add a few tablespoons of the vinaigrette, and toss gently.

10 Refill the saucepan with salted water, bring to a rapid boil, add the green beans, and parboil for 2 minutes. Drain and immerse in cold water to halt the cooking. Drain again, place in a separate bowl, and add a few tablespoons of the vinaigrette. Toss gently.

11 Skin and debone the chicken and shred or dice the meat, using any sauce that adheres to the meat.

12 Line a large platter with lettuce. Mound the chicken in the center. Surround with clumps of the dressed potatoes and the beans, the hard-cooked egg wedges, and the tomato wedges. Serve at room temperature.

Serves 6

Here is the Chinese philosophy of taste in a single recipe, a perfect balance of sweet, sour, spicy, and salty. Don't listen to anyone who would deter you from frying your own wonton skins. Any beginner cook can slice wonton skins into strips and fry them into the freshest crispy noodle ever. Watch out. They make an incredible munchie and might disappear before the salad is ready.

THE AUTHENTIC AND BEST
CHINESE CHICKEN SALAD

FOR THE FRIED WONTON SKINS:

10 wonton skins

Vegetable oil for frying

FOR THE DRESSING:

1 tablespoon shredded pickled ginger slices, plus 2 tablespoons juice from the jar

1 tablespoon Asian sesame oil

1 tablespoon thin soy sauce

1 tablespoon hoisin sauce or plum sauce

2 tablespoons crushed peanuts, walnuts, or almonds

White pepper to taste

FOR THE SALAD:

Assorted lettuces such as romaine, butter, and curly, torn into 1-inch pieces

2 cups shredded White-Cooked Chicken (page 50)

Fruits such as raisins, pineapple chunks, mandarin orange sections, and Asian pear slices

1 To prepare the fried wonton skins, stack the skins and cut into strips ¼ inch wide.

2 In a wok or saucepan, pour in oil to a depth of 2 inches and heat to 375°F. In batches, add the wonton strips and fry until they turn golden, 1 to 2 minutes. Using a slotted spoon, remove to paper towels to drain.

3 To make the dressing, in a bowl, whisk together all the ingredients. (Alternatively, shake well in a tightly covered jar.)

4 To assemble the salad, place the lettuces in a large bowl. Add the dressing and toss to coat evenly. Mound the lettuces on individual plates. Top with handfuls of the chicken, fried wontons, and fruits. Serve at once.

Serves 6

Note: The pickled ginger that's red and used for sushi cannot be used here. Go to an Asian market for pickled white ginger, because it's doubtful you'll find it in a supermarket. If you can't find pickled white ginger, use fresh ginger. Peel and mince a 2-inch piece ginger (about 2 ounces); add to a small pot with ⅓ cup distilled white vinegar and ⅓ cup sugar. Boil for 5 minutes to dissolve the sugar. Cool and add the remaining dressing ingredients.

The most expensive item in this salad is the dried cherries. Buy pliant cherries rather than ones so dry they're brittle. It is possible for a peach to be firm when it's ripe. The diced pieces stay shapely and add a little crunch to the salad.

CHICKEN SALAD

with DRIED CHERRIES, CELERY, and PEACHES

4 cups diced White-Cooked Chicken (page 50)

$^1\!/_2$ red onion, diced

$^2\!/_3$ cup dried pitted cherries

1 cup chopped celery (about 2 stalks)

1 large, firm but ripe peach, pitted and diced

$^3\!/_4$ cup mayonnaise

2 tablespoons fresh lemon juice

$^1\!/_2$ teaspoon curry powder

$^1\!/_2$ teaspoon salt

Black pepper to taste

Iceberg lettuce leaves

1 In a large bowl, mix together all the ingredients except the lettuce. (If you like, store in a large zip-style plastic bag in the refrigerator for up to 2 days.)

2 Line a platter or individual plates with the lettuce leaves. Spoon the salad on top and serve cold or at room temperature.

Serves 6 to 8

CHICKEN **17** NUGGET

First Steal a Chicken.
The title of an old cookbook about cooking chicken.

If the salad ingredients are ready as the chicken comes off the grill, the cream cheese will melt a little, and the warmth from the chicken will cause an eruption of flavors. If you are able to make the sauce ahead of time, such as a day before, this salad comes to the table in 15 minutes.

WARM CHICKEN BREAST SALAD
with TOMATILLO SAUCE and CREAM CHEESE

FOR THE SAUCE:

15 tomatillos, husked

1 jalapeño chile, seeded

4 fresh basil leaves

1 tablespoon fresh oregano leaves

2 tablespoons firmly packed fresh mint leaves

1/4 cup fresh cilantro leaves

2 garlic cloves

Juice of 2 limes

1/2 teaspoon salt

Black pepper to taste

FOR THE CHICKEN SALAD:

2 whole boneless chicken breasts, skin on

1/2 teaspoon salt

Black pepper to taste

1/2 pound cream cheese, at room temperature, diced

3 avocados, pitted, peeled, and diced

1 red onion, diced

Lettuce leaves for lining platter

1 Bring a saucepan of water to a boil. Drop in the tomatillos and cook until soft, about 20 minutes. (Alternatively, place the tomatillos in a 2-quart microwaveproof container, add a few tablespoons water, and microwave on High for 8 minutes.) Drain and rinse with cold water.

2 Meanwhile, prepare a direct-heat fire in a covered charcoal grill (pages 33–34).

3 Place the tomatillos in a blender with all the remaining sauce ingredients. Puree until smooth. Chill until ready for use.

4 To make the salad, rinse the chicken breasts and pat dry with paper towels. Sprinkle with salt and pepper.

5 Place the breasts, skin side down, on the grill rack, cover, open the vents fully, and grill, turning once, until well browned and cooked through, about 8 minutes on each side.

6 Remove from the grill. Remove the skin and discard. Immediately cut the hot chicken into 1-inch pieces and place in a bowl. Add the cream cheese, avocados, onion, and the prepared tomatillo sauce. Combine gently.

7 Line a platter with lettuce leaves. Mound the salad on the lettuce and serve.

Serves 6

When peaches flavored by cumin, fennel, ginger, tomatoes, and onion are cooked with chicken, the result is chutneylike.

CHICKEN with SUMMER PEACHES in SPICY LIGHT SAUCE

4 boneless chicken breasts, skinned

Salt and black pepper to taste

2 tablespoons butter or olive oil

¼ teaspoon ground cumin

1 teaspoon ground fennel

1-inch piece fresh ginger (about 1 ounce), peeled and minced

1 pound ripe tomatoes (about 3 medium), peeled, seeded, and chopped (see Peeling Tomatoes, page 177)

4 ripe peaches, peeled, pitted, and sliced

1 onion, sliced into rings

1 Rinse the chicken breasts and pat dry with paper towels. Sprinkle with salt and pepper.

2 Melt 1 tablespoon of the butter or olive oil in a wide heavy sauté pan over high heat. Add the cumin, fennel, and ginger and fry for about 30 seconds. Add the tomatoes and bring to a boil. Season with a little salt, and then pour into a bowl.

3 Melt the remaining 1 tablespoon butter or oil in the same pan over medium-high heat. Add the breasts, skinned side down, and sauté, turning once, until well browned, about 4 minutes on each side. Cover, reduce the heat to medium-low, and cook the chicken breasts for 6 minutes longer. Remove the breasts to a cutting board with a trough to catch the juices. Keep warm.

4 Add the peaches and onion to the pan and sauté over medium-high heat until slightly softened but still crisp-tender, about 5 minutes. If the peaches remain firm, cover the pan and steam the mixture for 1 minute longer. (The slices shouldn't get mushy.)

5 Slice the chicken breasts on the diagonal. Lift each breast as if in one piece to a serving platter. Stir the released juices into the peaches.

6 Top the chicken breasts with the tomato mixture and garnish with the onion-peach mixture.

Serves 4

Go all the way with a keep-the-kitchen-
cool attitude by poaching the chicken breasts
in the microwave.

154

CHICKEN and
SUMMER · FRUIT SALAD

4 boneless
chicken breasts, skinned

1 cup chicken stock

1 tablespoon chopped
fresh tarragon, or 2½ teaspoons
dried tarragon

½ pound big seedless red
grapes, halved

1 cantaloupe, peeled, seeded,
and diced

1 honeydew, peeled, seeded,
and diced

2 mangoes, peeled, pitted,
and diced

½ cup mayonnaise

Juice of 1 lime

1 teaspoon dried tarragon

½ teaspoon salt, or to taste

Bibb lettuce leaves for
lining plates

Fresh tarragon sprigs
for garnish (optional)

1 Set the chicken breasts in a microwaveproof baking dish or glass casserole with a cover. Add the stock and tarragon, cover, and microwave on High for 5 minutes. Remove the container from the microwave and let the chicken breasts cool in the liquid.

2 Dice the chicken breasts and place in a bowl. Add all the remaining ingredients except the lettuce. Toss gently. Cover and chill.

3 Line individual plates with the lettuce and spoon the salad on top. Garnish each plate with a small sprig of fresh tarragon, if desired. Serve cold.

Serves 6 to 8

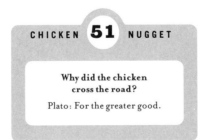

CHICKEN **51** NUGGET

**Why did the chicken
cross the road?**

Plato: For the greater good.

Nothing says California cuisine like the pairing of goat cheese and sun-dried tomatoes. What should seem tired after all these years of trendiness hasn't dimmed. Why? Because it's good. You may serve this salad while the chicken is still warm from grilling, or once it is cold.

THE CALIFORNIA CLICHÉ

1 jar (6 or 8 ounces) oil-packed sun-dried tomatoes

Olive oil, as needed

4 boneless chicken breasts, skinned

FOR THE DRESSING:

1/2 cup balsamic vinegar or sherry vinegar

1/2 cup chopped fresh cilantro

2 teaspoons minced fresh jalapeño

Reserved 3 tablespoons chopped tomato

1/2 teaspoon salt

Black pepper to taste

Reserved 1 cup oil

Mixed red and green salad greens, including arugula, radicchio, Bibb lettuce, and mâche

3 ounces fresh goat cheese such as Montrachet

1 Drain the jar of sun-dried tomatoes, capturing the oil in a measuring cup. Add olive oil as needed to measure 1 cup. Finely chop enough tomatoes to measure 3 tablespoons; reserve for use in the dressing. Reserve the remaining tomatoes for the salad.

2 Rinse the chicken breasts and pat dry with paper towels.

3 To make the dressing, in a food processor or blender, combine all the ingredients except the oil. Pulse until smooth. With the motor running, slowly pour in the oil. Pour half of the dressing into a jar, cover tightly, and reserve for the salad. Pour the remaining dressing into a bowl or zip-style plastic bag, add the chicken breasts, and marinate for 2 hours at room temperature or overnight in the refrigerator.

4 Prepare a direct-heat fire in an open charcoal grill (pages 33–34).

5 Lift the chicken breasts from the marinade and discard the marinade. Place the breasts on the grill rack, skinned side down, and grill, turning once, until browned and cooked through, about 6 minutes on each side. Transfer to a cutting board, then dice.

6 Line individual plates or 1 large platter with the salad greens.

7 In a bowl, toss the diced chicken with the reserved dressing. Using a slotted spoon, scoop out the chicken and arrange on the greens. Crumble the goat cheese over the top. Garnish with the reserved sun-dried tomatoes and serve.

Serves 6

scratch

At first, autumn is still very much like summer, with eggplants, tomatoes, green chiles, and corn. Then, the sun is no longer intense enough to ripen the tomatoes, so you use them green in a salsa. The last of the peppers can go in a pan of paprikash.

The heat waves still come and go, but a snap in the air brings us back to the stove. We rediscover the oven. Suddenly we've got apples and cider and an Oktoberfest mood. Chicken gets beer and mustard. That first vat of burbling stock almost prompts a rejoicing. Finally we're really cooking again—soufflés, timbales, roasts, casseroles of enchiladas.

As the season progresses, we see the fall crop of white and wild rices. Autumn's arugula, dandelion, mâche, mustard, radicchio, spinach, and chard return from their summer hiatus. The cruciferous foods—broccoli, cauliflower, and cabbage—grow nicely once the weather cools down. Cranberry beans you'd usually buy dried come along fresh. By the end of September the walnut harvest begins. Pomegranate seeds look beautiful in chicken salad, and the juice is another

choice for a braising liquid. Fennel bulb is dug up for the taste of licorice from a living food.

Stay sharp and you won't miss the fall boomlet of green beans. Soon the persimmons will hang like orange bulbs on their bare trees. Now that chicken is back roasting in the oven, might as well roast potatoes, too.

And who says you've got to eat turkey on Thanksgiving? A big chicken does nicely if it's just the two (or three) of you.

AUTUMN

CIPES

A quick dish with a robust sauce made in the same skil-let the chicken cooks in. Although a hearty whole-grain mustard is used here, just about any mustard—sweet-hot, Dijon, wine, tarragon—will work nicely.

164

SAUTÉED CHICKEN BREASTS
in BEER-MUSTARD SAUCE

4 boneless chicken breasts, skin on

½ cup flour

¼ teaspoon dry mustard

1 teaspoon salt

Generous black pepper to taste

2 eggs

2 tablespoons butter

1 cup flat beer

2 tablespoons German or other grainy mustard

2 tablespoons minced fresh chives

1 Warm a serving platter in a 150°F oven.

2 Rinse the chicken breasts and pat dry with paper towels.

3 In a shallow bowl, combine the flour, dry mustard, salt, and pepper. In another shallow bowl, beat the eggs.

4 Dredge the chicken in the seasoned flour, dip into the egg, then run through the flour again, shaking off the excess.

5 Melt 1 tablespoon of the butter in a large, heavy sauté pan with a lid over high heat. Add the chicken, sear briefly, reduce the heat to medium-high, and sauté, turning once, until golden brown and crusty, about 5 minutes on each side.

6 Add the beer, pouring it down the side of the pan rather than on top of the chicken. Cover, reduce the heat to low, and simmer until cooked through, about 15 minutes.

7 Remove the chicken to the warmed serving platter and keep warm. Bring the pan juices to a hard boil and boil until reduced by one-fourth. Remove from the heat and whisk in the mustard and remaining 1 tablespoon butter until the butter melts.

8 Pour the sauce over the chicken. Sprinkle with the chives and serve immediately.

Serves 3 or 4

Chicken fat is used here because of the high heat required to caramelize the eggplant. Peanut oil is the second choice. Butter would burn, as would olive oil. Safflower oil has a very high smoking point but imparts an undesirable flavor.

CHICKEN BREASTS
with CARAMELIZED EGGPLANT

4 boneless chicken breasts, skinned

¹/₂ cup flour mixed with 1 teaspoon salt and black pepper to taste

2 eggs

4 tablespoons rendered chicken fat (see Schmaltz, page 51) or peanut oil

1 large eggplant, peeled and cut into French-fry strips

¹/₄ cup packed brown sugar

CHICKEN **56** NUGGET

Why did the chicken cross the road?

Ronald Reagan: I forget.

1 Warm a serving platter in a 150°F oven.

2 Rinse the chicken breasts and pat dry with paper towels.

3 Place the flour mixture in a shallow bowl. In another shallow bowl, beat the eggs.

4 Dredge the chicken in the seasoned flour, dip into the egg, then run through the flour again, shaking off the excess.

5 Heat 1 tablespoon of the chicken fat or peanut oil in a wide, heavy sauté pan over high heat. Add the chicken, turning once, until well browned and cooked through, 6 to 7 minutes on each side. Remove to the warmed serving platter and keep warm.

6 Add the remaining 3 tablespoons chicken fat or peanut oil to the pan and heat over high heat until smoking. Add the eggplant and sauté until charred, about 10 minutes. Sprinkle with the brown sugar, toss, and cook until tender, about 2 minutes longer.

7 Top the chicken breasts with the eggplant, or mound the eggplant to the side. Serve hot.

Serves 4

What to do with green tomatoes? Pretend they're tomatillos and chop them up as the base for a piquant green salsa for grilled chicken.

166

GRILLED CHICKEN BREASTS
with AVOCADO and GREEN TOMATO SALSA

FOR THE SALSA:

1 green tomato, chopped

$^1/_2$ cup chopped red onion

$^1/_2$ jalapeño chile, minced

1 tablespoon minced garlic

2 tablespoons minced fresh cilantro

2 tablespoons fresh lime juice

Kernels from 1 ear of yellow or white corn

1 avocado, pitted, peeled, and cubed

$^1/_2$ teaspoon salt

4 to 6 boneless chicken breasts, skin on

Salt and pepper to taste

1 Prepare a direct-heat fire in an open charcoal grill (pages 33–34).

2 To make the salsa, mix together all the salsa ingredients in a bowl. Cover and chill.

3 Rinse the chicken breasts and pat dry with paper towels. Sprinkle with salt and pepper.

4 Place the chicken breasts on the grill rack and grill, turning once, until nicely charred and cooked through, 6 to 7 minutes on each side.

5 Serve the hot chicken breasts whole or sliced on the diagonal. Spoon the chilled salsa over the top.

Serves 4

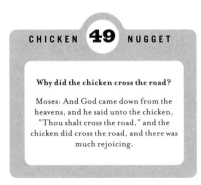

CHICKEN **49** NUGGET

Why did the chicken cross the road?

Moses: And God came down from the heavens, and he said unto the chicken, "Thou shalt cross the road," and the chicken did cross the road, and there was much rejoicing.

The wild rice and dark greens of autumn make a gorgeous and tasty team, especially with the Italian flavors smoked deep into the chicken.

SMOKED CHICKEN
and WILD RICE on SHREDDED AUTUMN GREENS

FOR THE WILD RICE:

1 cup wild rice

3 tablespoons butter

1 onion, chopped

3 cups boiling water

2 teaspoons salt

FOR THE VINAIGRETTE:

1/4 cup sherry vinegar or other wine vinegar

1 teaspoon Dijon mustard

Salt and black pepper to taste

1/2 cup olive oil

2 cups boned and diced Italian-Smoked Chicken (pages 48–49)

10 oil-packed sun-dried tomatoes, drained and sliced

3 cups shredded napa cabbage

3 green onions, chopped

3 tablespoons chopped fresh parsley

Assorted autumn salad greens such as arugula, dandelion, mâche, mustard, radicchio, and spinach, shredded

3 thin slices prosciutto, shredded

1 To cook the wild rice, rinse the rice and drain well. Melt the butter in a saucepan over medium-high heat. Add the onion and sauté until softened, about 4 minutes. Add the wild rice and sauté until well coated with the butter, about 3 minutes. Add the boiling water and salt, bring to a boil, cover, reduce the heat to low, and simmer until the kernels break open and become tender but not mushy, 50 to 60 minutes. Uncover, give a stir, and transfer to a large bowl to cool. If all the water hasn't been absorbed, taste the rice to make sure it's tender before draining off the excess liquid.

2 To make the vinaigrette, in a small bowl, whisk together the vinegar, mustard, salt, and pepper, then whisk in the oil.

3 Add the vinaigrette, chicken, tomatoes, cabbage, green onions, and parsley to the wild rice and mix together with your hands or a large spoon. Line a platter or individual plates with the shredded greens. Spoon the chicken and rice mixture on top and garnish with the prosciutto.

Serves 6

Fried green tomatoes are a Southern classic made
even more so when smothered with a bacon-based
cream sauce—a rich delight not enjoyed enough.

168

CHICKEN BREASTS
and POLENTA-FRIED GREEN TOMATOES
with CREAM GRAVY

4 bacon slices

4 large boneless chicken breasts, skin on

Salt to taste, plus ¼ teaspoon

Black pepper to taste

8 large green tomato slices, each ½ inch thick (about 2 tomatoes)

Brown sugar

2 eggs, separated

¼ cup water

⅓ cup polenta or regular white or yellow cornmeal

⅓ cup flour

FOR THE GRAVY:

2 tablespoons flour

1½ cups milk, heated

Salt and generous black pepper to taste

1 Warm a serving platter in a 150°F oven.

2 Fry the bacon in a heavy sauté pan over medium heat until crisp, 3 to 5 minutes. Transfer to paper towels to drain briefly, then crumble and set aside. Pour off all but 1 tablespoon fat from the pan.

3 Rinse the chicken breasts and pat dry with paper towels. Sprinkle to taste with salt and pepper.

4 Return the pan to high heat, add the chicken breasts, skin side down, and sauté, turning once, until browned and cooked through, 6 to 7 minutes on each side. Remove to paper towels to drain briefly, then transfer to the serving platter and keep warm. Leave the drippings in the pan.

5 Meanwhile, arrange the tomato slices on a plate in a single layer. Sprinkle with the brown sugar. In a bowl, beat together the egg yolks, water, polenta or cornmeal, flour, the ¼ teaspoon salt, and pepper to taste, until the mixture forms a pancakelike batter. If very thick, thin with a little more water. In another bowl, beat the egg whites until stiff peaks form. Fold the whites into the yolk-cornmeal mixture.

6 Reheat the drippings remaining in the sauté pan over medium-high heat. Working in batches, dip each tomato slice into the cornmeal batter, coating completely, and lower into the pan. Fry, turning once, until golden brown, about 4 minutes on each side. Remove to paper towels to drain.

7 To make the gravy, pour off all but 2 tablespoons of the fat from the pan. Place the pan over medium-high heat and whisk in the flour until a paste forms. Then gradually whisk in the milk to form a medium-thick gravy. Season with salt and pepper.

8 Arrange the chicken breasts in the center of the serving platter, surround with the tomatoes, and smother with the sauce. Top with the crumbled bacon. Serve immediately.

Serves 4

Pity that little of the cranberry design on these pretty beans remains after cooking. But their flavor and tender, buttery crunch is what eating these beans fresh is all about. They show up in late summer or early fall.

CHICKEN BAKED with
FRESH-SHELLED CRANBERRY BEANS

1½ pounds fresh cranberry beans in the pod

3 tablespoons olive oil

1 onion, chopped

1 tablespoon minced garlic

1½ cups chicken stock

1 chicken, 4 pounds, cut into serving pieces

Salt and generous black pepper to taste

½ cup dry white wine

2 bay leaves

1 or 2 fresh thyme sprigs

1 tablespoon chopped fresh parsley

1 Shell the beans. You should have between 1¼ and 1½ cups.

2 Heat 2 tablespoons of the oil in a saucepan over high heat. Add the onion and garlic and sauté, stirring so nothing burns, until the onion darkens to near-brown, a full 5 minutes.

3 Quickly pour in the stock and the beans and bring to a boil. Boil, uncovered, for 4 minutes.

4 Meanwhile, preheat an oven to 350°F. Hack the breasts in half crosswise. Rinse the chicken pieces and pat dry with paper towels. Sprinkle with salt and pepper.

5 Heat the remaining 1 tablespoon oil in a wide, heavy ovenproof sauté pan over high heat. Add the chicken, skin side down, and sauté, turning once, until well browned, about 4 minutes on each side.

6 With the heat still high, add the wine, let sizzle for 30 to 60 seconds, and then pour in the beans with all their liquid. Tuck in the bay leaves and thyme sprigs and bring to a boil. Cover, transfer to the oven, and bake until the chicken is cooked through, about 15 minutes.

7 If you like, serve directly from the pan sprinkled with parsley, or lift out the chicken with tongs, set in a wide shallow bowl (such as a pasta bowl), boil the sauce for a few minutes to concentrate its flavors, and pour it over the chicken.

Serves 4 to 6

By the end of September the walnut harvest begins. If you've never eaten them within 10 days off the tree, then you have no idea how a walnut really tastes. Look for new-crop nuts. Get them in the freezer as soon as possible, and they'll be "fresh" for a long time. This soup uses up any chicken stock you may have lurking in the freezer.

COLD CUCUMBER SOUP
with NEW WALNUTS

$^1/_2$ cup walnuts, chopped

2 cucumbers, peeled, seeded, and cut up

Juice of 1 lemon

2 tablespoons good-quality olive oil

2 cups chicken stock

1 cup buttermilk or thick plain yogurt

$^1/_2$ teaspoon salt

White pepper to taste

Dash of paprika

Chopped fresh mint or dill

1 In a food processor or blender, combine the walnuts, cucumbers, lemon juice, and oil. Process until pulverized.

2 Transfer the mixture to a bowl. Stir in the chicken stock, buttermilk or yogurt, salt, and white pepper. Cover and chill.

3 Serve in chilled bowls. Dust the tops with a little paprika and garnish with mint or dill.

Serves 4 to 6

A dazzling company dish that's light and tasty. The soup comes to the table with egg whites bobbing on top.

172

VELVET CHICKEN-CORN SOUP

1 tablespoon vegetable oil

1/4 pound ground chicken

4 cups chicken stock

1/8 teaspoon white pepper

1 tablespoon oyster sauce

1 1/2 cups corn kernels
(fresh or frozen)

2 1/2 tablespoons cornstarch
mixed with 3 tablespoons water

2 eggs

2 tablespoons
finely minced fresh cilantro

1 tablespoon
finely minced green onion

1 Heat the oil in a small sauté pan over medium-high heat. Add the chicken and sauté until cooked through, about 5 minutes. Pour into a sieve to drain; set aside.

2 In a saucepan, bring the chicken stock and white pepper to a boil. Add the oyster sauce and corn and bring to a boil.

3 Quickly stir the cornstarch-water mixture to combine, then pour it slowly into the boiling stock, stirring constantly. Boil until thickened and clear, about 1 1/2 minutes. Stir in the cooked chicken.

4 Break the eggs into a bowl, prick the yolks, and stir once. Remove the saucepan from the heat and slowly pour in the eggs while pushing them in the same direction with the back of a spoon or ladle.

5 Ladle into bowls and garnish with the cilantro and green onion. Serve immediately.

Serves 6 to 8

You'll need a hard apple that won't turn to mush during cooking.

CHICKEN BREASTS
with CURRY and APPLES

4 boneless chicken breasts, skin on

Salt and black pepper to taste

1 tablespoon butter

2 teaspoons curry powder

1 onion, diced

2 teaspoons minced garlic

2 firm apples such as Fuji or Granny Smith, peeled, cored, and cut into eighths

2 tablespoons fresh lemon juice

1/2 cup apple cider

1/4 cup heavy cream

1 Heat a serving platter in a 150°F oven.

2 Rinse the chicken breasts and pat dry with paper towels. Sprinkle with salt and pepper.

3 Melt the butter in a wide, heavy sauté pan with a lid over high heat. Add the breasts, skin side down. Sear briefly, reduce the heat to medium-high, and sauté, turning once, until well browned, about 4 minutes total. Remove the chicken to a plate.

4 Pour off all but 1 tablespoon fat from the pan and return the pan to medium-high heat. Add the curry, onion, and garlic and fry for about 1 minute until fragrant. Add the apples and sauté for about 1 minute longer.

5 Return the breasts to the pan skin side up, nestling them into the apples. Raise the heat to high and pour in the lemon juice and cider. Bring to a boil, cover, reduce the heat to low, and simmer until the breasts are cooked through, 8 to 10 minutes. Remove the breasts to the warmed serving platter and keep warm.

6 Bring the sauce to a boil and boil until thickened, about 2 minutes. Add the cream, return to a boil, and immediately pour the apples and sauce over the chicken. Serve hot.

Serves 4 or 5

The Normans may wish they'd had the Fuji all to themselves, but they were too early. A 1940s cross between a Red Delicious and a striped Ralls Janet, the Japanese created what many contend is the world's most wonderful apple. Sweet, crunchy, and juicy, the Fuji does a nice job alongside sautéed chicken. The degree of intensity in this dish rests entirely on how patient you are with the sauce. The longer you let it boil, the more concentrated the apple flavor will be.

SAUTÉED CHICKEN
with FUJI APPLES, NORMANDY STYLE

1 chicken, 4 pounds, cut into serving pieces

Salt and black pepper to taste

2 tablespoons butter

1/4 cup Calvados or other apple or grape brandy

3/4 cup apple cider

Peel from 1 lemon, cut off in wide strips

2 Fuji apples, peeled, cored, and cut into eighths

1/2 cup heavy cream

1 Warm a serving platter in a 150°F oven.

2 Hack the chicken breasts in half crosswise. Rinse the chicken pieces and pat dry with paper towels. Sprinkle with salt and pepper.

3 Melt the butter in a large, heavy sauté pan over high heat. Add the chicken, skin side down, and sauté, turning once, until well browned, about 4 minutes on each side.

4 With the heat high, pour in the brandy. Quickly ignite with a match and let the flame die out. Add the cider and the lemon peel, bring to a boil, cover, reduce the heat to low, and simmer for 15 minutes.

5 Uncover, scatter the apples around the chicken, re-cover, and simmer until the chicken is cooked through and the apples are tender, about 8 minutes longer. With tongs, remove the chicken pieces to the warmed serving platter, leaving the apples in the pan, and keep warm.

6 Bring the pan sauce to a boil and boil until reduced by half, about 2 minutes. Stir in the cream and return to a boil.

7 Pour the apples and sauce over the chicken. Serve hot.

Serves 4

A great reminder of autumn's healthiest bounty: dark leafy greens. Here is a two-step process that wilts chard before it's sautéed in olive oil with garlic. You can wilt the chard early in the day, or even a day or so before-hand.

SAUTÉED CHICKEN BREASTS
with TWICE-COOKED RED CHARD
and GARLIC

2 bunches red Swiss chard, rinsed and tough stalks removed

6 boneless chicken breasts, skin on

Salt and black pepper to taste

3 tablespoons olive oil

1 tablespoon minced garlic

½ cup dry red wine

1 tablespoon butter

1 Put the chard, its leaves still wet from rinsing, in a big pot over high heat. Cook, stirring frequently, until about three-fourths wilted, about 5 minutes. Drain, let cool, and squeeze out any excess water. Set aside.

2 Heat a serving platter in a 150°F oven.

3 Rinse the chicken breasts and pat dry with paper towels. Sprinkle with salt and pepper.

4 Heat 1 tablespoon of the oil in a wide, heavy sauté pan over high heat. Add the chicken breasts, skin side down, and sauté, turning once, until well browned and cooked through, 6 to 7 minutes on each side.

5 While the chicken cooks, heat the remaining 2 tablespoons oil in a another sauté pan over high heat. Add the wilted chard, stirring quickly. Season with salt and add the garlic. Sauté until glossy and hot, about 1 minute longer. Arrange the chard on the warmed serving platter and keep warm.

6 When the breasts are done, arrange them on top of the chard and keep warm. Bring the hot chicken juices remaining in the pan to a boil over high heat. Pour in the wine and cook, stirring, until reduced by half.

7 Remove from the heat, whisk in the butter until melted, and pour the sauce over the chicken. Serve hot.

CHICKEN **63** NUGGET

Why did the chicken cross the road?

Captain Kirk: To boldly go where no chicken has gone before.

Serves 4

Ask a dozen Hungarians for a recipe for paprikash and you'll get a different answer from each. "We Hungarians are very opinionated about our paprikash." That's my friend Eva Revesz talking. "Each one of us makes it the best." She explains that the dish varies by region. In one area, a heavy paprika taste might be preferred. She happens to add garlic. Watching her make this one afternoon I was most impressed with the subtlety from two pale yellow gypsy peppers instead of the usual stringent green bells. The gypsy pepper, Eva assures me, is the correct pepper. It is sort of heart shaped and has a distinctive pointed bottom and mild taste. The subtlety comes from adding the peppers to the sauce in large pieces, then fishing them out. The traditional accompaniment of this dish is a cucumber side salad.

CHICKEN PAPRIKASH
with CUCUMBER SALAD

1 chicken, 4 pounds, cut into serving pieces

2 onions, chopped

2 tablespoons vegetable oil

2 teaspoons minced garlic

3 rounded tablespoons sweet, or mild, paprika (see Note)

1 large, ripe tomato, peeled and chopped (see Peeling Tomatoes, page 177), or about 1 cup chopped canned tomatoes

Salt and black pepper to taste

1 cup chicken stock

2 small yellow gypsy peppers, seeded and quartered lengthwise

¾ cup sour cream

Cucumber Salad (recipe follows)

1 Hack the chicken breasts in half crosswise. Rinse the chicken pieces and pat dry with paper towels.

2 Heat I tablespoon of the oil in a skillet over medium heat. Add the onions and sauté until translucent but not browned, about 3 minutes. Set aside.

3 Heat the remaining I tablespoon oil in a wide, heavy sauté pan with a lid over high heat. Add the chicken, skin side down. Sear briefly, reduce the heat to medium-high, and sauté, turning once, until well browned, 5 to 7 minutes on each side.

4 Scatter in I teaspoon of the garlic, stir for a few moments, add the paprika, and turn the chicken pieces over to coat them. Add the cooked onions, tomato, salt, pepper, and stock. Allow to simmer, then tuck in the pieces of gypsy pepper.

5 Cover, reduce the heat to low, and simmer for 20 minutes. Uncover and continue to simmer until the chicken is cooked through, about 10 minutes longer. The sauce will thicken slightly.

6 Remove the chicken to a plate and discard the peppers. Add the remaining I teaspoon garlic to the juices in the pan. At this point, taste. If desired, add more salt and paprika. Remove from the heat.

7 In a little bowl, stir together the sour cream and a few table-spoons of the pan sauce. Stir the sour cream mixture into the sauce in the pan, mixing well.

8 Return the chicken to the pan and coat with the sauce. Serve directly from the pan or remove to a platter. Serve with the cucumber salad.

Note: Paprika was the one spice used so prominently by my mother, and for no reason except for color, that I grew to dislike it. I consider it an after-thought for the recipes she knew wouldn't amount to much. If you share this legacy, give paprika another chance. In the areas in which it is revered, it comes in many styles and degree of hotness. Sweet paprika means it's not hot rather than truly sweet. This recipe uses sweet paprika, which is often labeled "mild" in stores.

Cucumber Salad

1 cucumber, sliced paper-thin
1/4 cup white wine vinegar
1/4 cup water
1/8 teaspoon sugar
1/8 teaspoon salt
Black pepper to taste
1/2 teaspoon minced fresh dill or 1/8 teaspoon dried dill

1. In a bowl, combine all the ingredients, mixing well. Cover and chill until serving.

PEELING TOMATOES

No need to heat up the kitchen with a vat of boiling water just to loosen the skins on a couple of tomatoes. Here are two ways to get the job done. It also works well for peaches.

MICROWAVE METHOD

Set 1 to 3 tomatoes in a medium-sized plastic bowl, fill with water, and microwave on High, uncovered, until the water boils. Remove from the microwave. Leave the tomatoes in the water until you need them.

TEAKETTLE METHOD

Bring a teakettle filled with water to a boil. Load the tomatoes into a big bowl and pour the boiling water over them. In 30 to 60 seconds you'll be able to remove the skins easily. Drain and peel.

Apples and honey have always paired off nicely. Tarragon and mustard accentuate their sweetness, while the addition of a little cream subdues it— a lovely balance that's sophisticated yet easy.

178

CHICKEN BREASTS
with APPLES, TARRAGON, and HONEY

2 tablespoons butter

2 apples, peeled, cored, and cut into eighths

4 chicken breasts

Salt and black pepper to taste

1 cup apple cider

2 tablespoons honey

1 teaspoon Dijon mustard

1 tablespoon chopped fresh tarragon, plus extra for garnish

¼ cup heavy cream

1 Heat a serving platter in a 150° F oven.

2 Melt 1 tablespoon of the butter in a skillet over high heat. Add the apple wedges and sauté until softened, about 8 minutes. Remove from the heat and set aside.

3 Rinse the chicken breasts and pat dry with paper towels. Sprinkle with salt and pepper.

4 Melt the remaining 1 tablespoon butter in a wide, heavy sauté pan with a lid over medium-high heat. Add the chicken breasts, skin side down, and sauté, turning once, until nicely browned, about 5 minutes on each side.

5 Raise the heat to high and add the apple cider, honey, mustard, and 1 tablespoon tarragon. Bring to a boil, cover, reduce the heat to low, and simmer until the chicken is cooked through, about 10 minutes. Remove the chicken breasts to the warmed serving platter and keep warm.

6 Add the sautéed apples and their juices to the pan, stirring them into the chicken juices. Bring to a boil, add the cream, and boil for about 1 minute.

7 Pour the apples and sauce around the chicken breasts and garnish with a little more tarragon. Serve hot.

Serves 4

Pomegranates seem to just sit there and beg for inspiration. Use their acidic juice as the base for salad dressing. This unusual salad got raves the first time I made it. With its green and red colors, it appeared ready for the holidays.

CHICKEN SALAD
with AVOCADO, POMEGRANATE, and MINT

2 lemons

2 avocados

2 pomegranates

4 cups cubed cooked chicken meat such as Asian-Smoked Chicken (pages 48–49)

2 tablespoons finely minced shallots

FOR THE DRESSING:

2 tablespoons pomegranate juice (from above pomegranate; see Notes, page 189)

1 tablespoon plain vinegar

1 tablespoon chopped fresh mint

Pinch of sugar

1/4 teaspoon salt

White pepper to taste

1/4 to 1/3 cup olive oil

Salt and black pepper to taste

4 large iceberg lettuce leaves

Pita bread

1 Juice 1 of the lemons into a medium-sized bowl. Peel and section the other lemon into another larger bowl.

2 Pit and peel the avocados, then slice into the lemon juice. Toss gently and set aside.

3 Juice 1 of the pomegranates on a citrus reamer (see Notes, page 189); save the juice for the dressing.

4 Remove the seeds from the other pomegranate and add them to the sectioned lemon. Add the chicken, shallots, and the lemon juice and avocado, and toss lightly.

5 To make the dressing, combine all the ingredients except the oil and shake in a jar. Add 1/4 cup oil and shake again. If very sharp in taste, add a little more olive oil.

6 Toss the chicken mixture with the dressing.

7 Taste for salt and pepper, and add some if you think the salad needs it. Place a lettuce leaf on each individual plate, forming a cup. Spoon the salad into the lettuce cups and serve with the pita bread.

Serves 4

This is an anytime recipe, but I love it in fall when my rosemary has grown spiky. Start this 2 hours before you plan on serving it, even though the chicken is done before then. The extra time is for the chicken to rest and for the potatoes to cook fully in the pan drippings.

ROASTED
ROSEMARY CHICKEN
and POTATOES

Leaves from
2 fresh rosemary sprigs

4 or 5 garlic cloves

1/4 cup very good olive oil

1 chicken, 4 pounds

Salt and black pepper to taste

1 onion, cut into wedges

3 pounds White Rose or
other white skinned potatoes,
unpeeled, cut into
1 1/2-inch chunks

1/4 cup water, chicken stock,
or dry white wine

1 Set a rack inside an oblong roasting pan. Preheat an oven to 450°F.

2 Mince the rosemary leaves; you should have 2 tablespoons. Add 2 teaspoons of the rosemary to a food processor (reserve the remaining rosemary for the potatoes). With the motor running, drop in the garlic through the feed tube, then slowly pour in the oil and process until creamy. Strain the oil through a sieve reserving both the oil and the solids.

3 Using your fingertips, loosen the skin on the chicken's breast, thighs, and back, being careful not to tear it. Stuff portions of the garlic-rosemary mixture under the skin, smoothing it out by massaging it into place from the outside.

4 Place the chicken on the rack in the pan, breast down. Smear the backside with some of the strained oil. Sprinkle with salt and pepper.

5 Roast for 15 minutes. Remove from the oven, turn breast side up, smear the breast with the remaining oil, and sprinkle again with salt and pepper. Reduce the oven temperature to 350°F and roast for 30 minutes.

6 Meanwhile, put the onion, potatoes, the reserved rosemary, about ½ teaspoon salt, and pepper to taste in a bowl. Stir briefly to mix.

7 Add the water or other liquid to the roasting pan. Scatter the onion-potato mixture under the chicken. Continue to roast until the chicken is cooked through, about 40 minutes longer.

8 Remove the chicken to a cutting board with a trough for catching the juices. Raise the oven temperature to 450°F and finish browning the potato mixture, about 30 minutes longer, stirring now and then. If the chicken releases any juices, add them to the potatoes.

9 Carve the chicken and place on a platter. Serve surrounded with the hot rosemary potatoes. Use the hot juices from the potatoes to moisten the meat.

Serves 4

CHICKEN **57** NUGGET

Why did the chicken cross the road?

Ralph Waldo Emerson:
It did not cross the road.
It transcended it.

Fresh lima beans are the autumnal equivalent of spring fava beans—both have a season about as long as a doomed sitcom. The often-hated lima bean is the canned version, but fresh or fresh-frozen, it's a buttery beauty. Succotash always has corn, still abundant in fall. This succotash is a creamy companion for browned chicken.

CHICKEN BREASTS
with SUCCOTASH in CREAM

6 chicken breasts

Salt and black pepper to taste

4 tablespoons butter

1 hot banana pepper or other hot green or yellow chile, seeded and minced

Kernels from 6 ears of corn (about 2 cups)

2 cups fresh lima beans, or 1 package (1 pound) frozen lima beans, thawed

1/2 cup heavy cream

1/4 teaspoon fresh lemon juice

3 tablespoons flour

1 1/2 cups milk, heated

1 Preheat an oven to 325°F.

2 Hack the chicken breasts in half crosswise. Rinse the chicken pieces and pat dry with paper towels. Sprinkle with salt and pepper.

3 Heat 1 tablespoon of the butter in a heavy sauté pan over high heat. Add the chicken breasts, skin side down, and sauté, turning once, until well browned, 4 to 5 minutes on each side. Remove the chicken to a 9-by-13-inch baking dish, skin side up. Leave the collected cooking juices in the sauté pan.

4 Place the pan over medium-high heat, add the hot pepper, and sauté in the pan juices for 1 or 2 minutes. Add the corn and fresh lima beans (if using frozen, add 5 minutes later), and cook, stirring constantly, until limas are tender, 7 to 8 minutes. Remove from the heat.

5 Meanwhile, mix together the cream and lemon juice. In a saucepan, melt the remaining 3 tablespoons butter over medium heat. Add the flour and whisk until pale gold and bubbly, about 1 minute. Slowly whisk in the hot milk, then the lemon-cream mixture, to form a rather thick sauce. When the sauce bubbles, remove it from the heat. Pour the sauce over the vegetables, stirring gently to coat well.

6 Pour the succotash mixture over the chicken. Cover and bake until the chicken is cooked through, about 35 minutes. Serve the chicken directly from the baking dish.

Serves 6

I discovered many years ago how nicely figs, walnuts, and the flavor of coffee go together. I was experimenting with ice cream. The combination is now a household classic. Following this concept to a sauté pan gave me this fine dish of chicken—sweet, smoky, and dark with autumn's last figs and the season's new walnuts crunchy on top.

CHICKEN with WALNUTS and FIG SAUCE

6 dried Mission figs

$^1/_3$ cup Kahlúa or cold strong brewed coffee

1 cup walnut halves, preferably new crop

3 tablespoons packed brown sugar

Pinch of salt

1 chicken, 4 pounds, cut into serving pieces

2 tablespoons butter

Salt and black pepper to taste

$^3/_4$ cup chicken stock

1 In a small bowl, combine the figs and the Kahlúa or coffee and set aside to soak.

2 Lay a sheet of parchment paper or waxed paper on a baking sheet. Heat a small nonstick skillet over high heat. When hot, add the nuts and toss and stir constantly until they smell toasty, 1 to 3 minutes, depending on freshness. Quickly sprinkle the brown sugar and salt over the nuts, keeping them moving about 1 minute longer as the sugar melts. Immediately pour onto the paper and let cool completely before breaking apart.

3 Hack the chicken breasts in half crosswise. Rinse the chicken and pat dry with paper towels. Sprinkle with salt and pepper. Melt the butter in a wide, heavy sauté pan with a lid over high heat. Add the chicken pieces, skin side down. Reduce the heat to medium-high and sauté, turning once, until well browned, about 5 minutes on each side.

4 Mash the softened figs into the liqueur until a lumpy paste forms.

5 Remove the chicken to a plate. With the heat high, add the fig mixture to the pan and let it sizzle for a few moments, then douse with the chicken stock. Tuck the chicken back into the pan, skin side up, and bring to a boil. Cover, reduce the heat to low, and simmer until the chicken is cooked through, about 25 minutes.

6 Transfer the chicken to a serving platter. Boil the sauce for about 1 minute longer, to thicken slightly. Pour the sauce over the chicken. Break the walnuts apart and sprinkle on top. Serve hot.

Serves 4

White onions and white corn are staples of
Mexican and Southwestern cooking. Don't be fooled
by the sweetness of white onions. They can be quite
pungent during dicing, so work fast.

184

CHICKEN with GREEN CHILE, WHITE CORN, and CREAM

3 fresh poblano or Anaheim chiles or ¹/₂ cup canned mild green chiles

¹/₂ jalapeño chile, seeded and minced

1 chicken, 4 pounds, cut into serving pieces

Salt and black pepper to taste

2 tablespoons butter

1 white onion, chopped

¹/₄ cup chicken stock

³/₄ cup heavy cream

Kernels from 2 ears white corn

1 Preheat a broiler. Place the chiles on a baking sheet and broil, turning as needed, until the skins blister and blacken on all sides. Wrap in a kitchen towel or drop into a plastic or paper bag until cool, then peel, seed, and cut into 1-inch squares. If using canned chiles, seed and cut into 1-inch squares. Place the roasted or canned chiles in a bowl and add the jalapeño.

2 Hack the chicken breasts in half crosswise. Rinse the chicken pieces and pat dry with paper towels. Sprinkle with salt and pepper.

3 Heat a serving platter in a 150°F oven.

4 Melt 1 tablespoon of the butter in large sauté pan with a lid over high heat. Add the onion, reduce the heat to medium, and sauté until very soft, about 5 minutes. Remove to the bowl holding the chiles.

5 Add the remaining 1 tablespoon butter to the pan over medium-high heat. Arrange the chicken, skin side down, in the pan and sauté, turning once, until well browned, about 4 minutes on each side.

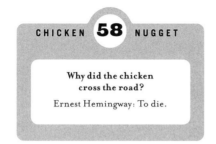

CHICKEN **58** NUGGET

Why did the chicken cross the road?

Ernest Hemingway: To die.

6 Pour off any excess fat from the pan. Raise the heat to high, add the chicken stock, and bring to a boil. Cover, reduce the heat to low, and simmer until the chicken is cooked through, about 20 minutes. Remove the chicken to the warmed serving platter and keep warm.

7 With the heat still on high, add the chile-onion mixture, stir for a few moments, and then add the cream. Bring to a boil and boil until reduced by half. During this time, taste and adjust the seasonings.

8 Add the corn and boil for 1 minute. Pour the sauce over the chicken and serve, scooping up corn and chiles with each portion.

Serves 4

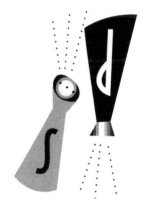

To be bourbon, it's got to be made from 51 percent corn. That's why bourbon goes so nicely in this chowder.

186

CHICKEN AND CORN
CHOWDER with BOURBON and GREEN BEANS

4 boneless chicken breasts, skinned

1 tablespoon butter

1 teaspoon salt

Black pepper to taste

1 white onion, chopped

3 cups yellow corn kernels (fresh or thawed frozen)

¼ cup bourbon

2 tablespoons flour

2 cups chicken stock, heated

½ pound green beans, trimmed and cut into ½-inch pieces

1 cup half-and-half

1 Rinse the chicken breasts and pat dry with paper towels. Cut into cubes.

2 Melt the butter in a Dutch oven over high heat. Add the chicken, sprinkle with ½ teaspoon of the salt and pepper to taste, and sauté for about 4 minutes without coloring. Reduce the heat to medium-high if the chicken begins to brown. Remove the chicken with a slotted spoon to a plate.

3 Add the onion to the fat remaining in the pan and sauté over medium-high heat until softened and lightly browned, about 3 minutes. Add the corn and stir for about 30 seconds.

4 Raise the heat to high and pour in the bourbon. Ignite with a match and let the flame die out.

5 Sprinkle the flour over the corn and stir for 1 minute. Add the hot stock and bring to a boil, stirring constantly. Add the green beans, the remaining ½ teaspoon salt, and pepper to taste. Return the chicken to the pot with any released juices and simmer the soup for 2 minutes to heat the chicken through and blend the flavors.

6 Add the half-and-half and heat through. Ladle into warmed bowls, grabbing up some soup, chicken, corn, and beans in each serving. Serve piping hot.

Serves 6

Here is a one-pot meal of chicken and autumn apples brightened with lemon juice and herbs. The chicken cooks in an old style—it just about falls off the bones.

CHICKEN POT ROAST
with APPLE and POTATOES

1 chicken, 4 pounds

Salt and black pepper to taste

4 tablespoons fresh lemon juice

1 apple, peeled and cored

3 russet potatoes (about 1½ pounds), peeled and quartered

1 onion, cut into eighths

5 garlic cloves, smashed

Few fresh sage sprigs

Few fresh parsley sprigs

½ cup chicken stock or dry white wine

1 Position a rack in the lower third of an oven. Preheat to 350°F.

2 Rinse the chicken and pat dry with paper towels. Rub the cavity with 2 tablespoons of the lemon juice and sprinkle with salt and pepper. Insert the apple.

3 Put the chicken in an oval roaster or an ovenproof Dutch oven. Rub the outside with the rest of the lemon juice and sprinkle with salt and pepper. Scatter the potatoes, onion, garlic, and sage and parsley sprigs around the chicken.

4 Cover and bake for 1 hour. Add the chicken stock or wine, and redistribute the vegetables if they are sticking or cooking unevenly. Continue baking until the chicken is cooked through, 30 minutes longer.

5 Using tongs, remove the chicken to a large, deep platter or a shallow bowl. Using a slotted spoon, scoop out the potatoes and onion and arrange around the bird. Strain the pan juices through a sieve placed over a small saucepan and set briefly in the freezer to force the fat to rise. Spoon off and discard as much fat as possible.

6 Place the saucepan over high heat, bring to a boil, and boil until reduced by one-fourth. Pour the sauce into a pitcher.

7 Cut the chicken into serving pieces with poultry sheers (it will probably fall off the bone). Pass the sauce at the table.

Serves 4

The dark, rich color of this sauce is the background for a sprinkling of ruby-red pomegranate seeds. Two well-known complements to pomegranate are basil and lemon. I got them both by using the leaves of fresh lemon basil, which I've grown with no problem just about every summer. Supermarket basil (probably the Genoese type) or Thai basil also provides great basil power and perfume. The most fascinating part of watching this recipe come to its conclusion is how ground almonds, if heated, thicken a sauce.

CHICKEN with POMEGRANATE JUICE, CARDAMOM, and BASIL in ALMOND-THICKENED SAUCE

1-inch piece fresh ginger (about 1 ounce), peeled and minced

1 tablespoon finely minced garlic

2 tablespoons finely minced fresh cilantro, plus sprigs for garnish

2 tablespoons finely minced fresh lemon basil or regular basil

4 cardamom pods

1/2 cup dry-roasted almonds

About 5 pomegranates

1 chicken, 3 1/2 to 4 pounds, cut into serving pieces

Salt and black pepper to taste

1 tablespoon olive oil

1/2 cup chicken stock

1 In a bowl, combine the ginger, garlic, minced cilantro, basil, and cardamom pods.

2 In a food processor, process the almonds to form a fine meal, at least 1 minute (see Notes). Leave in the work bowl.

3 Juice 4 of the pomegranates on a citrus reamer (see Notes). You should have about 2 cups. Remove the seeds from the remaining pomegranate and save for garnish.

4 Rinse the chicken pieces and pat dry with paper towels. Sprinkle with salt and pepper.

5 Heat the oil in a wide, heavy sauté pan with a lid over medium-high heat. Add the chicken pieces, skin side down, and sauté, turning once, until well browned, about 4 minutes on each side. Remove the chicken to a plate.

6 Pour off all but 2 tablespoons of the fat from the pan. Return the pan to medium-high heat, add the spice mixture, and fry until it starts to stick and emits a perfume, only about 30 seconds.

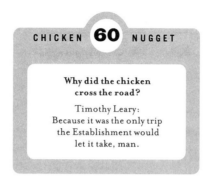

7 Sprinkle the ground almonds over the bottom of the pan. Top with the chicken pieces, skin side up. Add the pomegranate juice and stock, and a touch more salt and pepper. Bring to a boil, cover, reduce the heat to low, and simmer until the chicken is cooked through, about 20 minutes.

8 Remove and discard the cardamom pods. Arrange the chicken on a serving platter. Pour the sauce over the top. Sprinkle generously with the pomegranate seeds, top with cilantro sprigs, and serve.

Serves 4

Notes: To grind the dry-roasted almonds to a proper consistency, grind them in a food processor for at *least* 1 minute. You've reached the correct stage if the mixture clumps when lightly gripped in your palm. Stopping short of "ground" will give you chopped pieces. Going too far will give you almond butter—also good, but not for this recipe.

To extract the juice from a pomegranate, lightly juice it on a citrus reamer, preferably electric, no matter what you've heard about not doing this. If you're careful to avoid the white pith, which is bitter, the reamer method will give you the juice and strain it for you without a seedy mess.

If autumn puts you in the mood for a casserole, this Mexican border–styled combo is a meal in one pan. With chicken, rice, corn, and the last of the green chiles before they begin to turn red swirled with the richness of sour cream and cheese, a little goes a long way.

CHICKEN AND RICE
CASSEROLE with GREEN CHILES and CORN

4 fresh poblano or Anaheim chiles or about ³/₄ cup canned mild green chiles

4 boneless chicken breasts, skinned, or 8 boneless thighs, skinned

Salt and black pepper to taste

2 tablespoons vegetable oil

1 white onion, chopped

1 teaspoon minced garlic

1 cup long-grain white rice

2 cups boiling chicken stock

1 teaspoon pure chile powder such as New Mexico

¹/₂ teaspoon ground cumin

1 teaspoon dried oregano

1 tablespoon butter

2 cups yellow corn kernels (fresh or thawed)

2 cups (16 ounces) sour cream

1 pound Monterey Jack cheese, shredded

1 Preheat a broiler. Place the chiles on a baking sheet and broil, turning as needed, until the skins blister and blacken on all sides. Wrap in a kitchen towel or drop into a plastic or paper bag until cool, then peel, seed, and cut into long, narrow strips. If using canned chiles, seed and cut into long, narrow strips. Set aside.

2 Preheat an oven to 350°F. Lightly butter a baking dish.

3 Rinse the chicken pieces and pat dry with paper towels. Sprinkle with salt and pepper.

4 Heat I tablespoon of the oil in a wide, heavy sauté pan over high heat. Add the onion and garlic and sauté until softened, about 4 minutes. Remove from the pan.

5 Wipe out the pan with a paper towel and add the remaining I tablespoon oil. Place over medium-high heat, add the rice, and stir until toasty, about 2 minutes. Add the boiling stock, chile powder, cumin, oregano, salt, and pepper. Pour into the prepared baking dish, cover, and bake for 30 minutes.

6 Meanwhile, in the same pan, melt the butter over medium-high heat. Add the chicken breasts and sauté, turning once, until well browned, about 5 minutes on each side. Remove to paper towels to drain.

7 In a bowl, stir together the corn, reserved chiles, and sour cream. When the rice has cooked for 30 minutes, uncover and add the corn mixture to it, mixing well. Top with the browned chicken pieces, nestling them into the rice. Return to the oven and bake, covered, until the chicken is cooked through, about 15 minutes.

8 Remove from the oven and scatter the cheese evenly over the top. Return to the oven, uncovered, and bake until the cheese is thoroughly melted and bubbly, about 5 minutes. Bring to the table and serve hot.

Serves 4

The flavor of Dijon mustard from a leafy green! This soft, succulent chicken cooks slowly in broth with chopped leeks and chunks of White Rose potatoes. The mustard softens in the heat of the resulting sauce, so it is neither crunchy from undercooking nor army-green from overcooking. A homey early fall dish for an informal get-together or a family meal.

WHOLE CHICKEN
BRAISED with LEEKS, POTATOES, and SPICY LEAF MUSTARD

4 good-sized leeks, white part only, finely chopped

2 large celery stalks, chopped

5 White Rose or other white-skinned potatoes, peeled and cut into 1-inch cubes

1 chicken, 4 to 4½ pounds

Salt and black pepper to taste

About ¾ cup flour mixed with 1 teaspoon salt and black pepper to taste

1 tablespoon olive oil

1½ cups chicken stock

1 bunch mustard greens, tough stems removed

About 2 tablespoons minced fresh flat-leaf (Italian) parsley

1 In a bowl, combine the leeks and celery. Set aside. Hold the potatoes in another bowl.

2 Rinse the chicken inside and out and pat dry with paper towels. Season the cavity with salt and pepper. Dredge the whole chicken in the seasoned flour.

3 Heat the oil in a large pot or Dutch oven over high heat. When very hot, add the chicken and brown well—breast, back, both sides—about 10 minutes. Reduce the heat to medium-high if the chicken begins to burn. Remove the chicken to a large plate.

4 Pour off all but 1 tablespoon of the fat from the pot and return to medium-high heat. Add the leeks and celery and sauté until softened, about 5 minutes.

5 Return the chicken to the pot, breast up. Pour in the stock and drop the potatoes all around the bird. Sprinkle a little more salt and pepper over everything and bring to a boil.

6 Cover, reduce the heat to low, and simmer until a knife easily pierces the potatoes and the chicken is cooked through and very tender, 50 to 60 minutes. Remove the chicken and potatoes to a serving platter, setting the potatoes to one side of the bird.

7 Add the mustard leaves to the hot juices in the pot and swish them around until wilted, 2 to 3 minutes. Lift the mustard from the pot with a slotted spoon and place on the other side of the chicken. Boil the juices for 1 or 2 minutes, until somewhat thickened. Pour into a pitcher.

8 Sprinkle the chicken platter with parsley and serve hot. The chicken will not need carving so much as a gentle hand guiding it apart, as it will probably fall away on its own. Pass the pitcher of juices at the table.

Serves 6

CHICKEN **65** NUGGET

That'll Be 45 to 60 Days and the Usual Death Penalty
In Quitman, Georgia, it is illegal for a chicken to cross the road.

Of course, you can put any old cooked and shredded chicken into a tortilla and call it an enchilada. But where I come from along the Texas border, the chicken must be simmered very gently for the best results. It's nearly the same technique that produces the White-Cooked Chicken (page 50).

The sauce is for early fall, when the chiles are still fresh and green. The tortillas must be equally fresh. Remember, an enchilada is not a whale, but a cigar-sized roll containing just a little filling.

GREEN CHICKEN ENCHILADAS
with MONTEREY JACK CHEESE

FOR THE CHICKEN:

1 chicken, 4 pounds

2 garlic cloves

1 white onion, left whole, plus 1/2 white onion, grated

1 teaspoon dried Mexican oregano

2 bay leaves

1 teaspoon salt, plus salt to taste

Black pepper to taste

1/2 teaspoon dried thyme

1 To cook the chicken, place the bird in a large pot with a lid. Add water just to cover, add the garlic, the whole onion, the oregano, the bay leaves, the salt, and the pepper. Bring slowly to a simmer, uncovered, which may take as long as 30 minutes. Skim off any scum that appears.

2 Simmer the chicken gently for just 20 minutes. Cover the pot and remove from the heat. Let the chicken cool in the water for 2 hours. The meat will be tender and juicy.

3 Remove the chicken to a platter. Pour the stock through a fine-mesh sieve placed over a large bowl. Place briefly in the refrigerator to force the fat to rise, then spoon away the fat. Measure out 1 cup of the stock to use for the sauce; cover and refrigerate or freeze the remaining stock for future use.

4 When the chicken is cool enough to handle, remove and discard the skin, then remove the meat from the bones. Shred the meat into a big bowl. Add the thyme and grated onion and season with salt and pepper. Cover and set aside.

5 To make the sauce, preheat a broiler. Place the chiles on a baking sheet and slip under the broiler. Broil, turning as needed, until the skins blister and blacken on all sides. Wrap in a kitchen towel or drop into a plastic or paper bag until cool, then peel and seed. Set aside.

FOR THE SAUCE:

10 Anaheim or poblano chiles

20 tomatillos, husked

2 ripe tomatoes, peeled,
seeded, and quartered
(see Peeling Tomatoes, page 177)

1½ white onions, chopped

5 garlic cloves

3 jalapeño chiles, seeded

½ bunch cilantro

4 whole cloves

About 1 cup chicken stock
from cooking chicken

1 teaspoon salt

Black pepper to taste

Vegetable oil for frying

12 white corn tortillas,
6 inches in diameter

2 cups shredded
Monterey Jack cheese

1 cup sour cream,
plus extra for garnish (optional)

Chopped fresh cilantro,
diced avocado, and
grated radish (optional)

6 Meanwhile, bring a saucepan filled with salted water to a boil. Add the tomatillos and simmer until tender, about 10 minutes. Drain and immerse in a bowl of ice water to halt the cooking. Drain well again.

7 Working in batches, in a blender, combine the roasted chiles, tomatillos, tomatoes, onions, garlic, jalapeños, cilantro, and cloves. Pulse to chop finely. Add small amounts of the stock to get the blender going and to smooth out the sauce. Season with the salt and pepper.

8 Heat 2 tablespoons oil in a saucepan over high heat. Add the sauce, which will splash a little, and simmer, uncovered, until slightly thickened, about 15 minutes.

9 Preheat an oven to 350°F. Keep the sauce warm over very low heat. Ladle a thin layer of the sauce over the bottom of a 9-by-13-inch baking dish.

10 Pour about 4 tablespoons oil into a small sauté pan over medium-high heat. Using tongs, dip a tortilla into the hot oil to soften it for rolling, then immediately dip it into the warm sauce. Lay the tortilla on a work surface.

11 Place a few tablespoons chicken filling, plus a tablespoon or so of cheese across the bottom third of the tortilla. Roll up cigar fashion as tightly as possible. Place in the prepared baking dish, seam side down. Repeat until all the chicken filling and tortillas are used up.

12 Pour the remaining sauce evenly over the enchiladas. Bake for 10 minutes.

13 Remove from the oven and top evenly with the remaining cheese and the 1 cup sour cream. Return to the oven and continue to bake until the cheese melts and the sauce is bubbly, about 5 minutes longer.

14 Remove from the oven and top with more sour cream, cilantro, avocado, and grated radish, as desired. Serve piping hot.

Wild fennel grows near my house, but cultivated fennel bulbs should be easy enough to locate in season. If autumn is coughing up some late tomatoes, you can use them here. Otherwise, add the contents of a can of tomatoes, juice and all. Either way, the tomatoes will break up during the final phase of cooking.

CHICKEN BAKED
with BACON UNDER THE SKIN, with WINE, POTATOES, and FENNEL

1 chicken, 4 pounds

Salt and black pepper to taste

4 bacon slices

3 cups dry white wine

12 small red potatoes, unpeeled

4 carrots, peeled and cut into 1-inch chunks

1 fennel bulb, cut lengthwise into wedges

3 large tomatoes, peeled and cut into eighths (see Peeling Tomatoes, page 177), or 1 can (28 ounces) tomatoes, with juice

1 Position an oven rack in the lower third of an oven. Preheat to 350°F. Rinse the chicken and pat dry with paper towels. Sprinkle inside and out with salt and pepper.

2 Using your fingers, loosen the skin on the breast and slip the bacon slices under the skin. Put the chicken in an oval roaster or ovenproof Dutch oven and add the wine.

3 Cover and bake for 1 hour. Remove from the oven and add the potatoes, carrots, and fennel. Re-cover and continue baking for 30 minutes.

4 Add the tomatoes and continue baking until the vegetables are tender when pierced with a fork and the chicken is cooked through, about 30 minutes longer.

5 Using tongs, remove the chicken to a large platter or shallow bowl. Using a slotted spoon, scoop out the vegetables and place around the bird. Pour the pan juices into a saucepan and set briefly in the freezer to force the fat to rise. Spoon off and discard as much fat as possible.

6 Place the saucepan over high heat, bring the juices to a boil, and boil until reduced by half. Pour the sauce into a pitcher, or first strain through a sieve for a smoother sauce.

7 Cut the chicken into serving pieces with poultry shears or nudge apart with your hands. Pass the sauce at the table.

Serves 4

To modern tastes, the chicken overcooks in a sauce that defies ethnic origin. Curry from India with a western predilection to ground thyme? The dish was a favorite of Roosevelt's and of his era. Pro-FDR hosts liked to serve it to unsuspecting Republicans only to inform them of the dish's legacy after the usual round of compliments.

My friend Jim Spaulding is a wine maker in the Napa Valley town of Calistoga, and his tastes run to fine wine and Country Captain. His version is dark meat only and he changed the raisins to golden raisins. Special for his wife, my agent Martha Casselman, he leaves out the garlic and bell pepper. We all think this is an improvement over the original.

COUNTRY CAPTAIN

3 pounds chicken thighs

1 tablespoon vegetable oil

1 tablespoon butter

1 onion, thinly sliced

1 can (28 ounces) diced tomatoes, with juice

$^1/_2$ cup slivered blanched almonds

$^1/_2$ cup golden raisins

1 teaspoon salt

$^1/_2$ teaspoon white pepper

1 teaspoon curry powder

1 teaspoon chopped fresh parsley

1 teaspoon ground thyme

1 Position a rack in the lower third of an oven. Preheat to 350°F.

2 Rinse the chicken thighs and pat dry with paper towels.

3 Heat the oil in a large, heavy sauté pan over medium-high heat. Add the chicken, skin side down, and sauté, turning once, until well browned, about 5 minutes on each side. Remove to an ovenproof Dutch oven.

4 Pour off all but 1 tablespoon of the fat from the sauté pan. Add the butter and place over medium heat. When melted, add the onion and sauté until softened, about 5 minutes. Add the tomatoes and cook until broken up, about 10 minutes longer.

5 Meanwhile, in a small skillet, stir and toss the almonds over medium-high heat until toasted. Add to the sauté pan along with the raisins, salt, white pepper, curry powder, parsley, and thyme. Stir to mix well and cook for 5 minutes to blend the flavors.

6 Pour the sauce over the chicken pieces, cover tightly, and bake until the chicken is cooked through and very tender, 35 to 45 minutes. Serve hot.

Serves 4

A large skillet with a lid that can
go from the stove top to the oven and back again
is a must for this dish.

198

CHICKEN with PANCETTA,
DRIED TOMATOES, and OVEN-ROASTED CORN

1 chicken, 4 pounds, quartered or
cut into serving pieces

Salt and black pepper to taste

6 thin slices pancetta

1 onion, chopped

4 large garlic cloves, minced

¾ cup Pinot Grigio, Pinot Blanc,
or Sauvignon Blanc

¼ cup dried tomato pieces

3 ears of corn,
husks and silk removed

1 Position a rack in the lower third of an oven. Preheat to 450°F. Rinse the chicken pieces and pat dry with paper towels. Sprinkle with salt and pepper.

2 Fry the pancetta in a large ovenproof sauté pan with a lid set over medium heat until crisp, about 5 minutes. Remove to paper towels to drain, let cool, and crumble. Drain off all but 1 tablespoon of the fat from the pan.

3 Return the pan to high heat, add the chicken, skin side down, and sauté, turning once, until well browned, about 5 minutes on each side. Remove the chicken to a plate.

4 If excess fat has accumulated, drain off fat again until only 1 table-spoon remains. Return the pan to medium-high heat, add the onion and garlic, and sauté until soft, about 3 minutes. Remove the onion mixture to a bowl, and return the chicken to the pan, skin side up. Top with the cooked onions, wine, and dried tomatoes.

5 Cover and bake for 20 minutes. At the same time, place the ears of corn on the oven rack and bake until tender, about 15 minutes.

6 Remove the corn from the oven and reduce the oven temperature to 350°F. Continue baking the chicken until cooked through, about 30 minutes longer.

7 When the corn is cool, cut off the kernels and combine them with the crumbled pancetta.

8 Remove the chicken to a serving platter. Return the pan to the stove top, bring the juices to a boil, and boil until about ½ cup remains. Stir in the corn-pancetta mixture and briefly heat through. Pour the corn mixture over the chicken and serve at once.

Serves 4

This is a best-of-both-worlds dish to please light- and dark-meat eaters when company's coming.

200

VANILLA-and-MAPLE
MARINATED CHICKEN
with BOURBON SWEET POTATOES and MACADAMIA NUTS

6 chicken thighs

4 boneless chicken breasts, skin on

1/2 teaspoon salt

1/4 teaspoon white pepper

1/3 cup real maple syrup

2 tablespoons pure vanilla extract

3 or 4 sweet potatoes or yams, peeled and cut into chunks

4 tablespoons butter

1/2 cup packed brown sugar

1/3 cup bourbon

1/2 cup coarsely chopped unsalted macadamia nuts

1 Rinse the chicken pieces and pat dry with paper towels.

2 In a bowl, combine the chicken pieces, salt, pepper, maple syrup, and vanilla. Turn to coat evenly. Cover (or transfer to a zip-style plastic bag and seal the top) and marinate in the refrigerator for a few hours or as long as overnight.

3 Preheat an oven to 400°F. Butter two 9-by-13-inch baking dishes. Place the sweet potatoes in one of the baking dishes.

4 Melt the butter and brown sugar together just until liquefied (don't boil), which is easily accomplished in a microwave. Let cool slightly, add the bourbon, and pour over the sweet potatoes. Bake, uncovered, for 30 minutes.

5 Meanwhile, lift the chicken thighs from the marinade and arrange, skin side up, in the other baking dish. Pour over some of the marinade. Set in the oven with the sweet potatoes and bake for 30 minutes. By now the sweet potatoes have been baking for 1 hour, and are beginning to caramelize. Turn with tongs to coat with the cooking juices.

6 Now, add the breasts, skin side up, pour over the remaining marinade, and bake for 20 minutes longer.

7 Pour the sweet potatoes over the chicken. Top with macadamias and bake, uncovered, until the chicken pieces are cooked through, about 10 minutes longer. Serve hot.

Serves 6

This recipe comes closest to the thick, rich *juk,* the Cantonese term for rice porridge also known as congee, enjoyed by me and my husband when we visited Hong Kong. We ate it for breakfast every morning at the Can Do dim sum restaurant in Kowloon. Marinating chicken pieces in egg white gives them a pleasant velvety character.

GOOD JUK

2 cups medium-grain white rice such as Calrose variety

2 tablespoons vegetable oil

3 quarts chicken stock

3 quarts water

Salt to taste

1 quart plain soy milk

2 cups raw chicken slices marinated in 1 egg white, 1 teaspoon thin (light) soy sauce, and 1 tablespoon cornstarch for 20 minutes

Slivered green onion and chopped fresh cilantro for garnish

Oyster sauce and hot chile sauce for serving

1 Place the rice in a bowl with water to cover for 30 minutes. Drain, rinse well, and drain again.

2 Heat the oil in a large Dutch oven over high heat. Add the rice and sauté until it smells toasty, about 2 minutes.

3 Add the chicken stock and water and bring to a boil. Reduce the heat to low and simmer uncovered, stirring occasionally, for about 2½ hours. The soup should be thick and pasty.

4 Season with salt, and add the soy milk and chicken mixture. Simmer for 15 minutes longer.

5 Ladle into bowls and garnish with green onions and cilantro. Add oyster sauce and chile sauce to taste.

Makes 5 to 6 quarts

CHICKEN **66** NUGGET

Scratching Out a Living

Before the discovery of Elvis Presley, it was Col. Tom Parker and His Dancing Chickens.

Mini pumpkins make appealing receptacles for a filling of ground chicken so rich and satisfying you'd never guess it wasn't sausage. The pint-sized pumpkins show up in mid-September and go for a long season through November. The Fuyu persimmon is crisp and cuts like an apple.

This recipe is a complete make-ahead, to be heated through just before serving. Stuff the pumpkins, set on a baking sheet, wrap tightly with plastic wrap, and refrigerate for up to 1 day. Bring to room temperature before baking.

JACK·BE·LITTLES
STUFFED with GROUND CHICKEN, FUYU PERSIMMON, and DRIED CHERRIES

8 mini pumpkins, each about 6 inches in diameter

$1/4$ cup raw medium-grain white rice, or $1/2$ cup leftover cooked rice

1 tablespoon butter

1 onion, minced

$1/3$ cup finely chopped celery

1 tablespoon finely minced garlic

1 chicken (whole or cut up), $3 1/2$ to 4 pounds, boned and ground (see Grinding Chicken, pages 24–25), or 2 pounds store-bought ground chicken

1 Fuyu persimmon, chopped

$1/4$ cup quartered dried pitted cherries (about 12 cherries)

$1/4$ teaspoon ground sage

$1/8$ teaspoon ground allspice

$1/2$ teaspoon salt

Black pepper to taste

1 egg

$1/2$ cup grated Parmesan cheese

1 Position a rack in the lower third of an oven. Preheat to 375°F.

2 Using a large knife, slice the tops off the pumpkins. Use a soup spoon to scrape out the seeds. Set the pumpkins upside down on a baking sheet and roast for 20 minutes. Remove from the oven and let cool right side up. Reduce the oven temperature to 350°F.

3 If using raw rice, cook it as you would pasta. Bring a saucepan filled with water to a boil. Add the rice and boil until tender. Test for doneness after 5 to 8 minutes. Drain and reserve. You should have about $1/2$ cup. If using already cooked rice, set aside.

4 Melt the butter in a heavy skillet over high heat. Add the onion, celery, and garlic, reduce the heat to medium, and sauté until softened, about 5 minutes. Raise the heat to medium-high and add the chicken, persimmon, dried cherries, sage, allspice, salt, and pepper. Cook, stirring, for about 10 minutes. The chicken will end up looking like crumbled sausage.

5 Turn the chicken mixture into a sieve, draining well, then transfer to a bowl. Add the rice and the egg and stir to bind. You should have about 3 cups.

6 Fill the pumpkins, stuffing well and mounding the tops. Bake, uncovered, for 10 minutes. Top with the Parmesan cheese and return to the oven until the cheese melts, about 5 minutes longer. Serve hot.

Serves 8

Not everyone in America has 30 people for Thanksgiving dinner. Many are happy if a family of 2 or 3 can sit down together. For that occasion, a large chicken that still provides leftovers stands in for a turkey. Inside is a stuffing of corn bread, apple, sage, and sausage moistened with that Puritan mainstay, hard cider. Apple or pear hard cider is usually sold near the beer.

204

THANKSGIVING CHICKEN

FOR THE CORN BREAD:

4 tablespoons butter

2 cups yellow cornmeal

1 teaspoon salt

$^1/_2$ teaspoon baking soda

$^1/_2$ teaspoon baking powder

1 teaspoon sugar (optional)

$1^1/_2$ cups buttermilk or plain yogurt

2 eggs

FOR THE CHICKEN:

1 roasting chicken, 6$^1/_2$ pounds, with giblets

About 2 tablespoons butter, at room temperature

Salt and black pepper to taste

1 To make the corn bread, position a rack in the lower third of an oven. Preheat to 450°F. Put the butter into a 10-inch cast-iron skillet and set in the preheating oven to melt.

2 Meanwhile, measure the cornmeal, salt, baking soda, baking powder, and sugar, if using, into a bowl. Combine the buttermilk or yogurt and eggs in a small bowl and mix well. Add to the dry ingredients and blend lightly with a fork.

3 Pull the hot skillet from the oven, give it a swirl to coat the bottom and sides completely, then quickly pour the excess butter into the cornmeal batter, making it sizzle.

4 Mix the batter lightly, then pour it into the skillet. Return the skillet to the oven and bake until nicely browned on top, 20 to 25 minutes. Remove to a rack to cool. When cool, crumble enough of the corn bread to measure 4 cups crumbs (you will need a little more than half the loaf); slice the remaining corn bread and enjoy smeared with butter.

5 Leave the oven set at 450°F. To prepare the chicken, remove the giblets (heart, neck, gizzard, and liver) from the chicken cavity, set them in a saucepan with water to cover, and bring to a boil over medium heat. Reduce the heat to low and simmer, uncovered, until very tender, about 1 hour, then set aside until time to make the gravy.

FOR THE STUFFING:

¾ pound bulk Italian sausage

3 tablespoons butter

1 onion, chopped

1 celery stalk, chopped

2 apples, peeled, cored, and chopped

Reserved 4 cups corn bread crumbs

½ teaspoon ground sage

1 teaspoon salt

Black pepper to taste

½ cup apple or pear hard cider, or as needed

FOR THE GRAVY:

Reserved cooked giblets and cooking liquid

¼ cup flour mixed with ⅓ cup water

Splash of brandy (optional)

6 Meanwhile, rinse the chicken inside and out and pat dry with paper towels. Rub inside and out with the butter, salt, and pepper.

7 To make the stuffing, fry the sausage in a small skillet over medium heat, crumbling as you go, just until no longer pink, about 5 minutes. Transfer to a sieve to drain off the fat.

8 In another skillet, melt the butter over medium-high heat. Add the onion and celery and sauté until softened, about 5 minutes. Transfer to a big bowl. Add the apples, the drained sausage, the reserved crumbs, and the sage, salt, pepper, and ½ cup cider. If dry, moisten with a little more cider.

9 Stuff the neck and cavity of the chicken loosely. Skewer or sew closed the openings, tuck the wing tips under the bird's body, and truss the legs (see To Truss or Not to Truss, page 206). Set on a rack inside a shallow flameproof roasting pan. You'll have more stuffing than will fit into the chicken. Turn the extra into a buttered baking dish and cover with buttered foil. Set in the oven during the last 45 minutes of roasting, removing the foil the last 10 minutes.

10 Roast for 20 minutes. Reduce the temperature to 350°F and continue to roast for about 1½ hours longer. You don't have to baste. The chicken is done when the juices run clear at the "crotch" area between the thigh and body. If pink, keep roasting. Remove the chicken to a cutting board and let it rest for 10 minutes.

11 To make the gravy, pour the pan juices into a measuring cup, leaving behind any browned bits, and place the pan on the stove top. Set the juices briefly in the freezer to force the fat to rise.

12 Meanwhile, remove the giblets from their cooking liquid, reserving the liquid. Chop the giblets, discarding any skin and bones; set aside. Skim off and discard the fat from the pan juices.

continued...

13 Turn the heat to high under the roasting pan. When stuck-on bits sizzle, quickly pour in the pan juices and cooking liquid from the giblets. Bring to a boil, scraping up the bits and allowing them to be absorbed by the boiling liquid. Add the giblets.

14 Slowly add the flour-water mixture to the boiling liquid, stirring constantly until nicely thickened. (You might not need all of the flour solution.) Season with salt and pepper, and perhaps a splash of brandy. Return to a boil and pour the sauce into a pitcher.

15 Remove the stuffing to a serving dish. Carve the chicken by cutting off thin slices of breast meat, then pulling the thighs away from the bird's body, and cutting free, then the wings. Arrange on a platter. Pass the sauce at the table.

Serves 6

TO TRUSS OR NOT TO TRUSS

In the interests of being able to say that one of the easiest dinners you could ever make is to throw a whole chicken in the oven and leave it there for 1½ hours, I also have to admit that I've cooked probably hundreds of whole chickens without trussing them. The open cavity allows air to circulate and helps to cook the chicken faster.

The only time trussing a chicken is a good idea is when it's stuffed, if only for the sake of tradition and to keep the stuffing from leaking. The goal of trussing is to turn the chicken into a nice round package. Protrusions such as drumsticks or dangling wings cook faster and burn.

Here is one simple method: Put the bird on a cutting board with the drumsticks facing away from you. Push each wing tip down so it stays underneath the bird. Get a good piece of kitchen string and cut off a 2-foot length. Put the center of the string under the pope's nose. Holding the string evenly in both hands, make a sideways figure eight around the drumsticks. Pull tightly. Guide the string around the sides of the chicken toward you. If you use your thumbs behind the neck cavity to steady the bird, you'll be able to pull tightly on the string. Tie the string at the neck. It's done.

Just about everybody loves dumplings. These Chinese wontons stuffed with ground chicken and Chinese flavors are easy to make and once served, go fast. For the best results, boil the wontons in water, then add them to your favorite chicken stock.

CHICKEN WONTONS
with TANGERINE ZEST

FOR THE WONTONS:

5 dried shiitake mushrooms

About 1 pound raw ground chicken (about 3 cups from 2 to 3 breasts; see Grinding Chicken, pages 24–25)

5 water chestnuts, minced

1/2 cup chopped fresh cilantro, green onion, or chives

1 tablespoon cornstarch, plus extra for dusting baking sheets

1 1/2 tablespoons grated tangerine zest

1 tablespoon Asian sesame oil

1/2 teaspoon salt

1/8 teaspoon white pepper

1 package (12 ounces) wonton skins

1 egg, beaten

2 green onions, minced

3 quarts favorite chicken stock

1 To make the wontons, in a bowl, combine the mushrooms with warm water to cover and let stand until rehydrated, about 20 minutes. Drain, discard the stems, and chop coarsely.

2 In a bowl, combine the mushrooms, chicken, water chestnuts, cilantro or green onion or chives, cornstarch, tangerine zest, sesame oil, salt, and white pepper. Using your hands, mix until smooth and slightly tacky to the touch. (You can also mix this in a food processor until the mixture slaps around the sides of the work bowl.)

3 Place about 1 1/2 teaspoons filling in the center of a wonton skin. Moisten the edges of the skin with a little beaten egg and fold over to form a triangle, encasing the filling. Press the edges gently to seal and place on a baking sheet dusted with cornstarch. Repeat until you have used up all the filling. You should have about 3 dozen wontons. If you like, you can cover the baking sheet and refrigerate the wontons for up to 12 hours, or freeze them on the sheet, transfer to zip-style plastic bags, and freeze for up to 6 months.

4 To cook, bring a large pot of salted water to a boil. Lower the wontons into the water and cook until they float, about 10 minutes. Meanwhile, in a separate pot, bring the stock to a boil.

5 Remove the wontons with a Chinese strainer or slotted spoon and place in individual bowls, putting 4 or 5 wontons into each bowl. Ladle the boiling stock into the bowls, and sprinkle each serving with the green onions. Serve hot.

Makes about 3 dozen; serves 8

This old Chinese-American technique is foolproof, guaranteeing a moist, juicy bird every time. It came about in the forties, when Chinese chefs heading east from the West Coast, and French chefs heading west from the East Coast, ended up working together in kitchens in Chicago.

A Chicago-Chinese chicken doesn't have crispy skin, but the flavor is deep. Don't worry too much about the level of liquid. If it falls short of just submerging, simply cover the exposed parts of the chicken with foil.

CHICAGO-CHINESE CHICKEN

1 roasting chicken, 5 to 6 pounds

3 tablespoons vegetable oil

About 1 teaspoon coarse salt, plus salt to taste

½ teaspoon white pepper, plus pepper to taste

1 large onion, cut into chunks

2 large carrots, peeled and cut into 3-inch chunks

3 celery stalks, cut into 3-inch chunks

2 tablespoons pickling spice

2 cups white wine (sweet or dry)

2 cups chicken stock, heated

3 tablespoons flour mixed with ¼ cup water

1 tablespoon butter

1 Position a rack in the lower third of an oven. Preheat to 475°F.

2 Remove the giblets (heart, neck, gizzard, and liver) from the chicken cavity, set them in a saucepan with water to cover, and bring to a boil over medium heat. Reduce the heat to low and simmer, uncovered, until very tender, about 1 hour, then set aside until time to make the gravy.

3 Meanwhile, rinse the chicken inside and out and pat dry with paper towels. Rub inside and out with the vegetable oil, 1 teaspoon coarse salt, and ½ teaspoon pepper. Set aside.

4 Strew the onion, carrots, and celery in a deep roasting pan (I recommend a throw-away aluminum foil roasting pan). The vegetables will act as a bed for the chicken. Put the chicken on top of the vegetables, breast side down.

5 Roast for 20 minutes to brown. Flip the chicken (grasp the legs through a double thicknesses of paper towels) so the breast is up. Return to the oven for 20 minutes to brown the breast.

6 Reduce the oven temperature to 350°F. Sprinkle the bird with the pickling spice. Pour in the wine and stock. (Add water or a mixture of water and stock if necessary to fill to the rim of the pan.) Lay a sheet of foil loosely over all. Close the oven door and steam-poach until the drumsticks are loose, about 1¼ hours.

10 Carve as for Thanksgiving Chicken (page 206) and serve with lots of gravy.

9 Slowly add the flour–water mixture to the liquid, stirring constantly until nearly thickened. (You might not need all the flour solution.) Season to taste with salt and pepper. Return to a boil, remove from the heat, and whisk in the butter until melted. Pour into a pitcher.

8 Meanwhile, remove the giblets from their cooking liquid, reserving the liquid. Chop the giblets, discarding any skin and bones, and add them to the pan juices along with the giblet cooking liquid. Bring to a boil and boil down until 2 cups remain.

7 Transfer the chicken to a platter. Strain the pan juices into a medium saucepan and set briefly in the freezer to force the fat to rise. Skim off and discard the fat and set the pot on the stove top.

CHICKEN **42** NUGGET

Classical Chicken

Chicken Tetrazzini: Chicken in cream sauce poured over spaghetti and browned in the oven, named for Italian opera singer Luisa Tetrazzini.

Timbale comes from *thabal,* Arabic for "drum." The classic shape for a timbale is something along the lines of a fez, but today a Pyrex ramekin is suited nicely to the task. Usually something in the timbale is ground up, as the chicken is here (see Grinding Chicken, pages 24–25).

CHICKEN TIMBALES
with MUSHROOM SAUCE

FOR THE RAMEKINS:

A little butter

About ¾ cup dried bread crumbs

FOR THE CHICKEN FILLING:

3 tablespoons butter

1 tablespoon finely minced shallots

½ pound ground chicken (about 1½ cups from about 1½ breasts)

4 or 5 fresh white mushrooms, minced

1 teaspoon minced fresh parsley

1 teaspoon minced fresh thyme or sage

2 tablespoons flour

2 cups milk, heated

3 whole eggs

2 egg yolks

1 tablespoon sherry

Salt and white pepper to taste

1 Smear six 1-cup ramekins with a little butter, then coat with bread crumbs, tapping out any excess. Arrange the ramekins in an oblong baking dish. Position a rack in the lower third of an oven. Preheat to 325°F.

2 To make the filling, melt 1 tablespoon of the butter in a sauté pan over medium-high heat. Add the shallots, chicken, and mushrooms and sauté until the chicken is no longer pink, about 5 minutes. Stir in the parsley and thyme or sage and set aside.

3 Melt the remaining 2 tablespoons butter in a saucepan over high heat. Add the flour and whisk the resulting paste for 1 minute; do not allow to brown. Slowly add the milk, whisking constantly. Reduce the heat to low and simmer, stirring often, until thickened, about 3 minutes.

4 In a bowl, whisk together the whole eggs and egg yolks until blended. Whisk in a little of the hot sauce, then pour the eggs into the remaining sauce. Heat through without boiling. Finally, add the sherry, salt, and white pepper.

5 Add the sauce to the cooked chicken and stir to combine. Spoon into the prepared ramekins, dividing evenly.

FOR THE MUSHROOM SAUCE:

1 tablespoon butter

1 tablespoon olive oil

2 tablespoons chopped shallot

About 10 fresh white mushrooms, quartered

¼ teaspoon dried thyme

Salt and black pepper to taste

6 Pour boiling water into the baking dish to reach within ¼ inch of the rims of the ramekins. Bake until a knife inserted halfway between the edge and the center of a ramekin comes out clean, about 45 minutes.

7 Meanwhile, make the mushroom sauce: Heat the butter and oil in a skillet over medium heat. Add all the remaining ingredients and sauté until the mushrooms darken and wilt but still have a little crunch, about 6 minutes. Remove from the heat and keep warm.

8 Remove the timbales from the oven and let cool for 5 to 10 minutes. Gently reheat the mushroom sauce until hot. Run a knife around the edge of each timbale and invert onto individual plates. Top with the mushroom sauce and serve at once.

Serves 6

The key to winning the soufflé challenge is to prepare the soufflé dish ahead and to have the oven completely preheated. This soufflé puffs tall and is sure to inflate your sense of accomplishment. Chardonnay, anyone?

CHICKEN SOUFFLÉ
with SPINACH and EMMENTALER CHEESE

3 tablespoons butter

About 1/4 cup grated Parmesan cheese

1 pound spinach, rinsed and stemmed

2 tablespoons flour

1 cup milk, heated

4 eggs, separated

1/2 teaspoon salt

Black pepper to taste

1/3 pound Emmentaler, Jarlsberg, Swiss, or Gruyère cheese, shredded (about 1 1/2 cups)

1 cup neatly diced cooked chicken meat

1/8 teaspoon cream of tartar

1 Smear a 2-quart soufflé dish with 1 tablespoon of the butter. Sprinkle the bottom and sides with some of the Parmesan cheese to coat evenly. Cut a strip of waxed paper about 2 inches longer than the circumference of the soufflé dish and 5 inches wide. Fold the strip in half lengthwise, then smear one side with butter and coat with Parmesan cheese. Wrap the strip of paper, butter side in, around the rim of the dish so that it adds about 2 inches of height, and tie it securely in place with kitchen string.

2 Position a rack in the lower third of an oven. Preheat to 350°F.

3 Place the spinach, with the rinsing water still clinging to the leaves, in a large saucepan over high heat. Cook, stirring occasionally, until wilted, 3 to 5 minutes. Drain well and let cool, then squeeze between your palms to remove excess water. Chop roughly and set aside.

4 Select a saucepan large enough to hold the entire soufflé, add the remaining 2 tablespoons butter, and melt over high heat. Add the flour and whisk the resulting paste for 1 minute; do not allow it to brown. Slowly add the milk, whisking continuously. Reduce the heat to low and simmer, stirring often, until thickened, about 3 minutes.

**Why did the chicken
cross the road?**

Colonel Sanders:
I missed one?

5 In a bowl, whisk the egg yolks until blended. Whisk in a little of the hot sauce, then pour the yolks into the sauce. Season with the salt and pepper. Heat through without boiling, then remove from the heat and let cool slightly.

6 Stir in the shredded cheese until well blended, then stir in the chicken and spinach.

7 In a bowl, beat the egg whites and cream of tartar until medium-stiff peaks form. Pour into the soufflé base and gently fold the two elements together just until no white streaks remain.

8 Transfer the mixture to the prepared dish. Run the tip of a table knife through the soufflé batter about 1 inch from the sides of the dish. This will help the soufflé to rise higher in the middle.

9 Bake for 15 minutes. Raise the heat to 450°F and bake until the soufflé is nicely browned on top but still jiggly in the center, about 10 minutes. Serve at once.

Serves 4

scratch

The stove top and the oven are now in full swing. Did someone say comfort food? Making chicken pot pie will keep you in the kitchen, where it's warm, for a couple of hours, and then romance the family when it's done.

The stockpot is busy with potted chicken and stew, chili, and soups, all welcome both for the way they warm the body as much as for the extra heat and aroma their cooking spreads around the house. Chicken with red cabbage, beer, and what's left of the apple crop softens a cruel winter night.

Winter produce is defined by what has lived through the season and what got preserved when it was fresh. Now is the time for dried fruits, dried porcini and other mushrooms, dried tomatoes, and dried beans. Even olives, a late fall crop, must be cured and aren't ready until winter. Curry, honey, mustard, ginger, and red chile give chicken warmth without heat. Various fruits can be paired with chicken in winter— Anjou pears, Asian pears, and kiwifruits, plus there's plenty of citrus, particularly tangerines, to give winter a tropical aberration.

By winter's end, the strangest thing happens. Chervil pops up, a sign that the season is almost over.

WINTER

CIPES

My Israeli relatives use the term *comport* for stewed dried fruits—in other words, what most other folks know as compote. I thought this was because they make compote with port, which they do not. To honor the mispronunciation, I do. After you stuff all the chicken breasts, you'll have comport left over. This is deliberate. Eat the rest plain for dessert for days to come, or over pancakes or French toast.

CHICKEN BREASTS
STUFFED with DRIED FRUIT COMPORT

FOR THE COMPORT:

2 cups extra-fancy (top-grade) mixed dried fruits, including pears, pitted prunes, peaches, and apricots

¾ cup sugar

1 cup port

½ cup brandy

1 vanilla bean

2 cinnamon sticks

1 cardamom pod or ⅛ teaspoon ground cardamom

6 boneless chicken breasts, skin on

½ cup flour mixed with ½ teaspoon salt and ¼ teaspoon white pepper

2 tablespoons butter

¾ cup port

1 To make the comport, place all the ingredients in a heavy saucepan over medium heat. Cook gently, uncovered, stirring often, until the fruit is plumped but soft and most of the liquid has cooked away, about 45 minutes. The texture is correctable all the way through cooking. If the mixture goes dry before the fruits are plumped (the dryness of the fruits affects the absorption potential), add a little warm water to loosen the mix. If it is too loose, cook it down longer. If it is too thick, add water.

2 Remove from the heat, let cool, transfer to a covered container, and refrigerate for at least 1 day or up to a month before using. Leave the whole spices in the mixture until ready to use it.

3 When ready to use the comport, measure out 1½ to 1¾ cups. (See the recipe introduction for ways to use the remaining comport.)

4 Heat a serving platter in a 150°F oven.

5 Rinse the chicken breasts and pat dry with paper towels.

6 Place each breast skin side down on a cutting board. Carefully cut a horizontal slit into the thicker side of each breast, cutting about three-fourths of the way across. Stuff each pocket with about ⅓ cup of the comport. Pat each breast closed with your fingers.

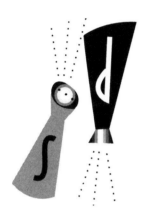

7 Dredge each breast in the seasoned flour, shaking off the excess.

8 Melt the butter in a large, heavy sauté pan over high heat. Add the breasts, skin side down, and sauté for 2 minutes. Reduce the heat to medium-high and sauté for 7 minutes. Turn and sauté on the second side until cooked through, about 8 minutes longer. Transfer to the warmed serving platter and keep warm.

9 Return the pan to high heat and pour in the port. Bring to a boil, scraping up browned bits from the pan bottom, and boil down until about only ¼ cup remains. Pour the sauce through a fine-mesh sieve into a small pitcher.

10 Either pour the sauce over the chicken breasts and serve immediately, or slice the chicken breasts on the diagonal to reveal the stuffing, fan out the slices, and top with the sauce. Serve immediately.

Serves 6

Ginger and pears are so well matched that it would be a shame to make this without so much as a hint of this magical spice. Don't let all the adding and taking from the sauté pan discourage you. This is simple, nutritious, and cheap. I prefer to sauté chicken breasts with the skin on, for nice browning. If you don't want the skin later, remove it when you're served.

CHICKEN BREASTS
with GINGERED ASIAN PEARS and CAULIFLOWER

6 boneless chicken breasts, skin on

½ teaspoon salt

Black pepper to taste

2 tablespoons butter

1 small onion, chopped

2 Hosiki or other Asian pears, peeled, cored, and sliced

⅛ teaspoon ground ginger

1 smallish head cauliflower, cut into florets

1 cup chicken stock

1 to 2 tablespoons Canton ginger liqueur (see Note)

1 Rinse the chicken breasts and pat dry with paper towels. Sprinkle with salt and pepper.

2 Melt the butter in a wide, heavy sauté pan over medium-high heat. Add the onion and sauté just until pale, about 5 minutes.

3 Add the pears and ginger, reduce the heat to medium, and shake and stir gently just until the pears are tender, 2 to 3 minutes. Scoop up the pears with a skimmer or slotted spoon and place in a bowl.

4 Return the pan to medium-high heat and add the chicken breasts, skin side down, to the fat remaining in the pan. Sauté, turning once, until well browned, 6 to 7 minutes on each side. Remove the chicken to a plate.

5 Add the cauliflower florets, arranging stems up. Raise the heat to high, add the stock, and bring to a boil. Cover, reduce the heat to low, and simmer the cauliflower until somewhat softened, about 5 minutes.

"He was like a cock who
thought the sun had risen to
hear him crow."

—*George Elliott*

6 **Remove** the cauliflower with a slotted spoon and add to the bowl with the pears. Raise the heat and boil the juices until they darken and reduce to about ¼ cup.

7 **Return** the chicken to the pan, top with the pears and cauliflower, and sprinkle with the ginger liqueur. Cover and simmer for 3 to 4 minutes longer.

8 **Place** the breasts on a platter with the sauce spooned over them.

Serves 6

Notes: Canton ginger liqueur tastes exactly what it sounds like, ginger booze. If you don't have any (and it's a good bet that you don't), prior to chopping the onion mix 2 tablespoons brandy with ¼ teaspoon ground ginger. Or simply dust the chicken breasts with ginger when they're salted and peppered.

If you find that after all the chicken breasts are consumed you have a bowlful of pears and cauliflower remaining, puree the mixture, thinning with a little chicken stock, cream, or milk, to make an exotic soup the next day.

Oranges and kiwifruits are the quintessential
winter combination. Put them together, and it feels
a little like summer.

226

CHICKEN BREASTS

with GARLIC, ORANGE, and KIWIFRUITS

3 kiwifruits, peeled and cut into
¾-inch pieces

1 tablespoon sugar

6 boneless chicken breasts,
skin on

1 tablespoon minced garlic

¼ teaspoon salt

Black pepper to taste

2 tablespoons butter

Juice of 1 large orange (½ cup)

1 Heat a serving platter in a 150°F oven.

2 In a bowl, combine the kiwifruits and sugar, toss gently, and set aside.

3 Rinse the chicken breasts and pat dry with paper towels. Smear the garlic over the side with skin. Sprinkle the same side with salt and pepper.

4 Heat the butter in a wide, heavy sauté pan over medium-high heat. Add the chicken breasts, garlic side down, and sauté, turning once, shaking the pan occasionally, and taking care not to burn the garlic, until nicely browned, about 4 minutes on each side.

5 Raise the heat to high and pour the orange juice over the chicken breasts. Bring to a boil, cover, reduce the heat to low, and simmer until the chicken breasts are cooked through, 4 to 5 minutes. Remove the chicken breasts to the warmed serving platter and keep warm.

6 Raise the heat to high, bring to a boil, and boil the sauce for about 30 seconds. Add the kiwifruits and cook until just heated through, 45 to 60 seconds longer.

7 Pour over the chicken breasts and serve immediately.

Serves 6

A number of features make this a winter recipe. One, if the weather is bad, you can probably pull the marinade together without going to the store. And two, in the frenzy of winter work and hectic schedules, you can marinate the chicken the night before and then come home the next evening, pour the marinade and chicken into a baking dish, and bake for 40 minutes.

As usual, I bake with the skin on. The marinade can squeeze itself between the skin and flesh easier than it can adhere to raw chicken flesh.

BAKED CHICKEN BREASTS
in HONEY-MUSTARD MARINADE
with MADRAS CURRY

½ cup honey

⅓ cup Dijon mustard

2 tablespoons soy sauce

1½ to 2 tablespoons Madras curry powder

6 boneless chicken breasts, skin on

1 The day before, in a bowl, stir together the honey, mustard, soy sauce, and curry powder. Pour into a zip-style plastic bag.

2 Rinse the chicken breasts and pat dry with paper towels.

3 Add the breasts to the bag, swish around, seal the top, and refrigerate overnight. (If you get a late start, you can marinate the chicken for just a couple of hours and it will still taste good.)

4 Preheat an oven to 350°F. Arrange the chicken breasts, skin side up, in an oblong baking dish pretty enough to bring to the table. They should fit snugly.

5 Bake until cooked through, about 40 minutes.

6 Serve from the baking dish, spooning sauce over each serving.

Serves 4

This recipe combines country French cooking with an American fondness for rhubarb (a distant relative of—are you ready for this?—buckwheat).

228

CORNISH GAME HENS
with PRUNES in RHUBARB·PORT SAUCE

8 pitted prunes

1 cup tawny port

1½ pounds rhubarb stalks, leaves removed and stalks chopped

1 large onion, sliced

1 tablespoon sugar

3 tablespoons butter

4 Cornish game hens

½ cup flour seasoned with 1 teaspoon salt, generous black pepper, and ½ teaspoon dried thyme

1½ cups dry red wine

2 garlic cloves, smashed

½ cup chicken stock

1 In a small bowl, combine the prunes and port and let soak.

2 In a saucepan, combine the rhubarb, onion, sugar, and 1 tablespoon of the butter. Bring to a simmer and cook, uncovered, for 30 minutes. Strain through a sieve placed over a bowl. The mixture will be light pink and slightly thick. Return to the same pan and set aside.

3 Lightly dredge the hens in the seasoned flour, shaking off the excess. Heat the remaining 2 tablespoons butter in a wide, deep sauté pan over high heat. Add the hens, breast side down, and sauté, reducing the heat to medium as needed, until well browned on all sides, about 8 minutes. Remove the hens to a plate.

4 Raise the heat to high, add the red wine plus the port from the prunes, and the garlic. Bring to a boil and boil until only ¼ cup remains.

5 Return the hens to the pan, breast side up. Add the stock, cover tightly, reduce the heat to low, and simmer until the juices run clear between the thigh and body, about 40 minutes. Remove the hens to a serving platter. Strain the pan juices into the rhubarb sauce, stir, and reheat gently.

6 Arrange the prunes around the hens. Cut the hens with poultry shears and serve with the rhubarb sauce.

Serves 4 to 6

You've seen Asians enjoying bowls of noodles in restaurants where you know only to order chow mein. They are eating this dish, in which stock and noodles have come together in a single bowl but were not cooked in the same pot. Noodles turn cooking liquid starchy, so the soup comes from the pot that makes soup and the noodles are boiled separately. This gives you a bowl of clear soup with the noodles of your choice.

ASIAN CHICKEN NOODLE SOUP

½ pound vermicelli, egg noodles, rice noodles, or soba noodles

1 tablespoon cornstarch mixed with 2 tablespoons cold water

1 egg

4 cups chicken stock

1 garlic clove or small piece of fresh ginger

2 teaspoons oyster sauce

A little shredded green onion

A little chopped fresh cilantro

Hot chile sauce

1 Bring a large pot of salted water to a boil. Add the noodles and boil, uncovered, until done (no crunchiness). The timing will depend on the type of noodles.

2 Have the cornstarch and water mixture ready in a little cup. Crack the egg into another cup, but don't beat it, yet.

3 Bring the stock to a boil with the garlic or ginger and the oyster sauce. Boil for 1 minute. Quickly stir the cornstarch mixture, then add it to the boiling stock, stirring it in to mix well. Boil for 1 minute longer.

4 Remove from the heat. With a fork, stab the yolk of the egg, then stir once or twice. Slowly pour the egg into the hot liquid, pushing it through the soup with a big spoon.

5 When the noodles are done, drain and divide them evenly among 2 or 3 soup bowls. Ladle the soup over the noodles.

6 Garnish each serving with green onion and cilantro. Serve immediately, making sure that the table is equipped with a bottle of chile sauce.

Serves 2 or 3

Sugars in the honey and pears continuously
caramelize the components in the recipe, from
the skin of the chicken to the sauce. Avoid cast
iron; it will discolor the pears.

230

CHICKEN SAUTÉED

with HONEYED PEARS
in CARAMELIZED SAUCE

1 chicken, 3½ to 4 pounds,
cut into serving pieces

½ teaspoon salt,
plus salt to taste

Black pepper to taste

4 Bosc pears, peeled (see Note)

3 tablespoons butter

2 tablespoons honey

1 cup Riesling or
Gewürztraminer

1 cup chicken stock

½ cup heavy cream

1 Heat a serving platter in a 150°F oven.

2 Hack the breasts in half crosswise. Rinse the chicken pieces and pat dry with paper towels. Sprinkle with ½ teaspoon salt and pepper to taste.

3 Halve each pear and, with a melon baller, scoop out the cores. Cut the halves lengthwise into ½-inch slices.

4 Melt the butter in a wide, heavy sauté pan over medium heat. Add the pears and sauté until well browned on all sides, about 10 minutes. Remove to a bowl. Add the honey and toss together.

5 Add the chicken to the pan, skin side down, and sauté, turning once and sprinkling with salt and pepper to taste, until well browned, about 5 minutes on each side.

6 Raise the heat to high, pour the wine over the chicken, and then add the stock. When the liquid comes to a boil, cover, reduce the heat to low, and simmer until the chicken is cooked through, about 15 minutes.

7 Add the pears to the chicken, scattering in and around the pieces. Cover and simmer until the liquid around the pears is very caramelly, about 2 minutes longer. Transfer the chicken and pears to the serving platter and keep warm.

8 Raise the heat to high, bring the pan juices to a boil, and boil until reduced to 1 cup. Add the cream and boil, stirring, for about 30 seconds. Spoon over the chicken and pears and serve right away.

Serves 4

Note: To keep peeled pears from turning brown before you have a chance to cook them, have ready a big bowl of water with a couple of tablespoons of lemon juice added. As you peel the pears, drop them into the water.

This quick and highly flavored combination starts on the stove and finishes by being baked in the oven.

232

CHICKEN BAKED
with ORANGE, GINGER, and RED CHILE

1 chicken, 4 pounds, cut into serving pieces

½ teaspoon salt, plus salt to taste

¼ teaspoon white pepper, plus pepper to taste

2 tablespoons butter

2 tablespoons flour

2 tablespoons honey

2 tablespoons peeled and finely minced fresh ginger

1 ancho chile

Juice of 4 oranges (about 1½ cups)

2 oranges, sectioned

1 Place a rack in the lower third of an oven. Preheat to 350°F.

2 Rinse the chicken and pat dry with paper towels. Sprinkle with the ½ teaspoon salt and the ¼ teaspoon white pepper.

3 Melt the butter in a wide, heavy ovenproof sauté pan with a lid over high heat. Add the chicken, skin side down, and sauté, turning once and reducing the heat to medium-high as necessary until well browned, 4 to 5 minutes on each side. Remove the chicken to a plate.

4 Drain off all but 1 tablespoon of the fat from the pan and return the pan to medium-high heat. Add the flour, honey, ginger, ancho chile, and a touch more salt and white pepper. Fry until somewhat dry, about 1 minute, then add the orange juice, raise the heat to high, and bring quickly to a boil. Boil for a full minute.

5 Return the chicken to the pan, skin side up, cover, and bake for 20 minutes. Scatter the orange sections around the chicken, re-cover, and bake until the chicken is cooked through, about 10 minutes longer.

6 Remove the chicken to individual plates or a platter and spoon the sauce over the top. Serve immediately.

Serves 4

Honey tangerines are big, juicy fruits with a taste that leaves no doubt as to how they got their name. They're especially popular during Lunar New Year in the Chinese community on the West Coast. A tablespoon or two of oyster sauce lifts most any dish to noteworthiness. Select a good-quality brand—not the cheapest one.

GINGER CHICKEN BAKED
with HONEY TANGERINES and OYSTER SAUCE

1 chicken, 4 pounds, cut into serving pieces

Zest of 2 honey tangerines or other variety

Juice of 3 honey tangerines (about 1½ cups)

2 tablespoons oyster sauce

¼ cup honey (see Note)

2 green onions, sliced

2-inch piece fresh ginger (about 2 ounces), peeled and minced

2 small fresh red chiles

1 Rinse the chicken pieces and pat dry with paper towels.

2 In a large bowl or zip-style plastic bag, combine the chicken with all the remaining ingredients, turning to coat. Cover or seal securely and marinate in the refrigerator a couple of hours or as long as overnight.

3 Position a rack in the lower third of an oven. Preheat to 350°F. Arrange the chicken pieces, skin side up, in their marinade in an oblong baking dish pretty enough to bring to the table.

4 Cover and bake for 35 minutes. Uncover and continue baking until the chicken is cooked through, about 10 minutes longer.

5 Serve directly from the baking dish, spooning some of the sauce over each serving.

Serves 4

Note: Look for eucalyptus honey, orange blossom honey, buckwheat honey, sage honey, alfalfa honey, or star thistle honey.

From my friend Dotty Griffith of the *Dallas Morning News* comes this ultimate Texan winter dish. Except for mashed potatoes, there's not a vegetable in sight. (Texans will actually eat this during any season.)

234

CHICKEN-FRIED CHICKEN
with CREAM GRAVY and MASHED POTATOES

4 boneless chicken breasts, skinned

1 cup buttermilk

2 or 3 drops Tabasco sauce or other hot-pepper sauce

1 cup flour

1 teaspoon salt, or to taste

1 teaspoon black pepper, or to taste

Vegetable oil for frying

FOR THE MASHED POTATOES:

4 russet potatoes, peeled and cut into chunks

2 tablespoons butter

½ cup milk, heated

½ teaspoon salt

Generous black pepper to taste

1 Rinse the chicken breasts and pat dry with paper towels. One at a time, sandwich the chicken breasts between two sheets of waxed paper and pound (a rolling pin works great) to an even thickness.

2 In a shallow bowl, combine buttermilk and pepper sauce. Add the chicken breasts, turn to coat, and let stand for at least 20 minutes or up to 1 hour.

3 Combine the flour, salt, and pepper in a zip-style plastic bag. Shake the bag to mix well. One at a time, lift the chicken breasts from the buttermilk, draining well, add to the bag, seal closed, and shake to coat the chicken evenly. Repeat until each breast is coated. As the breasts are coated, place in a single layer on a sheet of waxed paper and allow the batter to set for about 20 minutes.

4 Warm a serving platter in a 150°F oven.

5 Pour oil to a depth of 1 inch in a heavy sauté pan over medium heat. Heat to 350°F to 375°F. Working in batches, gently slide the chicken breasts into the hot oil. Do not crowd and do not allow their sides to touch, or they'll stick. Fry until golden and crisp on one side, about 5 minutes. Turn and cook until golden and crisp on the second side, 3 to 5 minutes longer. Using tongs, transfer to paper towels to drain. Transfer to the warmed serving platter and keep warm.

FOR THE CREAM GRAVY:

¼ cup flour

1 cup milk

Salt to taste

¼ teaspoon black pepper

CHICKEN **19** NUGGET

The first poultry magazine,
The Poultry Bulletin,
was published in 1870.

6 While preparing and cooking the chicken, cook the mashed potatoes: Bring a saucepan filled with salted water to a boil. Drop the potato pieces into the boiling water, cover, reduce the heat to medium, and cook until a knife easily glides into a potato chunk, 12 to 15 minutes. Drain, return to the pan, and place over medium heat, shaking the pan once or twice, for 1 or 2 minutes to dry out the potatoes somewhat. Remove from the heat. In the same pan, mash the potatoes with a potato masher or whip with a handheld mixer, adding the butter, milk, salt, and pepper. The potatoes should be smooth with no lumps at all. (Why are lumpy mashed potatoes considered an achievement? To me they seem like a sign of a lazy cook.) Cover and keep warm.

7 When all the chicken is cooked, make the cream gravy: Pour off all but 3 tablespoons of oil from the pan. Place over medium-high heat, add the flour, and whisk until completely smooth and golden, about 1 minute. Be sure to loosen and scrape any crusty bits that may be stuck to the pan bottom. Slowly whisk in the milk and season with the salt and pepper. Reduce the heat to low and simmer, stirring, until slightly thickened, about 5 minutes.

8 Arrange the chicken breasts on individual plates. Spoon the potatoes on the side and smother all with gravy.

Serves 4

With the hint of parsley-licorice from the chervil, the sauce's elements combine into a flavor that's soft and pleasing, which is a great way to enjoy a roast chicken. Serve with mashed potatoes.

CHICKEN ROASTED with WHOLE SHALLOTS and FRESH CHERVIL in CHARDONNAY SAUCE

1 chicken, 4 pounds

2 tablespoons butter

½ teaspoon salt, plus salt to taste

Black pepper to taste

1 onion, diced

2 celery stalks, diced

1 carrot, peeled and diced

1 pound shallots, peeled and root ends trimmed but left whole

1¼ cups Chardonnay

2 tablespoons fresh lemon juice

¼ cup minced fresh chervil, plus sprigs for garnish

2 tablespoons flour

1 Position a rack in the lower third of an oven. Preheat to 450°F.

2 Rinse the chicken and pat dry with paper towels. Smear 1 tablespoon of the butter and the ½ teaspoon salt inside the chicken. Rub the outside of the chicken with the remaining 1 tablespoon butter and salt and pepper to taste.

3 Strew the onion, celery, and carrot in the bottom of a flameproof roasting pan. Top with the chicken breast, skin side up. Scatter the shallots around the chicken.

4 Roast the chicken and shallots for 20 minutes.

5 Meanwhile, combine 1 cup of the Chardonnay, the lemon juice, half of the minced chervil, and a touch more salt and pepper. After 20 minutes, pour the wine mixture over the chicken, reduce the temperature to 350°F, and continue roasting, basting occasionally with the pan juices, until the juices between the thigh and the body cavity run clear, about 1¼ hours longer.

6 Remove the chicken to a cutting board that has a trough to catch the juices. Lift out the shallots with tongs and reserve.

7 Pour the juices of the roasting pan through a sieve placed over a 2-cup measuring cup, leaving the glazed brown bits on the pan's bottom. Discard the vegetables. Set the measuring cup in the freezer briefly to force the fat to rise. Skim off and discard the fat. If there are less than 2 cups juices, add water as needed to achieve measure.

8 Place the roasting pan on the stove top over medium-high heat. Sprinkle with the flour and whisk well, dislodging the browned bits and cooking the resulting paste for I minute. Slowly add the remaining ¼ cup wine, then the pan juices. Bring to a boil and boil until the sauce is as thick as you like. Remove from the heat and add the remaining minced chervil. Pour into a warmed sauce boat.

9 Garnish the chicken with the reserved shallots and the chervil sprigs and carve at the table. Pass the sauce at the table.

Serves 4

This is an old-fashioned recipe that takes me back to my days in Louisville. Friends there hunted doves, gave them to me to cook, and loved them prepared in a classic hearty way but with a certain finesse. Doves deserve fine brandy, port, and sherry and buttery-soft liver pâté as backdrops. Using thighs gets you pretty close to doves, as I discovered when substituting them in this earthy, showy dish.

THIGHS COOKED LIKE DOVES
with WILD RICE and LIVER PÂTÉ

FOR THE LIVER PÂTÉ:

3 tablespoons rendered bacon fat

3/4 pound chicken livers

Salt and black pepper to taste

1 teaspoon dried thyme

3 tablespoons dry sherry or Armagnac, or as needed

2 tablespoons dry sherry or Armagnac or rendered bacon fat, if needed to thin mixture

8 to 10 toast points, crusts removed

FOR THE WILD RICE:

1 cup wild rice

3 cups water

2 teaspoons salt

2 tablespoons butter

1 To make the liver pâté, heat the bacon fat in a sauté pan over medium heat. Add the livers and sauté, turning as necessary, just until no longer pink at the center, about 15 minutes. Remove from the heat and let cool.

2 Puree the livers and their pan juices in a food processor or blender (or mash finely with a fork), adding the salt, pepper, thyme, and 3 tablespoons sherry or Armagnac. Use additional sherry or Armagnac or bacon fat to thin the pâté to a spreading consistency, if necessary.

3 Scrape into a small bowl, cover tightly with plastic wrap, and refrigerate until needed. The pâté will firm up as it chills. When ready to serve, spread the pâté generously onto the toast points.

4 To cook the wild rice, rinse the rice and drain well. Place all the ingredients in a heavy saucepan. Cover and bring to a boil over high heat. Reduce the heat to low and simmer until the kernels break open and become tender, not mushy, 50 to 60 minutes. Uncover and give a stir. If all the water hasn't been absorbed, taste the rice to make sure it's tender before draining off excess liquid.

5 While the rice is cooking, prepare the chicken: Fry the bacon in a wide, heavy sauté pan, over medium-high heat until crisp, 5 to 8 minutes. Remove to paper towels to drain, the, basting often with the red pan juices, for 30 minutes longer.

FOR THE CHICKEN:

8 slices bacon

8 to 10 boneless
chicken thighs, skin on

½ cup flour mixed
with 1 teaspoon salt
and black pepper to taste

3 green onions,
mostly white part only, minced

¾ cup dry sherry

1 cup beef stock

1 tablespoon butter

3 cups sliced fresh
white mushrooms

¾ cup port

1 bunch watercress,
tough stems removed

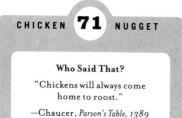

6 Rinse the chicken thighs and pat dry with paper towels. Dredge in the seasoned flour, shaking off the excess.

7 Return the pan to medium-high heat. Add the thighs, skin side down, and sauté, turning once, until well browned, about 4 minutes on each side. Remove to paper towels to drain; set aside.

8 Again pour off all but 1 tablespoon of the fat from the pan and return the pan to high heat. Add the green onions and sauté for 1 minute, stirring constantly. Add the sherry, bring to a boil, and boil until the liquid becomes syrupy and is reduced to about ¼ cup, 5 to 6 minutes.

9 Return the thighs to the pan, skin side up, nestling them in the onions. Add the stock, cover, reduce the heat to low, and simmer gently until cooked through, 20 to 25 minutes.

10 Meanwhile, melt the butter in another sauté pan over high heat. Add the mushrooms and sauté until they shrink and are tender, 6 to 8 minutes. Add the port and cook, uncovered, until the liquid becomes syrupy and is reduced to about ¼ cup, 5 to 6 minutes.

11 Remove the thighs to a plate and keep hot. Transfer the mushrooms and their liquid to the pan juices that remain. Stir well, then bring to a boil over high heat and boil until thickened, about 3 minutes.

12 To serve, mound the wild rice in the center of a large serving platter. Encircle the rice with the toast points spread with the pâté. Place a thigh on each toast. Pour the mushroom sauce over or around the thighs. Garnish with the crumbled bacon and watercress. Serve immediately.

Serves 6 to 8

What an incredible dish to make for company. It's so rich that only a little is eaten at a time. The tradition is to pass the "sandy pot" it is cooked in so guests can pick up their portions with chopsticks. By the time the chicken makes it around the table it looks ravaged, but the eating is good. Use good-quality soy sauce for the best results. Serve with sautéed bok choy or spinach and lots of rice to sop up the aromatic sauce.

DRUNKEN CHICKEN

1 chicken, 3½ pounds (not much bigger)

¼ cup soy sauce

¼ cup rice wine or dry sherry

1 teaspoon five-spice powder

4 cups vegetable oil or solid vegetable shortening

6 or 7 green onions, sliced, plus shredded green onions for garnish

3 to 3½ cups chicken stock

3 tablespoons black soy sauce (see Note)

3-inch piece fresh ginger (about 3 ounces), peeled, cut into chunks, and smashed

4 or 5 garlic cloves, smashed

4 fresh cilantro sprigs, plus extra for garnish

¾ cup dry sherry, port, or rice wine

½ cup good gin

3 big chunks yellow rock sugar, or ½ cup packed dark brown sugar

1 Rinse the chicken and pat dry with paper towels. Place in a large bowl and add the soy sauce, rice wine or sherry, and five-spice powder. Turn the chicken several times to coat with the mixture. Cover and marinate in the refrigerator for 3 to 4 hours or as long as overnight.

2 Preheat an oven to 350°F. Put the vegetable oil or shortening in a wok and heat to moderately hot, between 350°F and 375°F. Using a large Chinese mesh sieve, lift the chicken from the marinade and carefully lower into the hot oil. Ladle the oil over the chicken, then, using the sieve and a large wok spoon, turn the chicken in the oil several times until it is evenly and darkly browned. This will take about 5 minutes.

3 Lift the chicken out of the oil. Stuff with the sliced green onions, then transfer to a Chinese sandy pot or other deep lidded casserole. Add the stock, black soy, ginger, garlic, and 4 cilantro sprigs. Cover tightly and bake for 1 hour.

4 Add the sherry or port, gin, and rock sugar. If using brown sugar, pat it thickly on the exposed parts of the chicken, then drop the rest into the cooking liquid. Cover tightly and bake until the chicken meat nearly falls off the bone, about 20 minutes longer.

5 Bring the chicken to the table in the cooking pot. Garnish with shredded green onion and a few cilantro sprigs.

Serves 6

Note: Black soy sauce has molasses and is more strongly flavored and more viscous than regular soy sauce. It is used when deep coloring is desired.

Here's a dish that browns on top of the stove, then bakes silently, out of sight, to give you a half hour to get the rest of dinner ready. Fennel goes nicely with the cinnamon and cloves in this richly red sauce.

CHICKEN WITH ITALIAN TOMATOES and TWO VERMOUTHS

1 chicken, 4 pounds, cut into
serving pieces
¹/₂ cup flour mixed with
1 teaspoon salt and
black pepper to taste
2 tablespoons olive oil
³/₄ cup sweet red vermouth
2 teaspoons minced garlic
1 fennel bulb, sliced
1 can (1 pound) crushed
Italian tomatoes
¹/₂ teaspoon ground cinnamon
5 whole cloves
Salt to taste
¹/₂ cup dry vermouth

CHICKEN **61** NUGGET

**Why did the chicken
cross the road?**

Bill Gates: For the release
of ChickenOffice 3.0.

1 Preheat an oven to 350°F.

2 Hack the breasts in half crosswise. Rinse the chicken pieces and pat dry with paper towels. Dredge each piece in the seasoned flour, shaking off the excess.

3 Heat the oil in an ovenproof Dutch oven or wide, heavy sauté pan with a lid over high heat. Add the chicken, skin side down, and sauté, turning once, until well browned, 4 to 5 minutes on each side. Remove the chicken to a plate.

4 Pour off all but 1 tablespoon of the fat from the pan. Return the pan to high heat and pour in the sweet vermouth. Bring to a boil, scraping up the browned bits on the pan bottom, then boil until reduced to 2 tablespoons.

5 Return the chicken to the pan, skin side up. Scatter the garlic, fennel, and tomatoes over the chicken, sprinkle with the cinnamon, and then drop the cloves on top. Give it a sprinkling of salt. Finally, pour the dry vermouth on top of the chicken.

6 Cover, transfer to the oven, and bake for 20 minutes. Uncover and spoon some of the pan sauce over the chicken. Re-cover and continue baking until the chicken is cooked through, about 10 minutes longer.

7 Serve the chicken with sauce spooned over each portion.

Serves 4

Regardless of whether the chicken gets seared, which vegetables show up or when they're added, or whether the dish is simmered or baked, the classic chicken-in-a-pot should always end up in your bowl as soft shreds of boiled chicken in a rich, golden broth. You get golden broth from a lot of carrots, two to one over celery. Serve with toasted rye bread.

CHICKEN·IN·A·POT

1 chicken, 3½ to 4 pounds

3 tablespoons vegetable oil

12 small (pearl) onions, yellow or white skinned, peeled but left whole

2 large carrots, peeled and cut into 1-inch chunks

1 celery stalk, cut into chunks

¼ teaspoon paprika

2 teaspoons salt

⅛ teaspoon white pepper

2 white-skinned potatoes, peeled and cut into chunks

1 Rinse the chicken and pat dry with paper towels.

2 In a large pot or skillet, heat the oil over high heat. When it's very hot, add the chicken and turn to sear on all sides until golden but not browned, about 10 minutes.

3 Remove the chicken to another large pot, such as a Dutch oven. Add water to cover. Bring slowly to a simmer over medium heat, uncovered. This may take up to 45 minutes. Skim off any scum as it appears.

4 When the water simmers, add the onions, carrots, celery, paprika, salt, and white pepper. Return to a simmer, cover partially, and simmer for 30 minutes.

5 Add the potatoes and continue cooking until the potatoes are soft, 20 to 30 minutes longer.

6 Remove the chicken to a bowl. Taste the broth for a good salt flavor. For a more condensed flavor, simmer, uncovered, for another 20 minutes. (If there is time, set briefly in the refrigerator to force the fat to rise, then skim off and discard the fat.)

7 When the chicken is cool, skin and debone it (although some people may prefer that you leave some of the skin in there) and put the meat back into the soup.

8 Ladle the soup into warmed bowls and serve at once.

Serves 6

This is the simple, warming chicken-in-a-pot that makes sick kids and grown-ups feel better, and makes anyone who isn't at all sick feel fine. The best benefit is that as the chicken cooks in the pot, it makes the house smell good.

CHICKEN-IN-A-POT,
COMFORT-FOOD STYLE

1 chicken, 3½ to 4 pounds

1 onion, peeled but left whole

2 large carrots, peeled and halved

1 celery stalk, halved

Handful of fresh parsley sprigs, tied in a bundle with kitchen string

2 teaspoons salt

⅛ teaspoon white pepper

1 Rinse the chicken. Set it in a large pot and add cold water to cover by 1 inch. Bring to a simmer over medium heat, uncovered. This may take 45 minutes. Skim any scum as it appears.

2 After all the scum disappears, add all the remaining ingredients. Cover partially and simmer until the chicken meat falls off the bone, about 1 hour. Taste for a good salt flavor.

3 Remove the chicken to a large bowl, let cool, skin, debone, and shred into rather large pieces. Remove the vegetables from the broth with a slotted spoon and reserve.

4 Return the bones and skin to the pot and simmer, uncovered, for 15 to 30 minutes longer to intensify the flavor.

5 Strain the skin and bones from the soup. Ladle the soup into bowls, capturing pieces of carrot or onion and adding pieces of the shredded chicken. Or, if there is time, refrigerate the strained soup until the fat rises, then skim it off, reheat, and serve.

Serves 8

The same humble ingredients that create an ordinary chicken-in-a-pot become a fashionable bowl of trendy components. The first departure is to roast the onions and garlic. The cooked vegetables that flavor the broth are pureed, while the strained broth simmers with mushrooms, which intensifies the soup's flavor. The puree holds its shape to one side of a serving bowl as the mushroom broth is ladled over and fresh spinach leaves float by. A tall pile of boiled chicken finishes the dish.

CHICKEN-IN-A-POT
with ROOT VEGETABLES and ROASTED ONIONS and GARLIC

2 onions, peeled but left whole

1 head garlic, root end trimmed

3 tablespoons vegetable oil

1 chicken, 4 pounds

4 large carrots, peeled and cut into chunks

1 turnip, peeled and cut into chunks

1 parsnip, peeled and cut into chunks

2 celery stalks, cut into chunks

12 black peppercorns

2 1/2 teaspoons salt

1/4 teaspoon white pepper

2 russet potatoes, peeled and cut into chunks

1/2 pound fresh white mushrooms, sliced

1/2 bunch spinach, rinsed and stemmed

1 Preheat an oven to 350°F. Rub the onions and garlic with 1 tablespoon of the oil. Set in a pie plate, cover with foil, and roast until the garlic is soft to the touch, about 1 hour. Remove the garlic and continue roasting the onions until soft, about 15 minutes longer. When the garlic is cool enough to handle, squeeze the pulp from the skin and reserve.

2 Rinse the chicken and pat dry with paper towels.

3 Heat the remaining 2 tablespoons oil in a large pot or skillet over high heat. Add the chicken and turn to sear on all sides until golden but not browned, about 10 minutes.

4 Remove the chicken to another large pot, such as a Dutch oven. Add water to cover by 1 inch. Bring slowly to a simmer over medium heat, uncovered. This may take up to 45 minutes. Skim any scum as it appears.

5 When the liquid is simmering, add the roasted onions, garlic pulp, carrots, turnip, parsnip, celery, peppercorns, 2 teaspoons of the salt, and white pepper. Return to a simmer, cover partially, and simmer for 30 minutes.

6 Add the potatoes and continue simmering until the potatoes are soft, about 30 minutes longer.

7 Remove the chicken to a large bowl, let cool, skin, debone, and shred into rather large pieces. Pour the broth through a sieve into a clean saucepan, reserving the vegetables. Skim off any fat from the surface of the broth.

8 Puree the vegetables in a blender, adding the remaining ½ teaspoon salt. Keep warm.

9 Add the mushrooms to the broth and bring to a simmer, uncovered, while you prepare the final steps.

10 Put the spinach into a saucepan with the rinsing water still clinging to the leaves. Place over high heat and cook, stirring occasionally, until just wilted, about 3 minutes. Drain well.

11 To serve, place about ½ cup of the vegetable puree to the side of each serving bowl. Drop a pile of spinach next to the puree. Ladle the hot mushroom broth over all, then pile the shredded chicken in the center. Serve hot.

Serves 4

Here, I use rendered chicken fat (see Schmaltz, page 51) for its high-heat properties. It browns the chicken darker and faster than butter or other mortal oil does, both of which could burn. The fat is drained away just as it is in any other sauté, and you're left with the same tablespoon of fat that everyone seems to think is okay.

HINDQUARTERS
with PRUNES and LEMON

6 chicken hindquarters

1 teaspoon salt

Black pepper to taste

3 tablespoons rendered chicken fat or vegetable oil

2 onions, chopped

1/4 teaspoon ground cardamom or ginger

2 cups chicken stock

1 cup pitted prunes

Zest of 1/2 lemon

Juice of 1 lemon

1 Preheat an oven to 350°F.

2 Rinse the chicken pieces and pat dry with paper towels. Sprinkle with the salt and pepper.

3 Melt the chicken fat in a very wide, heavy sauté pan over high heat. (Or use 2 smaller sauté pans set over 2 burners simultaneously.) When the fat shimmers, add the chicken, skin side down, and sauté, turning once, until well browned, 4 to 5 minutes on each side. Remove the chicken to a plate. Drain off all but 1 tablespoon fat.

4 Return the pan to medium heat and add the onions. Sprinkle with the cardamom or ginger and fry until translucent and pasty, about 5 minutes.

5 Raise the heat to high, and add the stock. Return the chicken to the skillet, and add the prunes and lemon zest and juice. Bring to a boil and check for a good salt flavor.

6 Cover, transfer to the oven, and bake until the chicken is cooked through, about 25 minutes. Remove the chicken pieces to a serving platter.

7 Return the pan to the stove top and bring the juices to a boil over high heat. Boil until the sauce is as thick as you like. Pour the sauce and prunes over the chicken and serve hot.

Serves 8 easily

The simple, deep flavors of Eastern Europe are the essence of comfort food. Kasha is buckwheat groats. Sometimes grocery stores like to think too much. That's why you might not find buckwheat logically situated near other grain products, such as couscous, pilaf mixes, and quinoa. No, kasha is so identified with Jewish cooking that you'll probably locate it near the matzo.

CHICKEN with KASHA and MUSHROOMS

1 chicken, 4 pounds, cut into serving pieces

1 teaspoon salt, plus salt to taste

¼ teaspoon white pepper, plus pepper to taste

3 tablespoons rendered chicken fat (see Schmaltz, page 51) or vegetable oil

1 pound fresh white mushrooms, cut into chunks

2 onions, chopped

2 cups chicken stock, boiling

1 cup kasha

1 tablespoon chopped fresh flat-leaf (Italian) parsley

1 Preheat an oven to 350°F. Hack the chicken breasts in half crosswise. Rinse the chicken pieces and pat dry with paper towels. Sprinkle with the 1 teaspoon salt and ¼ teaspoon pepper.

2 Heat 2 tablespoons of the chicken fat or oil in a large oven-proof sauté pan with a lid over medium-high heat. Add the mushrooms and onions, reduce the heat to medium, and sauté until the onions are very soft gold but not crisp and the mushrooms have shrunk, about 15 minutes.

3 Meanwhile, in another large sauté pan, heat the remaining 1 tablespoon fat over high heat. Add the chicken, skin side down, and sauté, turning once, until well browned, about 5 minutes on each side. Remove the chicken to a plate. Pour off all the fat from the pan. Return the pan to high heat and pour in the stock. Bring to a boil.

4 When the mushrooms are done, scrape them out of the pan into a bowl. Add the kasha to the pan and stir and toss over medium-high heat until the grains smell toasty, 2 to 3 minutes.

5 Stir the boiling stock into the kasha. Add the mushrooms, folding them in completely. Add a touch more salt and white pepper. Nestle the chicken pieces in the kasha, skin side up. Cover and bake for 30 minutes. Uncover, stir in the parsley, and bake until all the liquid is absorbed, the kasha is tender, and the chicken is cooked through, about 5 minutes longer.

6 Serve directly from the pan, spooning kasha and chicken together.

Serves 4 easily

An earthy dish for a cruel winter night. I love the sweet-sour notes and mustard spice in German cuisine, not to mention the beer. These two recipes interplay ingredients. Start the cabbage first. While the cabbage simmers, you'll have plenty of time to prepare the chicken.

BEER-BRAISED CHICKEN
with RED CABBAGE and APPLES

FOR THE RED CABBAGE
AND APPLES:

1 head red cabbage

3 bacon slices

½ onion, minced

3 apples, peeled, cored, and sliced

¼ teaspoon salt

½ cup boiling water

2 tablespoons flour

¼ cup distilled white vinegar or cider vinegar

FOR THE CHICKEN:

1 chicken, 4 pounds, cut into serving pieces

Salt and white pepper to taste

Reserved 2 tablespoons bacon fat

1 bottle (12 ounces) dark German beer, somewhat flat

1 tablespoon German dark grainy mustard

½ cup raisins

1 bay leaf

Dusting of ground nutmeg

2 tablespoons fresh lemon juice

1 To make the cabbage and apples, discard the outer leaves of the cabbage head if they appear ragged. Shred the cabbage or slice thinly. Place in a big bowl of cold water.

2 Fry the bacon in a Dutch oven or other big pot over medium-high heat until crisp, 3 to 5 minutes. Remove to paper towels to drain. Crumble and reserve.

3 Spoon out 2 tablespoons of the fat from the pot and set aside to use for the chicken. Then pour off all but 2 tablespoons of the remaining fat from the pot. Place the pot over medium-high heat, add the onion, and sauté for 1 minute.

4 Lift the cabbage from its water with tongs, letting excess water drip back into the bowl, and add to the onion. Bring to a simmer and cook, uncovered, for 10 minutes.

5 Add the apples and boiling water, stirring well. Cover, reduce the heat to low, and cook, lifting the lid to give an occasional stir, until everything is very tender, about 1½ hours.

6 Near serving time, in a little cup, mix together the flour and vinegar until smooth. Pour into the cabbage and simmer, uncovered, 10 minutes longer.

7 While the cabbage is cooking, prepare the chicken. Hack the breasts in half crosswise. Rinse the chicken pieces and pat dry with paper towels. Sprinkle with salt and pepper.

8 Warm a deep serving platter or shallow bowl in a 150°F oven.

9 Heat the 2 tablespoons reserved bacon fat in a wide, heavy sauté pan over high heat. Add the chicken pieces, skin side down, and sauté, turning once, until well browned, about 5 minutes on each side. Remove the chicken to a plate.

10 Pour off all but 1 tablespoon of the fat from the pan. Return the pan to high heat. Stir in the beer and mustard and bring to a boil. Return the chicken to the pan, skin side down. Add the raisins, bay leaf, nutmeg, and lemon juice. Cover, reduce the heat to low, and simmer until the chicken is cooked through, about 20 minutes.

11 Uncover and taste the chicken for a good salt flavor. Arrange the cabbage in the warmed serving platter or bowl; top with the chicken pieces, skin side up.

12 Bring the pan juices, including the raisins, to a boil and boil until thick and shiny, at least 1 full minute. Spoon some of the sauce and raisins over each piece of chicken. Garnish with the crumbled bacon and serve at once. (If you are not quite ready, you can cover and keep hot in a warm oven for 15 minutes.)

Serves 4 or 5

Braising chicken in cream makes it tender, juicy, and rich. You'll be surprised at how little cream actually shows up when the bird is finally served. I like to serve this on a bed of twice-cooked red and green chard as prepared on page 175 but without the garlic. You'll need a pan that can go from the stove top to oven.

CHICKEN BRAISED
in SWEET CREAM

1 chicken, 4 pounds,
cut into serving pieces

½ teaspoon salt,
plus salt to taste

⅛ teaspoon white pepper,
plus pepper to taste

3 tablespoons butter

1 teaspoon sugar

1½ cups heavy cream

3 bay leaves

1 Preheat an oven to 350°F.

2 Hack the chicken breasts in half crosswise. Rinse the chicken pieces and pat dry with paper towels. Sprinkle with the ½ teaspoon salt and ⅛ teaspoon white pepper.

3 Melt the butter in a large ovenproof sauté pan with a lid or a Dutch oven over high heat. Add the chicken, skin side down, and sauté, turning once, until lightly browned, about 4 minutes on each side.

4 In a measuring cup, stir the sugar into the cream. Pour over the chicken. Sprinkle with a touch more salt and pepper. Tuck in the bay leaves.

5 Cover and bake until the chicken is cooked through, 30 to 35 minutes. Two or three times during baking, uncover and spoon the pan sauce over the chicken. Remove the chicken to a platter.

6 Place the pan on the stove top over high heat. Boil the pan juices until thick and reduced to about ¾ cup. Spoon over the chicken and serve hot.

Serves 4

CHICKEN HINDQUARTERS
and TOMATO BITS BRAISED
in WHITE WINE

4 chicken hindquarters

$\frac{1}{2}$ teaspoon salt

Black pepper to taste

1 tablespoon butter

1 onion, chopped

1 tablespoon minced garlic

1 cup dry white wine

1 cup chicken stock

1 tablespoon dried tomato bits

Few fresh parsley sprigs,
plus 1 tablespoon minced parsley

Few fresh thyme sprigs

1 Preheat an oven to 350°F. Rinse the hindquarters and pat dry with paper towels. Sprinkle with the salt and pepper.

2 Melt the butter in a wide, heavy ovenproof sauté pan over high heat. Add the chicken, skin side down, and sauté, turning once, until well browned, about 4 minutes on each side. Remove the chicken to a plate.

3 Pour off all but 1 tablespoon of the fat from the pan. Return the pan to medium-high heat, add the onion and garlic, and sauté until softened, about 3 minutes.

4 Return the chicken to the pan, skin side up. Raise the heat to high and pour in the wine and then the stock. Add the dried tomato bits and tuck in the herb sprigs. Bring to a boil.

5 Cover, transfer to the oven, and bake until the chicken is cooked through, 35 to 40 minutes. Remove the chicken to a serving platter.

6 Strain the sauce through a sieve into a bowl, keeping the pan handy. If there is time, set the sauce in the freezer briefly to force the fat to rise, then skim off and discard the fat.

7 Pour the sauce back into the sauté pan and place over high heat. Bring to a boil and boil until thick and richly brown, about 5 minutes. The longer it boils, the less you'll have, but the richer it will taste.

8 Pour the sauce over the chicken. Sprinkle with the minced parsley and serve hot.

Serves 4

THIGHS in CABERNET-PORCINI SAUCE

4 bacon slices

8 boneless
chicken thighs, skin on

½ cup flour mixed
with 1 teaspoon salt
and black pepper to taste

1 large shallot, minced

1 cup Cabernet Sauvignon

1½ cups chicken stock

1½ ounces dried
porcini mushrooms soaked
in warm water to cover

2 tablespoons butter

1 Fry the bacon in a large sauté pan over medium-high heat until crisp, 3 to 5 minutes. Remove to paper towels to drain. When cool, crumble and reserve. Pour off all but 2 tablespoons of the fat from the pan.

2 Preheat an oven to 400°F.

3 Rinse the thighs and pat dry with paper towels. Dredge in the seasoned flour, shaking off the excess.

4 Heat the reserved bacon fat in the sauté pan over medium-high heat. Add the thighs, skin side down, and sauté, turning once, until well browned, 4 to 5 minutes on each side. Transfer to an 8-inch square baking dish and bake until the chicken is cooked through, about 30 minutes.

5 Meanwhile, again pour off the excess fat. Return the sauté pan to medium-high heat, add the shallot, and sauté for 30 seconds or so. Quickly pour in the wine, scraping up the browned bits on the pan bottom. Bring to a boil and boil until just 2 or 3 tablespoons of syrupy wine remain.

6 Pour in the chicken stock. Drain the mushrooms, reserving the soaking liquid, and add the mushrooms to the pan. Quickly strain the soaking liquid through a fine-mesh sieve and add ½ cup of it to the pan. Bring the liquid to a boil and boil until reduced by half.

7 Remove from the heat and whisk in the butter until melted. Arrange the thighs on plates and spoon the sauce over them. (If you are serving polenta, spoon some of the sauce over it, too.) Garnish with crumbled bacon.

Serves 8

Green olives are harvested until early winter. Unable to be eaten pleasantly straight off an olive tree, they've got to be brined. It doesn't make any difference if they're fresh; you still have to buy them in jars or cans. Even so, this being olive season, I used big stuffed ones in this hearty braised chicken dish made in one pan.

CHICKEN in LEMON-TOMATO SAUCE with GREEN OLIVES

1 chicken, 3½ to 4 pounds, cut into serving pieces

½ cup flour mixed with 1 teaspoon salt and black pepper to taste

2 tablespoons olive oil

2 teaspoons finely minced garlic

1 onion, chopped

2 celery stalks, chopped

1 tablespoon minced fresh parsley

½ cup fresh lemon juice

1 can (1 pound) crushed Italian tomatoes

1 cup chicken stock

Salt to taste

15 pimiento-stuffed green olives ("queen size"), quartered

1 Hack the chicken breasts in half crosswise. Rinse the chicken pieces and pat dry with paper towels. Dredge the chicken lightly in the seasoned flour, shaking off the excess.

2 Heat the oil in a wide, heavy sauté pan with a lid over high heat. Add the chicken, skin side down, and sauté, turning once, until well browned, about 5 minutes on each side. Remove the chicken to a plate.

3 Drain all but 1 tablespoon fat from the pan. Return the pan to medium-high heat and add the garlic, onion, celery, and parsley. Sauté until softened, about 8 minutes.

4 Raise the heat to high, pour in the lemon juice, and stir well, scraping up any browned bits from the pan bottom. Bring to a boil and boil down until the vegetables are sitting in about 2 tablespoons liquid.

5 Nestle the chicken back into the vegetables, skin side up. Pour in the tomatoes and stock, and sprinkle with a touch of salt. Cover, reduce the heat to low, and simmer until the chicken is cooked through, about 25 minutes.

6 At the end of cooking, swish the chicken pieces though the sauce to coat them nicely. Remove the chicken to a platter.

7 Raise the heat to high, bring to a boil, and boil the sauce for 2 minutes. Add the olives and boil until thickened, 2 to 3 minutes longer. Spoon the sauce over the chicken and serve hot.

Serves 4

Talk about nutrition! 254
And with the colors of orange and green against
the browned chicken, lovely to look at.

CHICKEN and GENTLY SPICED MOROCCAN CARROTS

FOR THE CARROTS:

1¼ cups chicken stock

1 pound carrots, peeled
and cut into 1-inch chunks

Pinch of sugar

2 teaspoons chile powder
such as New Mexican

¼ teaspoon ground cumin

Dash of salt

FOR THE CHICKEN:

1 chicken, 4 pounds,
cut into serving pieces

½ cup flour mixed with
1 teaspoon salt and
½ teaspoon black pepper

1 tablespoon rendered chicken
fat (see Schmaltz, page 51)
or butter

2 tablespoons fresh lemon juice

2 bay leaves

2 green onions, minced

1 To prepare the carrots, in a saucepan, bring the stock to a boil. Add the carrots and sugar, reduce the heat to low, and simmer, uncovered, until crisp-tender, about 10 minutes. Scoop out the carrots with a slotted spoon into a bowl. Reserve the hot liquid. Toss the carrots with the chile powder, cumin, and salt.

2 Warm a serving platter in a 150°F oven.

3 Meanwhile, prepare the chicken: Rinse the pieces and pat dry with paper towels. Dredge in the seasoned flour, shaking off the excess.

4 Heat the chicken fat or butter in a wide, heavy sauté pan with a lid over high heat. Add the chicken pieces, skin side down, and sauté, turning once, until well browned, 4 to 5 minutes on each side.

5 Drain off the excess fat from the pan. Raise the heat to high and add the reserved carrot liquid. Sprinkle the chicken with the lemon juice, tuck in the bay leaves, and bring to a boil. Cover, reduce the heat to low, and simmer for 10 minutes.

6 Uncover and add the spiced carrots. Re-cover and continue simmering until the chicken is cooked through, about 10 minutes longer. Remove the chicken to the warmed serving platter.

7 Bring the carrots and pan juices to a boil for 1 minute. The carrots are done if the point of a knife easily glides into a chunk.

8 Pour the carrots and pan juices over the chicken. Sprinkle with the green onions and serve hot.

Serves 4

By the time this comes from the oven, the rice will have fattened up and the liquid around it will have cooked into a light custard, almost like a rice pudding but with velvety-soft chicken and aromatic spices. If you've got something gorgeous to bake this in, it can come straight from the oven to a table of important invited people.

An EXOTIC
CHICKEN AND RICE CASSEROLE

FOR THE CHICKEN:

1 chicken, 3½ pounds

1 onion, peeled but left whole

Few celery stalks, cut into chunks

1 tablespoon salt

White pepper to taste

FOR THE CASSEROLE:

Cooked chicken and stock

1 cup raw medium-grain white rice such as Calrose variety

½ cup whole buttered almonds (see Note)

1 tablespoon finely minced garlic

½ cup golden or dark raisins

¼ teaspoon ground cardamom

Rounded ¼ teaspoon ground cinnamon

About ⅛ teaspoon saffron threads

¼ teaspoon hot paprika

4 eggs, beaten

1 To cook the chicken, first rinse it, then place in a big pot with water to cover by 1 inch. Bring to a simmer over medium heat, uncovered. Skim off any scum as it appears. This may take up to 45 minutes.

2 When the broth is clear, add the onion, celery, salt, and pepper. Cover partially and simmer until cooked through, about 1 hour.

3 Remove the chicken (tongs work well) to a colander set in a big bowl. Strain the broth through a fine-mesh sieve into the bowl, preferably one with a spout. You will need 5 cups.

4 To assemble the casserole, preheat an oven to 350°F. Lightly butter a 3-quart baking dish, preferably one with a lid.

5 Debone and skin the chicken, then shred the meat roughly. Drop the meat into the 5 cups stock.

6 Add all the remaining ingredients except the eggs, mixing gently. Then stir in the eggs. Pour into the buttered casserole.

7 Cover and bake until the rice is tender and the "custard" is set, about 1 hour and 10 minutes. Serve hot directly from the dish.

Serves 6

Note: To prepare buttered almonds, sauté the ½ cup whole, unskinned almonds in 2 tablespoons butter in a skillet over medium-high heat, moving and tossing them constantly, until you hear 1 almond crackle. Quickly pour the contents of the skillet into the chicken-rice mixture.

This is real Chinese restaurant–quality chicken. A marinade that mixes quickly and takes effect in 20 minutes makes this one of my weekday workhorse recipes. If you have bamboo steamers, you'll need two. Otherwise, rig up your own steaming apparatus, making sure the chicken and marinade cook in a shallow bowl to capture all the juices. To rig up a steamer, see Chicken Cooking Equipment on pages 38–39. Serve with steamed white rice.

CHINESE-STYLE
STEAMED THIGHS

FOR THE MARINADE:

1 tablespoon vegetable oil

3 tablespoons rice wine vinegar

2 tablespoons oyster sauce

2 tablespoons brandy or dry sherry

Pinch of sugar

1/4 teaspoon white pepper

1 teaspoon minced garlic or ginger

1/4 cup sliced green onion

1/4 cup chopped fresh cilantro

2 tablespoons cornstarch

1 teaspoon Asian sesame oil

8 chicken thighs

1 Combine all the marinade ingredients in a big bowl. Add the chicken thighs, mix with your hands, and let marinate for 20 minutes at room temperature.

2 Ready 2 bamboo steamers or rig up a steamer (see recipe introduction). Put the chicken in 1 or more shallow bowls and place in the steamer. Steam until the chicken is cooked through, 40 to 45 minutes.

3 Remove the chicken with tongs to a serving dish. Pour the cooked marinade and collected juices over the chicken and serve at once.

Serves 4 to 6

Special for dark-meat lovers, a batch of comfort food best made on a cold weekend afternoon to be enjoyed at dinner and again as leftovers in the week ahead.

BAKED CHICKEN STEW with WHITE BEANS and HERBS

2 cups small dried white beans

6 cups water

8 chicken thighs

Salt to taste,
plus 1¹/₂ teaspoons

White pepper to taste,
plus ¹/₂ teaspoon

2 tablespoons vegetable oil or
olive oil

1 tablespoon minced garlic

1 white onion, chopped

2 cups chopped celery
(about 4 stalks)

¹/₃ cup chopped fresh flat-leaf
(Italian) parsley

1 can (1 pound)
plum tomatoes, drained

1¹/₂ teaspoons dried thyme

1 Pick over the beans, then place in a colander and rinse well. Place the beans in a large saucepan with the water, bring to a boil, and boil for 2 minutes. Remove from the heat, cover, and let stand for 1 hour.

2 Meanwhile, prepare the rest of the stew. Preheat an oven to 325°F. Hack the thighs in half crosswise. Rinse the pieces and pat dry with paper towels. Sprinkle with salt and pepper.

3 Heat the oil in a heavy sauté pan over high heat. Add the thighs, skin side down, and sauté, turning once, until well browned, 4 to 5 minutes on each side.

4 Scatter the garlic over the thighs, give a few stirs, then drain off the excess fat. Set the pan of thighs aside.

5 Butter or oil a large, heavy baking dish, preferably with a lid. Add the onion, celery, parsley, tomatoes, thyme, the 1¹/₂ tea-spoons salt, and the ¹/₂ teaspoon pepper to the beans and their liquid. Stir well, breaking up the tomatoes, then add the thighs, scraping all the garlic out of the pan. Stir once or twice and pour all into the prepared baking dish.

6 Cover and bake until the beans are tender and the chicken is cooked through, about 2 hours. Taste for salt during the last 30 minutes of cooking.

7 Ladle into warmed bowls, as you would a stew or soup, and serve hot.

Serves 6

Root vegetables give an unexpected sweetness to stew. Parsnips, especially, surprise with their impact of pleasant, sweet flavor. The browning of the vegetables is the most time-consuming part of this dish, but it's important. It guarantees that the sauce will have rich color. After you've completed all the stove-top work, the stew is in the oven long enough for you to clean up, set the table, decide on some bread, and relax.

BAKED CHICKEN STEW
with WINTER VEGETABLES

1 chicken, 3½ to 4 pounds

2 to 3 tablespoons butter

Salt and black pepper to taste

2 onions, peeled and cut into eighths

2 large carrots, peeled and cut into 1-inch chunks

1 large yam (about 2 pounds), peeled and cut into 2-inch chunks (see Notes)

2 parsnips, peeled, halved lengthwise, and cut into 1½-inch chunks

1 celery root, peeled and cut into 1-inch cubes (see Notes)

2 cups chicken stock

1 fresh thyme sprig

1 fresh rosemary sprig

1 Hack the chicken into bite-sized pieces. Rinse the chicken pieces and pat dry with paper towels. Sprinkle with salt and pepper.

2 Melt 1 tablespoon of the butter in a wide, heavy sauté pan over medium-high heat. Add the chicken, skin side down, and sauté, turning once, until well browned, about 8 minutes. Transfer the chicken to an ovenproof Dutch oven.

3 Pour off all but 1 tablespoon fat from the pan. Add the onions and carrots and sauté until well browned, about 10 minutes. Remove to the Dutch oven, spooning the mixture around all the chicken pieces.

4 If the sauté pan is dry, add another tablespoon butter. Add the yam, parsnips, and celery root, and sauté, turning as needed, until lightly browned, about 12 minutes. Transfer to the Dutch oven.

5 Raise the heat to high and pour in the stock, scraping up any browned bits from the pan bottom. Bring to a boil and boil until reduced by half, about 2 minutes. Pour the pan juices over the chicken. Sprinkle with a touch more salt and pepper. Tuck in the herb sprigs.

6 Cover and bake for 30 minutes. (For mushier vegetables, bake for 45 minutes.)

7 Uncover and continue baking until the chicken is cooked through and the vegetables are tender, about 10 minutes longer.

8 Spoon out the vegetables and chicken either onto a serving platter or into individual stew bowls. If the sauce remaining in the Dutch oven is thin, place on top of the stove and boil over high heat for 2 to 3 minutes. Pour the sauce over the chicken and vegetables and serve.

Serves 6

Notes: The Garnet is the best yam I've ever used. Try to locate them during the Thanksgiving food–shopping days. They'll keep in a cold garage or cellar for a couple of months.

Celery root is the hairy monster of the produce department. It's yanked from the ground covered in a damp mottling of roots spewing everywhere. To tame it, cut off the top and bottom so it stands flat. With a sharp knife poised at the top and holding on with your other hand, carve down, following the contour of the root and cutting off strips of the dirty skin until the celery root is a nice white ball.

What a nice, warming, and economical brew of a stew.
To bone an entire chicken, see Boning an Entire
Chicken, page 24. I gave it my best shot the first time
and got a decent showing of boneless pieces. If your
initial attempts at boning result more in shreds than in
perfect cubes, they'll be camouflaged by the rest of the
stew, and you'll do better next time. Also, please taste
for salt. Stew usually takes more than you think,
particularly when tomatoes are present.

CHICKEN STEW
with PIMIENTO DUMPLINGS

1 chicken, 3½ to 4 pounds

½ cup flour mixed
with 1 teaspoon salt,
½ teaspoon black pepper,
and ½ teaspoon paprika

2 tablespoons chicken fat
(see Schmaltz, page 51)
or vegetable oil

1 onion, chopped

2 teaspoons minced garlic

¼ cup dry sherry

2 cups chicken stock

1 can (28 ounces)
crushed Italian tomatoes

1 jar (4 ounces)
chopped pimientos, drained

2 carrots, peeled
and cut into ½-inch slices

1 bay leaf

Salt to taste

2 russet potatoes, peeled
and cut into 1-inch dice

½ pound fresh
white mushrooms, sliced

1 cup frozen peas

1 Rinse the chicken, then skin and bone it (see recipe introduction). As soon as possible, get the bones into a pot, add water to cover by 1 inch, bring to a boil, and simmer for 30 minutes while you pull the rest of the recipe together. You'll have usable stock by the time it's called for in Step 5.

2 Cut the chicken meat into 1½-inch cubes. Combine the ingredients for the seasoned flour in a paper bag. Then add the chicken cubes and shake until evenly coated.

3 Heat 1 tablespoon of the chicken fat or oil in a heavy Dutch oven over high heat. Add the chicken and sauté until the pieces are golden on all sides, about 5 minutes. Remove the chicken to a bowl.

4 Add 1 tablespoon more fat to the Dutch oven and reduce the heat to medium-high. Add the onion and garlic and sauté until golden, about 3 minutes.

5 Raise the heat to high, pour in the sherry, and ignite with a match. Let the flame die out and let the sherry cook away. Then immediately add the stock, tomatoes, pimientos, carrots, bay leaf, and a little more salt. Bring to a boil uncovered, then cover partially and simmer for 20 minutes.

FOR THE PIMIENTO DUMPLINGS:

2 cups flour

4 teaspoons baking powder

¼ teaspoon paprika

½ teaspoon salt

4 tablespoons chilled butter

1 tablespoon chopped fresh parsley

1 jar (4 ounces) chopped pimentos

Milk, as needed

6 Add the potatoes, cover tightly, and simmer for 20 minutes.

7 When time's up, add the mushrooms and the reserved chicken. Re-cover and cook over medium-low heat for 15 minutes, giving a few stirs and checking that the bottom doesn't scorch. You should have plenty of gravy, a necessity to puff the dumplings.

8 Meanwhile, make the dumpling batter: In a bowl, stir together the flour, baking powder, paprika, and salt. Cut the butter into pieces and rub them into the flour with your fingers until a fine meal forms. Add the parsley and toss to mix.

9 Pour the pimientos from their jar into a 1-cup measure. Add milk as needed to equal ⅞ cup. Add the pimiento-milk mixture to the flour, stirring well with a fork until the sides of the bowl come clean. If necessary, knead gently—just a few times—to pick up excess flour from the bottom of the bowl.

10 Stir the peas into the stew. Drop the batter by ¼ cupfuls onto the surface of the stew. You should have about 8 dumplings. Cover tightly and cook over medium heat until the dumplings are puffed to triple their original size, about 15 to 20 minutes.

11 Ladle into bowls, including at least 1 dumpling in each bowl. Serve at once.

Serves 6

A pot pie must have juicy pieces of chicken, or it's a failure. The best way to make chicken incredibly moist and succulent is to let it simmer and sit, Chinese style, in a technique called "cooking a chicken white." The chicken never boils, only simmers. Then it cools in its liquid, allowing the chicken's juices to flow back into the chicken's meat.

CHICKEN POT PIE
with BUTTER CRUST

FOR THE BUTTER CRUST:

3/4 cup chilled butter

4 tablespoons chilled solid vegetable shortening

2 cups flour

1 teaspoon salt

3 tablespoons ice water

FOR THE FILLING:

5 cups cubed White-Cooked Chicken (page 50)

2 cups reserved chicken-cooking stock

6 tablespoons butter

1 cup peeled and finely diced carrots (about 3 medium)

1 cup corn kernels (fresh or frozen)

1 cup finely diced celery (2 medium stalks)

5 tablespoons flour

1/2 cup heavy cream

1/2 teaspoon salt

1/4 teaspoon white pepper

2 tablespoons dry sherry

3 green onions, minced

1/2 cup chopped fresh flat-leaf (Italian) parsley

1 To make the crust, chop the butter and shortening into chunks, set on a plate, and put in the freezer for a few minutes.

2 Place the flour and salt in a food processor. Pulse once or twice to mix. Top with the pieces of cold butter and shortening, and pulse until the mixture looks like sand. Then, with the motor running, add the ice water. The dough should just hold together in a rough mass. Stop the machine immediately.

3 Gather the dough into a ball. Divide in half and flatten each half into a thick disk. Wrap separately in plastic wrap and chill for 2 hours.

4 Prepare the chicken as directed. Strip 5 cuts of meat from the bones; set aside. Measure out 2 cups of the stock, bring to a simmer, then remove from the heat, cover, and keep hot.

5 Melt 2 tablespoons of butter in a large sauté pan over medium heat. Add the carrots, corn, and celery and sauté until the carrots are softened, 15 to 20 minutes. Remove from the heat.

6 Melt the remaining 4 tablespoons butter in a large pot over medium-high heat. Whisk in the flour, then continue whisking for 2 minutes until a paste forms. Gradually pour in the hot stock, whisking constantly to prevent lumps from forming. Simmer until the sauce thickens, about 5 minutes. Remove from the heat and stir in the cream, salt, and pepper.

FOR ASSEMBLING THE PIES:

A little more sherry

1 egg yolk mixed with
1 tablespoon water

7 Add the chicken, the sautéed vegetables, and the sherry and mix well. (At this point, you can cover the mixture and refrigerate for 3 days before continuing.) Add the green onions and parsley, mix well, and taste and correct the seasoning.

8 Preheat an oven to 400°F. To assemble the pies, on a lightly floured work surface, roll out 1 piece of the dough ⅛ inch thick. Cut out rounds to line six 1½-cup ramekins. Line the ramekins with the rounds. Trim to leave a ¼-inch overhang. Prick the bottoms with fork tines.

9 Fill with the chicken mixture, dividing evenly. Make a small well in the center of each portion and add a drop of sherry.

10 Roll out the second piece of dough ⅛ inch thick. Cut out rounds to cover the ramekins. Transfer each round to a ramekin, trim the excess overhang, then tuck the edge of the top round under the overhang of the bottom round and flute together.

11 Brush the tops with egg yolk–water mixture. If you like, cut any dough scraps into decorative shapes and use to embellish the tops of the pies. Brush again with the yolk mixture.

12 Set all the ramekins on a baking sheet. Bake until the pastry is golden, 20 to 25 minutes. Serve hot.

Makes 6

When you lift the plumped porcini from their soaking liquid, you'll be tempted to add it to your stock for extra mushroom flavor. No matter how tempting, and forgetting all thoughts of waste, you won't need it. The flavor of the mushrooms alone is very powerful; adding the soaking liquid would be overkill.

I've made this with Sauvignon Blanc, Chardonnay, and Pinot Grigio, all with good results. The stock used is usually fairly full flavored. I've sneaked in some of the chicken's cooking juices as part of the quantity of stock, too. When stock is used hot, risotto cooks faster.

RISOTTO with ROSEMARY-SMOKED CHICKEN and PORCINI

1 ounce dried porcini mushrooms

1½ tablespoons butter

1 onion, chopped

1 bay leaf

2 teaspoons fresh thyme leaves

2 tablespoons dried tomato bits

1 cup Arborio rice

1 cup dry white wine

¼ teaspoon salt

Black pepper to taste

6 cups chicken stock, heated

½ cup frozen peas

2 cups shredded Italian-Smoked Chicken (pages 48–49) or deli-bought smoked chicken

¾ cup grated Parmesan cheese

1 Place the porcini in a bowl with warm water to cover and set aside to soak while you ready the rest of the ingredients. Drain, discard the liquid, and rinse the mushrooms. Squeeze out excess moisture and slice.

2 Melt the butter in a wide, heavy skillet over medium-high heat. Add the onion and sauté until softened, about 5 minutes. Add the bay leaf, thyme, and tomato bits and sauté for 1 minute longer. Add the mushrooms and sauté about 3 minutes longer.

3 Add the rice and sauté until coated with the butter and toasty, about 2 minutes. Add the wine, raise the heat to high, and boil until nearly evaporated. Season with the salt and pepper.

**Bulletin! Chicken Is Second Animal
to Cross Brooklyn Bridge!**

The maiden trip taken across the Brooklyn Bridge,
just as the foundation was in place but before the structure was complete, was made by Emily Roebling, wife of
bridge architect Washington Roebling.
The engineers decided to test the bridge with a trotting
horse pulling a carriage with Mrs. Roebling,
who carried with her a symbol of victory, a rooster.

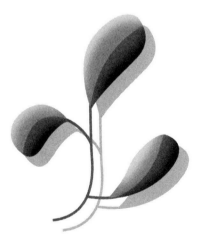

4 Add 1 cup of the hot stock and cook, stirring, until the liquid is nearly absorbed. Reduce the heat to medium, add another cup of stock, and again cook, stirring until the liquid is absorbed. Continue adding the stock in this manner, 1 cup at a time and allowing it to be absorbed before adding more, until the kernels are tender but still slightly firm at the center and the rice is creamy. You may not need all of the stock, or you may need a little more liquid, in which case more hot stock or water can be added.

5 Just before you anticipate the last addition of stock, stir in the peas and chicken. Add the final cup of stock, cook for a few minutes, stirring well, and turn the risotto into a serving bowl.

6 Serve immediately topped with the Parmesan cheese.

Serves 4 to 6

No, it's not sissy chili but plenty spicy and tasty! This is a recipe adapted from my friend Dotty Griffith's book, *Wild About Chili*. It's from Bo Pilgrim, an East Texas chicken rancher made famous by two things: 1) this chili and 2) an invention that sucks all the bones out of a chicken for a clean deboning.

Bo's recipe, naturally, uses all that boneless meat. I like the contrast of how the small pieces of white and dark meat cook into contrasting textures, although the dark meat acts and feels more like beef. As is decreed in Texas, there are no beans in this chili. If you want beans, make 'em on the side.

CHICKEN CHILI

1 chicken, 4 pounds

¼ cup rendered chicken fat (see Schmaltz, page 51) or vegetable oil

1 onion, chopped

4 cloves garlic

⅓ cup New Mexico chile powder

2 tablespoons ground cumin

½ teaspoon cayenne pepper

2 teaspoons dried Mexican oregano

1 teaspoon salt

2 tablespoons flour

1 can (15 ounces) Hunt's brand chunky Mexican tomato sauce or plain tomato sauce

2½ cups chicken stock, or as needed

1 teaspoon sugar

1 fresh jalapeño chile, seeded and minced (optional)

2 tablespoons masa harina mixed with ¼ cup water

FOR GARNISH:

Chopped fresh cilantro

Chopped yellow onions or green onions

Shredded Cheddar cheese

Sliced pickled jalapeños

1 Skin and bone the chicken (see Boning an Entire Chicken, page 24). Grind the meat coarsely in a food processor, about 20 short bursts, or cut it into ¼-inch cubes with a knife.

2 Heat the chicken fat or vegetable oil in a Dutch oven or other heavy pot with a lid. Add the onion and garlic and sauté until softened but not browned, about 5 minutes.

3 Add the chicken and sauté until no longer pink, 5 to 7 minutes. Add the chile powder, cumin, cayenne, oregano, and salt, and stir to coat the chicken. Add the flour and stir well again. Stir in the tomato sauce, 2½ cups stock, and sugar. If the meat isn't covered by 1 inch of liquid, add more stock or water.

4 Bring to a boil, cover, reduce the heat to low, and simmer for 30 to 40 minutes. Uncover and add the fresh jalapeño, if desired, and the masa harina–water mixture. Continue to simmer, uncovered, until thickened, about 30 minutes longer. Stir from time to time to prevent scorching.

5 Set out the garnishes in separate small bowls. Ladle the chili into warmed bowls and let the diners add the garnishes to taste.

Serves 4 to 6

My friend Marcie Rothman, known as the
5-Dollar Chef, can make any meal fit a budget.
This white chili is based on one of her spicy,
sustaining suppers.

WHITE CHICKEN CHILI

1 pound (2¼ cups) dried large white beans, or 3 cans (15 ounces each) white beans

2 large onions, chopped

2 teaspoons minced garlic

2 celery stalks, chopped

1 tablespoon New Mexico chile powder

1½ teaspoons ground cumin

1½ teaspoons dried oregano

3 ancho chiles, or 1 teaspoon red pepper flakes

1 can (7 ounces) chopped green chiles, drained

6 to 8 cups chicken stock or water

1½ pounds coarsely ground chicken (see Grinding Chicken, pages 24–25)

½ teaspoon salt

Black pepper to taste

FOR GARNISH:
Shredded Monterey Jack cheese
Chopped fresh cilantro
Chopped green or white onions
Finely minced jalapeño chiles

1 If using dried beans, pick over the beans, then place in a colander and rinse well. Place the beans in a large saucepan, add water to cover by 1 inch, bring to a boil, and boil for 2 minutes. Remove from the heat, cover, and let stand for 1 hour. Drain. If using canned beans, drain, rinse, drain again, place in a large saucepan, and proceed with recipe.

2 Add the onions, garlic, celery, chile powder, cumin, oregano, whole anchos or red pepper flakes, and enough stock or water to cover the beans. Bring to a boil over high heat. Cover, reduce the heat to low, and simmer until the beans begin to soften, about 1 hour.

3 Meanwhile, in a skillet, sauté the chicken over high heat, sprinkling with the salt and pepper, until no longer pink, 5 to 7 minutes.

4 When the beans have cooked about 1 hour (or 30 minutes, if using canned), add the sautéed chicken to the chili pot and simmer until the chicken and beans are done, about 20 minutes longer.

5 Set out the garnishes in separate bowls. Ladle the chili into warm bowls and let the diners add the garnishes to taste.

Serves 4 to 6

Here is a quick way to make salad using winter fruits. "Poach" the breasts submerged in stock and white wine in the microwave oven. They come out moist and tender every time. During the time you're not worrying about the chicken, you can cut and chop the fruits and vegetables.

CHICKEN
and WINTER-FRUIT SALAD

1 cup walnut halves or pecans

3 tablespoons packed brown sugar

Salt to taste

4 boneless chicken breasts, skinned

1 cup chicken stock

³/₄ cup dry white wine

4 kiwifruits, peeled and sliced

2 tangerines, peeled and sectioned

¹/₂ cup Muscat raisins

2 Anjou pears, peeled, cored, and cubed

1 banana, peeled and sliced

¹/₂ cup mayonnaise

Juice of 1 lemon

1 to 2 teaspoons curry powder

FOR ASSEMBLING THE SALAD:

2 cups shredded cabbage

1 cup shredded spinach

¹/₄ cup shredded mustard greens

1 Lay a sheet of parchment paper or waxed paper on a baking sheet. Heat a small nonstick skillet over high heat. When hot, add the nuts and toss and stir constantly until they smell toasty, 1 to 3 minutes, depending on freshness. Quickly sprinkle the brown sugar and salt over the nuts, keeping them moving about 1 minute longer as the sugar melts. Immediately pour onto the paper and let cool completely before breaking apart.

2 Set the chicken breasts in a microwaveproof dish with the stock and wine. Cover well and place in the microwave on High for 10 minutes. Remove from the microwave and let cool slightly in the cooking liquid.

3 Dice the chicken and place in a bowl. Add the kiwifruits, tangerines, raisins, pears, and banana. Toss gently.

4 In a small bowl, stir together the mayonnaise, lemon juice, and curry powder. Add to the chicken mixture and stir gently to coat evenly. Add the sugared nuts and toss again to mix.

5 To assemble the salad, in a bowl, toss together the cabbage, spinach, and mustard greens. Divide among individual plates, to form beds. Spoon the salad on top, again dividing evenly. Serve at once.

Serves 6

scratch

Bibliography

American Poultry Historical Society, Inc. *American Poultry History 1974–1993.* Mount Morris, Ill.: Watt Publishing Co., 1996.

Batty, Dr. J. *Lewis Wright's Poultry.* Hindhead, Surrey, England: Triplegate Ltd., 1983.

Belko, Vivian. *Historic Adamsville: Its People and Its Places.* Adamsville, R. I.: Adamsville Historical Association, 1992.

Bullock, Helen Duprey, comp. *National Treasury of Cooking: Victorian Era.* New York: Heirloom Publishing Co., 1962.

Cole, H. H., and W. N. Garrett, eds. *Animal Agriculture: The Biology, Husbandry, and Use of Domestic Animals.* Second edition. San Francisco: W. H. Freeman and Company, 1974, 1980.

Huston, Jan. *The Chicken Ranch: The True Story of the Best Little Whorehouse in Texas.* South Brunswick, N.J.: A. S. Barnes, 1980.

Jones, Judith, and Evan Jones. *The L. L. Bean New New England Cookery.* New York: Knopf, 1987.

Lobel, Leon, and Stanley Lobel. *All About Meat.* New York: Harcourt, Brace, Jovanovich, 1975.

MacDonald, Margaret Read, ed. *The Folklore of World Holidays.* Detroit: Gale Research, Inc., 1992.

Mieder, Wolfgang, ed. *A Dictionary of American Proverbs.* New York: Oxford University Press, 1992.

Perdue, Mitzi. *The Perdue Chicken Cookbook.* New York: Pocket Books, 1991.

Smith, Page, and Charles Daniel. *The Chicken Book, Being an Inquiry into the Rise and Fall, Use and Abuse, Triumph and Tragedy of Gallus Domesticus.* Boston: Little, Brown and Company, 1975.

Stromberg, Loyl. *Poultry Oddities, History, Folklore.* Pine River, Minn.: Stromberg Publishing Co., 1992.

———. *Poultry of the World.* Port Perry, Ontario, Canada: Silvio Mattacchione & Co., 1996.

Thomas, Gertrude I. *Foods of Our Forefathers.* Philadelphia: F. A. Davis Company, 1941.

Whiting, Bartlett Jere. *Early American Proverbs and Proverbial Sayings.* Cambridge, Mass.: The Belknap Press, 1977.

Index

Table of Equivalents

The exact equivalents in the following tables have been rounded for convenience.

LIQUID/DRY MEASURES

U.S.	Metric
¼ teaspoon	1.25 milliliters
½ teaspoon	2.5 milliliters
1 teaspoon	5 milliliters
1 tablespoon (3 teaspoons)	15 milliliters
1 fluid ounce (2 tablespoons)	30 milliliters
¼ cup	60 milliliters
⅓ cup	80 milliliters
½ cup	120 milliliters
1 cup	240 milliliters
1 pint (2 cups)	480 milliliters
1 quart (4 cups, 32 ounces)	960 milliliters
1 gallon (4 quarts)	3.84 liters
1 ounce (by weight)	28 grams
1 pound	454 grams
2.2 pounds	1 kilogram

LENGTH

U.S.	Metric
⅛ inch	3 millimeters
¼ inch	6 millimeters
½ inch	12 millimeters
1 inch	2.5 centimeters

OVEN TEMPERATURE

Fahrenheit	Celsius	Gas
250	120	½
275	140	1
300	150	2
325	160	3
350	180	4
375	190	5
400	200	6
425	220	7
450	230	8
475	240	9
500	260	10

Artificial light is introduced to stimulate egg production.

First electric candler developed to gauge egg quality.

The commercial broiler chicken industry begins on Delmarva Peninsula in Sussex County, Delaware.

Commercial chicken feed is introduced, in Chicago.

Chicken research in Java identifies vitamin A.

The USDA establishes standards for eggs.

A.D. 1892

A.D. 1898

A.D. 1911

A.D. 1918

A.D. 1926

A.D. 1935

A.D. 1889

A.D. 1895

A.D. 1909

A.D. 1914

A.D. 1923

A.D. 1934

Rhode Island State College offers a course on poultry.

The U.S. Post Office first ships baby chicks by mail.

Poultry are artificially inseminated.

Cornell University offers a course on poultry.

Researchers coin the word "vitamin" to describe chicken feed components.

The USDA establishes the Federal Poultry Inspection Service.